HV5840.A8K74 1982

KRIVANEK
DRUG PROBLEMS, PE

WITHDRAWN FROM THE EVAN'S LIBRARY AT FMCC

FULTON-MONTGOMERY COMMUNITY COLLEGE LIBRARY

DRUG PROBLEMS, PEOPLE PROBLEMS

Drug problems, people problems

Causes, treatment and prevention

JARA A. KRIVANEK

GEORGE ALLEN & UNWIN
Sydney London Boston

© Jara A. Krivanek 1982
This book is copyright under the Berne Convention. No
reproduction without permission. All rights reserved.

First published in 1982 by
George Allen & Unwin Australia Pty Ltd
8 Napier Street, North Sydney NSW 2060 Australia

George Allen & Unwin (Publishers) Ltd
18 Park Lane, Hemel Hempstead, Herts HP2 4TE, England

Allen & Unwin Inc.
9 Winchester Terrace, Winchester, Mass 01890, USA

National Library of Australia
Cataloguing-in-Publication entry:
Krivanek, Jara A.
   Drug problems people problems.
   Bibliography.
   Includes index.
   ISBN 0 86861 364 9.
   ISBN 0 86861 372 X (pbk.).

   1. Alcoholism   2. Alcoholism counseling.
   3. Drug abuse.   4. Drug abuse counseling.
   I. Title

362.2' 9' 02436

Library of Congress Catalog Card Number: 82-71783

Phototypeset in Linotron 202 Plantin 10/11 pt by
Graphicraft Typesetters, Hong Kong

Printed in Hong Kong

Contents

Contributors	9
Preface	11

1 Drugs and their use: some basics — 15
- What is a drug? — 15
- How do drugs act? — 17
- What determines the observable drug effect? — 20
  - Dose — 20
  - Time since the drug was taken — 22
  - Purity of the drug — 23
  - Status of the user — 25
- References — 27

2 Symptoms of drug use and misuse — 29
- Anatomy of a drug: alcohol — 30
  - Pharmacology — 31
  - Physiological effects — 32
  - Behavioural effects — 35
  - Symptoms of alcohol misuse — 37
- How well can drug effects be recognised? — 41
- How well are the signs of drug use recognised in practice? — 43
  - Why do clients not present their problems as due to drugs or drinking? — 43
  - Why do professionals fail to recognise drinking and other drug problems? — 44
- What is recognised—is 'diagnosis' desirable? — 46
- References — 50

3 Epidemiology: assessing the problem *L.R.H. Drew* — 51
- Introduction *Jara A. Krivanek* — 51
- Patterns of drug use and drug-related problems in Australia — 53
  - Levels of drug consumption — 54
  - Individual drug use — 58
  - Outcomes of drug use — 66
  - Conclusion — 70
- Notes — 72

4 Bases of addiction — 73
Why drugs? — 74
- Biomedical factors — 74
- Commercialism and the mass media — 75
- Societal factors — 76

Which drugs? — 77
Drug use, misuse and addiction — 80
- The use-misuse continuum — 81
- The misuse-addiction continuum — 83

Some characteristics of addiction — 85
Determinants of addiction: who becomes an addict? — 87
- Genetic factors — 88
- Personality factors — 89
- Societal factors — 91

References — 98

5 Approaches to treatment — 99
Should abstinence or controlled drug use be the goal? — 100
Should addicts be treated by specialists or non-specialists? — 103
Treatment strategies — 105
- Drug emergencies — 105
- Self-referral — 107

Therapeutic success — 114
- Client-related variables — 114
- Therapy-related variables — 116

References — 118

6 Individual and group counselling *J. Howard* — 121
Introduction *Jara A. Krivanek* — 121
Counselling adolescents with drug-related problems — 122
- Assessment — 124
- A counselling model — 126
- 'Real life' counselling — 129
- A treatment model — 135
- Alternatives theory — 136
- Family work — 138
- Group work — 138
- Conclusion — 142

References — 143

7 Drug and alcohol services in Australia *P. Stolz* — 145
Introduction *Jara A. Krivanek* — 145
Providing drug and alcohol services in Australia — 147
- Services available — 147
- Finding appropriate services — 150
- Setting up and operating a referral service — 155

8 Preventive strategies: primary prevention and the community	161
General problems in prevention	161
What are we trying to prevent?	161
What strategies are feasible?	163
Which strategies are effective?	165
Primary prevention	167
Educational approaches	167
Environmental manipulation	179
References	189
9 Preventive strategies: secondary prevention and professional training	191
Current strategies	191
Problems of implementation	195
Professionalism and multidisciplinarity	195
Status of existing services	198
Provision of training: what makes a successful professional?	200
References	205
10 Main non-government and government contacts for drug and alcohol information	207
Index	213

Contributors

Dr L.R.H. Drew, BSc, MB, BS, DPM, FRANZCP, is Senior Medical Adviser in Mental Health and Adviser on Drugs of Dependence to the Commonwealth Department of Health. He was in private psychiatric practice and specialised in the treatment of drug problems. He is the prime author of *Alcoholism–A Handbook*, and has made major contributions to the literature on drinking problems. He is an occasional consultant to the World Health Organisation and is President of the Australian Medical Society on Alcohol and Drug-Related Problems.

John Howard, BA, MA (Counselling), Dip Crim, is Senior Counsellor at the Community Youth Centre, Stanmore, of the NSW Department of Youth and Community Services. Formerly a school counsellor and specialist school counsellor (delinquents), he has worked with delinquent and drug-involved youth for some 10 years in school, residential and community facilities.

Pierre Stolz, BA, has been Executive Director of the Australian Foundation on Alcoholism and Drug Dependence since 1974. Born in France of Swiss parents, he has extensive experience and qualifications in general and psychiatric nursing, therapeutic communities, and school and community education. He has always been especially concerned with early intervention techniques and programs.

Preface

Humans do not like complexity, and they tend to seek easy answers and ready-made solutions whenever possible. Unfortunately, the subject of drug use and misuse really is complex. First, the drug problem is a 'people' problem, and before we can deal with it we must be prepared to understand and deal with people. In doing so, we deal both with the inherent complexity of individual human beings and their behaviour, and with the influence on them of society, culture and history. No one of these is fully understood and the effects of their interaction are virtually unexplored.

Anyone who wants to understand drug use must be prepared for complicated answers. 'Is marijuana (or heroin or alcohol) harmful?' It depends. A number of other questions must be answered first. Under what circumstances is it harmful? To whom? In what dosage? And what do you mean by 'harmful'?

Similarly, the question 'How many people misuse drugs?' has no simple answer. What drugs? What do you mean by misuse? How do you propose to survey the population to identify these people?

Finally, 'Do we, today, have a drug problem?' Yes, but with qualifications. First, the drug problem is not unique to our time. Drug use is very much a part of our cultural history; indeed, a substantial part of our technological progress has come about as a result of the search for more and newer psychoactive substances. Drugs have been used therapeutically for centuries. They have also been misused, both legally and illegally. What is new in our time is their greater availability, the generality of their use, and the increasing involvement of progressively younger age groups.

Second, we need to distinguish between legal and illegal drugs. We have a considerable problem with drugs that may be purchased without restriction (pain killers, laxatives and vitamins) and with those that are relatively freely available on prescription (antianxiety drugs, stimulants and sleeping tablets). The problem with illegal drugs is statistically very much smaller. Consider the following figures. In 1978, the Sydney City Coroners Court, which has jurisdiction over an area inhabited by about three million people, performed 1308 inquests into cases of unnatural death. A total of 172 of these deaths were attributed either to suicide through drug overdose or to accidental poisoning by drugs liable to illegal use. Drug-related deaths, therefore, form some 15 per cent of the unnatural deaths, a significant figure. On the other hand, while no one would consider mortality statistics alone an adequate estimate of the size of the drug problem, 172 drug-related deaths among three million people does not seem to be very many, especially when we compare it with an annual road toll several times that, for the same population.

Nevertheless, the prevention and treatment programs directed at illegal drugs are already sizeable and there is periodic pressure to expand them further despite evidence that the upsurge in drug use seems to have lost impetus. At the same time, Australia, like many other countries, is experiencing a large alcohol problem. About a half of our annual road deaths are directly attributable to misuse of alcohol. Yet the alcohol problem has so far not elicited particularly determined counter-measures, and the treatment programs available are not especially innovative.

Third, we must maintain a proper perspective. Drug misusers are a heterogeneous group and they show a continuum of problems from minimal to severe. More importantly, most people do not have *problems* with either illegal drugs or alcohol. This is not to suggest that they do not use drugs or alcohol. It it essential to realise that legitimate use and even experimentation with drugs is quite different from misuse. So we must not over-react. For those who misuse any drug, legal or illegal, the problem is personal, often tragic and has widespread repercussions for their families, friends and others who may be victimised by this behaviour. All these people deserve our compassion and care and there are enough of them to strain our presently available resources. Nevertheless, they are a statistical minority and there is no evidence to suggest that society as a whole is plunging headlong into intoxication.

Drug misuse is a highly emotional issue. Few topics arouse more anxiety, anger or irrationality. Drug use is a favorite subject for the mass media and always provides good political capital. Some people discuss it with open-mindedness but far too many react with a mixture of morbid fascination and moral outrage that makes even the simplest examination of facts difficult. Lack of sophistication or ignorance cannot fully explain this phenomenon, for it may be found equally among professionals and the public. The answers must be sought not in the nature of drugs or drug users but in the forces that have shaped society. Drug problems are people problems and each person who intends to address this issue seriously, whether from an intellectual or a practical perspective, must be prepared to take a hard look at his or her own attitudes, beliefs and values.

This book was prepared for those individuals who will be dealing directly with people who use and misuse drugs. It arose from a Continuing Education program offered jointly by Macquarie University and the Australian Foundation for Alcohol and Drug Dependence especially for people who intend to work in this field in some helping capacity. This includes not only professional drug and alcohol counsellors but teachers, employers, union officials, doctors, clergy, police officers, parents and concerned members of the public.

For these reasons, this book is neither a manual nor a handbook. Its approach is multidisciplinary because that is the nature of the problem, but it is not intended to give expertise in any of the many relevant areas. Nor is any attempt made to provide a compendium of the drugs subject to misuse or of the many strategies that might be used in treatment or prevention. Rather, the aim has been to demystify the technical aspects and present the broadest possible range of facts, attitudes and opinions on the drug problem and solutions to it. No prior information is needed to study this field, but an open mind is essential.

No book can pretend to be unbiased. In this one, my own biases—as a neuro-psychobiologist, a psychopharmacologist, a university teacher and an administrator concerned with the professional training of alcohol and drug workers—will be apparent, as will be the biases of a private person who has made certain decisions and developed particular attitudes about the use of psychoactive chemicals. Within these biases, I have nevertheless made every effort to follow the rules of scientific evidence in presenting the issues. My primary goal has been simply to separate and discuss the facts and themes, and help each reader to reach a rational point of view on the subject.

Many people helped produce this book. I owe much to my colleagues, especially those in the sociological and anthropological areas, who have guided me from the narrow confines of hard science to a broader and I hope clearer view of the world.

My students throughout the years have contributed more than they know, and to them must go my special thanks. They were the guinea-pigs on whom these ideas were first tested, and without that none of this would have been possible.

My co-authors, Les Drew, John Howard and Pierre Stolz gave me the greatest co-operation an editor could ask for in producing excellent chapters within tight deadlines. Kathy Hyland expertly typed the manuscript, and Bill Farber patiently read and re-read it and saved me from myself on countless occasions.

To all these people, my sincere thanks.

Jara Krivanek

1 Drugs and their use
Some basics

Almost every aspect of drug use and misuse produces controversy. Beliefs about drugs are sometimes without real foundation, often irrational and always maintained with tenacity and passion. Despite the ready availability of reasonably unbiased information, ignorance about drugs remains widespread. Public attitudes are dominated by oversimplification. People generally fail to distinguish one drug from another; substances as diverse as marijuana and heroin may be spoken of as 'narcotics'. More importantly, there is a general failure to distinguish one drug user from another. Many people sincerely believe, for example, that an alcoholic must drink spirits if not methyl alcohol and must resemble the social derelicts of skid row. Very few alcoholics fit this image. Many are young, highly successful and attractive—the exact opposite of the popular stereotype.

Definitions of drugs are largely traditional and only partly scientific. Understanding their actions requires at least as much knowledge of drug users and their society as of chemistry or physiology. Patterns of drug use differ markedly with social standing, and each subculture has a characteristic attitude to both the general phenomenon and specific aspects of it. Each subculture also develops and perpetuates different though overlapping bodies of 'drug lore'. As with all mythologies, such lore contains elements of fact, fiction and value judgement, and the meaning of the word 'drug' is neither simple nor straightforward.

What is a drug?

Drugs are chemicals, but not all chemicals are drugs. Popular definitions normally exclude substances naturally present in the body, though some of these, for example the hormones, may be used medically. In the first instance, therefore, drugs are substances introduced into the body. From this category we further exclude foods in whatever form, and necessary components of the diet such as vitamins and salt, even though these may be taken in forms and ways unrelated to ordinary eating. Also excluded are chemicals used to flavour, colour and preserve food. Among non-food substances, we exclude from the definition chemicals which may be accidentally or unwittingly consumed, breathed or otherwise absorbed into the body in the course of everyday living, even though these might be called drugs in other contexts. Initially, therefore, a drug might be defined as *a substance introduced into the body knowingly and not as a food.*

It is already apparent that designation of a substance as a drug depends importantly on the purpose for which it is used. This may be stated quite specifically. One of the most influential definitions is that set out in the Pure Food and Drug Act of 1906, in which a drug is ' ... *any substance or a mixture of substances intended to be used for the cure, mitigation or prevention of disease* ... '.

A number of problems arise from such a definition. First, are we to assume that a substance used for any other purpose is not a drug? Second, what do we mean by disease and who decides whether it is present or not?

Disease usually implies over- or under-activity relative to some normal state, but how is this to be defined? Are we referring to individuals or to populations? Relative to his or her own subjective standards, a person may feel ill or well, but this may or may not be accepted as illness or health relative to some population norm. Middle-class adolescents caught in the alienating bind of pressure to achieve in a world that seems to offer no predictable future may feel mentally and even physically ill, but the message from society is that they have every reason to be well: youth, education, money, all the trimmings of the good life. Conversely, the manic person, brimming over with subjective elation and grandiose plans, will generally be considered ill and may be institutionalised. In such cases, are we to accept society's definition of health or the individual's? If we accept the former, unwanted drugs may be forced on manic persons and adolescents may be penalised for using drugs they subjectively feel they need.

Further complications arise because there are often alternative and equally acceptable normalities. Thus, pregnancy and non-pregancy are both normal states and drugs exist to help achieve either. Which will be chosen depends on personal and social factors. In addition, although normality may be typical, it is not necessarily the most desirable. A certain level of anxiety may be normal, but less may be desirable; some degree of alertness may be normal, but more may be desirable.

Given all these problems, it is not surprising that most scientifically-minded people retreat behind very broad definitions of drugs as *any substances that alter structure or function in living organisms.* Such definitions will undoubtedly stand the test of time, but they seem too general to be practically useful. The alternative is simply to define as a drug *any substance that people consider to be a drug,* with the understanding that this will change from culture to culture and from time to time.

In current Western cultures, the word 'drug' is likely to evoke one of two images. One is that of medication for sickness. Implicit in this concept is the idea that the drug is prescribed by some knowledgeable person such as a doctor, chemist or mother, and that it is to be used in specified amounts and ways. In this context, the terms 'medicine' or 'the prescription' are as likely to be used as 'drug'. The second and probably more common image is that of illegally obtained substances used irresponsibly for hedonistic purposes by people stereotyped as young, antisocial and at least amoral if not actually immoral.

Few people think of alcohol and nicotine as drugs and even fewer see tea or coffee in this way. Nevertheless, the use of coffee was banned in seventeenth century England, and as recently as 1920 it was illegal for New York City women to use tobacco in public. Alcohol has been prohibited at various times in the West and continues to be so in the Muslim world and in certain Western subcultures. There is also strong evidence that alcohol and tobacco are the primal drugs in the progression from non-use to illegal drug use.

The important point is that most societies accept the use of some substances for social, recreational purposes and these substances will not ordinarily be seen as drugs. What these substances are and under what conditions they are used is very much a matter of history and cultural attitudes. Their chemical properties or effects are relatively unimportant. Consider alcohol, a preferred recreational substance in Western cultures. Many of its supposed benefits as a food, medicine and aphrodisiac have little basis in fact. Most of its value is either symbolic or directly attributable to its tranquillising and disinhibiting actions. Other tranquillisers (Valium, for examply) duplicate its tension-reducing properties, but they have no similar social connotation. Other intoxicants (marijuana, for instance) also seem to facilitate social intercourse, but these appear alien and dangerous to most people. Such alternatives are 'drugs', their bad effects are exaggerated and their positive effects ignored or denied. Exactly the reverse is true of alcohol, which is entrenched in the popular mind as a substance that promotes enjoyment and conviviality. Its bad effects tend to be ignored, minimised or diffused in jokes.

These arguments about definition are not just academic niceties. How drugs, their use and misuse are defined has the greatest impact on who is to be held responsible for dealing with these issues and in what ways.

How do drugs act?

The primary action of a drug is the triggering of a series of chemical changes, but only the physiological or behavioural result of these changes is usually designated the drug effect. Because almost all drugs produce several such results, definition of a drug effect depends on the frame of reference and/or the interest of the investigator. The intended result of a drug is usually designated the *main effect*, and drugs are often classified according to its nature. Thus, barbiturates are sedative-hypnotics: their main effect is depressant and sleep-producing. Unwanted results are *side effects*. These are not necessarily smaller or less important. The distinction is always relative and depends on the purpose for which the drug is used. When morphine is used as an analgesic, the reduced intestinal motility it produces is a side effect. However, morphine is also used to treat diarrhoea, without any specific intent to relieve pain.

Historically, a substance produced its effects in one of three ways. It could physically resemble or have some of the characteristics of the desired object or state. The aphrodisiac properties of mandrake root were attributed to its supposed likeness to the human form, and ancient drug pushers were apparently no more honest than modern ones: the author of the *Grete Herball* (published in England in 1526) commented that 'nature never gave form or shape of mankind to an herb. But it is of truth that some hath shaped figures by craft'.

A substance could also be effective by virtue of its physical location. In sixteenth century England, Dr Stone experimented with extracts of willow bark as a cure for rheumatism—not because he was aware of the anti-inflammatory properties of the salicylic acid it contains but because willows grow in wet places where aches and pains abound, and 'many natural maladies carry their cures along with them, or... their remedies lie not far from their causes'.

Finally, a substance might have good or evil powers granted it by gods or demons. Medieval herbals are filled with catalogues of them. Dr Stone believed that the presence of willow trees in wet land was the 'intention of Providence', and the Native American Church, which is a variant of Christianity, now teaches that Christ endowed the peyote cactus with its mystical powers.

The general modern concept of drug action, however, is that drugs achieve their effects by interacting with one or more 'receptor' sites somewhere in the body. Receptors can be various, but they are usually normal chemical components of tissues. A drug adds nothing new to the body: it merely accentuates or suppresses activities that are already occurring. No drug can produce an effect of which the body or brain is incapable. The essentially chemical reaction of drug and receptor triggers more complex reactions of tissues and eventually manifests as some physical or behavioural change.

These changes can take several forms. First, some pre-existing physical or psychological condition may be exacerbated. Drugs can act synergistically with a variety of heart conditions and epilepsies, for instance. A perennially controversial issue is whether they can precipitate psychosis. When drug-related psychosis occurs, it is not specific to the drug and typically takes the form of paranoid schizophrenia. It is uncommon in narcotics users, but occurs relatively frequently in association with misuse of all other recreationally used drugs. Can drugs cause psychosis in a mentally healthy individual? There is no clear answer, but an honest approach seems to be to ask whether anyone is free of conscious or unconscious fears and anxieties. The evidence is overwhelming that if a drug user's pre-drug adjustment is marginal the probability of such a reaction is very much higher.

Second, the drug may directly alter organ function. The organs may be peripheral (eyes, lungs, skin and so on), or the target of drug action may be the brain. Alterations in brain function may show up as peripheral organ change. For instance, both opiates and barbiturates produce respiratory depression not by direct action on the lungs but by inhibition of the breathing centers in the brain. More usually, however, drug effects on the brain take the form of some sort of behavioural change.

The nature of the behavioural change varies. Sensory and motor functions are usually altered quite specifically and predictably. Thus coordination disorders, disturbance of gait and alterations in reflexes will appear quite generally when the sedatives are misused. Effects on more complex functions, however, show much less regularity. The physical arrangement of the brain is partly responsible. Different areas show a good deal of functional specialization. We can speak of areas concerned with emotion, memory, intellect and so on, and because of this localization quite dissimilar drugs can produce comparable effects. For instance, all higher brain function depends on the operation of centres concerned with arousal. If a drug has a direct action here, as the barbiturates, alcohol and amphetamine do, it will have a general depressant or stimulant effect on *all* activities.

At the same time, the brain's functional systems are both interdependent and plastic. The function of each depends on what is going on elsewhere and the functional modes change over time. This means that the effects of drugs, however specific in terms of chemistry or location of action, will not be readily predictable from the standpoint of individual behaviour. Thus, the highest brain centres generally operate by inhibiting the more primitive, lower ones. Developmental maturation involves increasing inhibition of certain thoughts, feelings and behaviours by the cerebral cortex. Removal of such inhibition will result in re-emergence of the inhibited material. Alcohol, barbiturates and the depressant drugs all inhibit the cortex and therefore disinhibit behaviour. Socially appropriate actions, normal critical thinking and emotionality will all be disrupted, but the exact form this will take depends on what was inhibited originally in that individual. The old adage of 'in vino veritas' is based on sound physiology.

The effects of drugs on the brain, then, can be described in terms of general depressant or stimulant actions. It is also possible to isolate a generalised 'acute brain syndrome' of delirium, confusion and disorientation. This clears quickly, has few if any long-term effects and presumably reflects a temporary derangement of general brain function. By contrast, the 'organic brain syndrome' of lessened acuity, short attention span, emotional lability and impaired recent memory is thought to reflect direct damage. It is clinically similar to senile dementia, may have similar causes and is largely irreversible. Apart from these syndromes, behavioural changes produced by drugs are highly individual and vary with the personality, mood, past experience and present situation of the user.

What determines the observable drug effect?

The nature of drug effects varies in size and quality with four major factors: dose, time since the drug was taken, the purity of the drug and status of the user.

Dose

Other things being equal, the larger the dose the greater the effect. However, this is somewhat modified by the way the drug is given. Smaller doses are required if the drug is injected directly into the bloodstream because delivery to receptor sites is rapid and there will be less chance of either binding to irrelevant sites or destruction of the drug by the body's normal metabolic processes.

Dose also to some extent determines the type of symptoms. In general, the effect seen with very high doses is so different from that produced by low or moderate ones that different families of receptors are probably being affected in each case.

Interacting with all these dose-related factors is the degree of *tolerance* developed. Tolerance is defined as a decreased responsiveness to any effect of a drug. Tolerance may develop simultaneously to shared effects of related drugs ('cross-tolerance'), but it does not usually develop equally to all the effects of a drug. Thus, tolerance to the analgesic and euphoriant effects of the narcotics develops quite rapidly, and increasing amounts of the drug are needed to maintain the initial level of these effects. Much less tolerance develops to the constipating effects and almost none to the effect on the pupils of the eyes. The development of tolerance is not necessarily undesirable: long term therapy with many drugs is made much easier because the initial nausea they produce is subject to tolerance.

The rate at which tolerance develops depends on both dose and frequency of administration. Ordinarily, a fair number of reasonably closely spaced exposures is required. The degree of tolerance developed varies from drug to drug, and depends partly on the specific effects involved. With narcotics, tolerance to the respiratory and cardiac depressant effects parallels that to the analgesic and euphoriant effects, and tolerant individuals can receive doses that would be lethal in ordinary people. With barbiturates, tolerance develops rapidly to the sedative effects but this is not matched by an equal tolerance to depression of various vital functions and the potentially lethal dose for tolerant people is not much greater than that for non-tolerant ones.

Some degree of tolerance develops with repeated exposure to most drugs and many produce it to a marked extent, but there are also some reports of 'reverse' tolerance. It is claimed, for example, that less marijuana is required by experienced users. Presumably this reflects a learning process (in how to smoke or how to focus on the drug effect), but more physiological explanations are possible. The active principle of marijuana is highly fat-soluble, and it is likely that a significant percentage of it will remain dissolved in body fat (including that of the brain) for a considerable time after the first dose. Additional doses taken soon after the first build on the drug still present in the body, and a smaller amount will be needed to produce the effect. Tolerance disappears gradually when drug use is discontinued.

The nature of tolerance is not fully understood. Usually, the effect to which tolerance has developed can be restored by an increase in drug dose. This suggests that the sensitivity of the receptors responsible for the drug effect is unimpaired, but that the drug's access to them is altered ('drug disposition tolerance'). Decreased absorption and increased elimination might be responsible, but the best documented mechanism is increased metabolic rate. Most drugs induce their own metabolism. When a drug is taken repeatedly, its breakdown becomes increasingly efficient and more of the drug must be taken to maintain the desired level of effect. In addition, some drugs, especially the barbiturates, can act as general metabolic inducers. Other drugs taken with them will have smaller and briefer effects unless their dose is appropriately adjusted.

In some cases of tolerance, however, the original effect cannot be restored at any dose for a considerable time ('cellular tolerance'). This may happen with amphetamines. Such tolerance can only be explained by assuming basic changes in tissue sensitivity.

Time since the drug was taken

In general, symptoms diminish with time, but the various effects of a drug may show quite different time courses. For example, the physiological effects of the hallucinogenic drugs peak about two hours after ingestion and are generally gone after three hours. The psychedelic effects peak four to five hours after ingestion and decline after about eight hours.

The time course of a drug's effects may be complicated by the presence of *psychological and/or physical dependence*. The two forms of dependence are unrelated, and although they often occur together either can be present alone.

Psychological dependence is a state in which the presence of the drug or some behaviour or situation associated with its use is essential to normal psychological functioning. It can be produced by any drug, with or without concomitant tolerance.

Physical dependence is a state in which the presence of the drug is essential to normal physiological functioning, and it is produced to a marked degree by relatively few classes of drugs: narcotics, sedatives, alcohol and antianxiety agents. Again, tolerance may or may not be associated with the phenomenon.

The physiological basis of physical dependence is poorly understood. Several different mechanisms are probably involved. At present, we infer the presence of physical dependence from the occurrence of a distinct physical *withdrawal syndrome when the drug is discontinued*. Definition is critical here. The withdrawal syndrome from narcotics or barbiturates is obvious and dramatic. On the other hand, when amphetamine is discontinued abruptly there is a vague but regularly recurring syndrome that includes changes in the electroencephalogram, fatigue, anorexia and depression. The person is clearly not 'normal', but whether this qualifies as a 'withdrawal syndrome' is a matter of opinion.

The withdrawal syndrome consists of purposive and non-purposive symptoms. The *purposive symptoms* appear first, generally at about the time when the next dose of the drug would ordinarily be taken. They are directed at getting the drug and include complaints, pleas, simulation and manipulation. They are in general as varied as the imagination of the drug-using population, and their intensity, type and frequency varies with the setting.

The *non-purposive symptoms* form the definable withdrawal syndrome. They are relatively constant from one person to another, independent of both setting and observer, and include both physiological and psychological features. In general, the symptoms are opposite to the usual effects of the drug and their timing is reasonably predictable. With heroin, for instance, non-purposive symptoms first appear about eight hours after the last dose as yawning, perspiration, tear and nasal secretion. A period of sleep usually follows at about 14 hours. The major withdrawal symptoms of cramps, vomiting, diarrhoea, muscle spasm and disorganisation of temperature, blood pressure and cardiac function peak between 48 and 72 hours and subside slowly over the following several days.

Withdrawal from drugs that produce physical dependence is not necessarily more difficult or more dangerous than from drugs that produce only psychological dependence. Gradual withdrawal from the narcotics, although uncomfortable, is relatively safe. Withdrawal from amphetamine, however gradual, is often dangerous because of the depression and suicidal thinking that frequently accompany it. Psychological dependence is also more enduring and it is this, not physical dependence, that leads the ex-user to resume use after a period of abstinence.

Two further points about physical dependence are noteworthy. One is the phenomenon of *cross-dependence*. If physical dependence develops to a particular drug, the withdrawal syndrome triggered by its abrupt discontinuation may be terminated not only by that drug but by related ones. The degree to which another drug may substitute may be partial or complete, and seems to be related more to the drug's physiological effects than to its chemistry. Thus methadone, with its broad spectrum of physiological effects, substitutes completely for heroin. Codeine, although closely related, has a much narrower range of effects and would only partly substitute for heroin. Once substitution has been made, any withdrawal effect will be that of the substitution drug, not of the drug that initiated the physical dependence.

The second point is the fact that although the character of physical dependence (as measured by the withdrawal syndrome) depends on drug and dose, it also varies significantly with the drug's rate of elimination from the body. Short-acting drugs produce the most severe dependence (withdrawal syndrome). This is apparently less a question of the effects of the drug itself than of the time the tissues have to adjust to its presence or absence. Methadone, a long-acting drug, ordinarily produces a relatively mild withdrawal syndrome. If, however, it is abruptly displaced from its receptors by a competing drug such as nalorphine, the resulting withdrawal is as severe as that from, say, the much shorter-acting heroin. The principle has obvious relevance to the concept of substitution discussed above.

Purity of the drug

Multiple versus single drug administration. Multiple drug administration is becoming the rule. Such use may be deliberate. The specific effects of different drugs may be desired simultaneously. The 'speedball' mixture (formerly heroin and cocaine; now more usually heroin and amphetamine) is one example. Alternately, two drugs may be taken together to potentiate each other, particularly if one is more expensive or more difficult to obtain than the other. Barbiturates will potentiate the narcotics. Almost all sedative-hypnotics potentiate each other and the antianxiety drugs as well. In its pharmacological actions, alcohol closely resembles the sedative-hypnotics and will markedly potentiate them, a fact that is unfortunately not generally appreciated. Finally, one drug may be taken to counteract the effects of another. A frequent combination is a sedative followed by a stimulant.

A number of problems arise from such practices. One is the increasing prevalence of simultaneous dependence on more than one drug. This makes diagnosis and treatment more complex, especially as, for reasons not completely understood, multiple drug users tend to over-estimate the amount of stimulants or narcotics they take, and underestimate their intake of sedatives. Another problem is drug interaction. Barbiturates, for example, are general metabolic inducers. A drug taken with a barbiturate will have to be taken in larger than normal doses to be effective. Should the barbiturate then be discontinued and the dose of the second drug not adjusted appropriately, there is be a real danger of overdose.

Serious problems arise when multiple drug use is not deliberate, that is, when the user is not consciously attempting to potentiate or counteract drug effects or obtain several effects simultaneously. The use of over-the-counter medication or social drugs such as alcohol with prescribed or illegally obtained drugs presents special difficulties. For instance, about 500 mg/day for 30 days is the intake of hypnotic drugs required to produce physical dependence, and withdrawal from these drugs can be life-threatening. The 'barbiturate equivalents' of hypnotics are as follows: 100 mg barbiturate = 300 mg Mandrax = 80 mg Librium = 20 mg Valium = 1360 ml (4 cans) beer = 2/3 bottle wine = 170 ml spirits = indeterminate (and individually variable) amount of depression and/or fatigue. Physical dependence of the hypnotic type could thus be achieved without taking a particularly large amount of any one substance.

Adulteration. 'Street' drugs are almost never what they are advertised to be. Sometimes the actual drug obtained is different from the one sought, though in the same general category. Thus, two-thirds of drugs sold as mescaline or psilocybin are LSD; THC, the active principle of marijuana, is almost never available and phencyclidine is the usual substitute. More usually, the required drug is adulterated with another active drug with dissimilar actions. Psychedelics are commonly adulterated with strychnine and the anticholinergics; cocaine with local anaesthetics; amphetamine with caffeine or strychnine; heroin with barbiturates, quinine or strychnine. Such adulteration can produce potentiation, counteraction, masking and general confusion of effects.

Even if not adulterated, street drugs are invariably 'filled' to some extent. In general, if a 'hit' of LSD offered is big enough to see, it has been filled. The fillers are various: sugars, talc and cornstarch are common. Insoluble fillers (most commercially available tablets are also filled) are especially problematic if the drug is destined for intravenous injection. Even if the crushed material is drawn up through cotton wool some solid material will still be injected. This will lodge in the narrowest blood vessels, especially those of the lungs, and over time the amount is significant. Breathing will be reduced and irreversible damage may result. Unsterile procedures can also give rise to an assortment of infections, some with major complications.

The problem in all these cases is to separate the symptoms that arise from the actions of the drug and those that derive from other factors surrounding its use.

Status of the user

This includes all aspects of functioning, both physical and psychological. Such factors as age, sex, genetic background and presence or absence of disease interact in significant ways with the action of drugs to produce unique symptoms. However, psychological and environmental variables are especially relevant, and a few generalizations may be made.

First, the type of activity the person is engaged in is important. The more complex or abstract the behaviour, the more likely it is to be affected by drugs. An individual suspected of driving under the influence of alcohol and requested to 'walk the line' is being given the benefit of every doubt. Alcohol levels that would disrupt this relatively simple task are considerably higher than those that would impair one's ability to react appropriately to an emergency on the road.

Second, one must consider the person's familiarity with the task in question. Some behaviours are so well learned that only coma will disrupt them. Reacting to one's own name would be an example. Simple activities that are part of an individual's life, especially physical tasks, are relatively insensitive to drug effects.

Motivation is important in two ways. The first is a matter of degree. Within limits, the more important the outcome of an act to the drug user, the less will the drug affect it. The drink-driving suspect walking the line may actually do better than a non-drinker.

The second factor is type of motivation. The pleasure and pain systems of the brain are anatomically and chemically distinct, and different drugs tend to affect these differentially. The chemical affinities of amphetamine, for example, suggest that it would excite the pleasure system. This is, on reflection, a very mixed blessing. Unspecific pleasure system activation would mean that all activities would seem more desirable, with the result that the user would not stay with any one for very long before another claimed his or her attention. Opiates such as heroin seem to exert part of their action by blocking the receptors of the pain system. The result would be not so much active pleasure as relief from physical or mental discomfort.

Expectation about the drug experience—a person's 'mental set'—is critical. Such expectations can be solely responsible for the type of effect experienced. 'Placebo' is the term generally used for inert substances that, in the words of an 1811 medical text, are 'given to please rather than benefit the patient'. With an appropriate setting, such substances can produce a real pharmacology, complete with main and side effects and even symptoms of physical dependence. Major physiological changes and many psychological changes can occur. When the substance has some discernible physiological effects, the possibilities are multiplied enormously. At the height of the psychedelic drug scene, some teenagers 'tripped' (presumably to their satisfaction) on strychnine. The muscle twitches which low doses of this drug produce were being taken as indicative of the effects of LSD, which none of them had experienced.

This does not mean that the effects of different drugs cannot be distinguished, but simply that different substances can serve the same purpose in different people. The converse is also true: the same substance can have contrasting effects on different people. For instance, over-the-counter sleep inducers and tranquillisers contain generally identical chemicals. In the USA, about one million people use sleep inducers each week and about half a million use tranquillisers, but the groups are entirely different. The sleep inducer users are distributed evenly over race and socio-economic level and the major consumers are housewives of all ages and people over 50. The tranquilliser takers are predominantly white, middle-to-upper socio-economic level females, employed women rather than housewives, and frequency of use decreases sharply after age 50. Only a small proportion would qualify as 'drug addicts'; the important point is that physically and socio-economically different persons are at risk for addiction to the same substances advertised as having different effects.

'Placebo effects', once narrowly defined as those arising from the giving of inert medication, have taken on a broader meaning. Most recent definitions extend the term to include the effects of any non-drug variable such as personal set, the physical or social setting and the ritual associated with drug taking. Observers are as susceptible to such placebo effects as drug users. It is all too easy to attribute symptoms to a supposed drug user that are more appropriate to some stereotype that exists in the observer's mind than to the reality of the situation. It is a regrettable fact that an expectation of misuse of alcohol or marijuana can create evidence of such misuse. An open mind is as important, indeed perhaps more so, than highly developed powers of observation.

References

Barchas, J., Berger, P., Ciaranello, R.D. & Elliott, G. (eds.), *Psychopharmacology: from Theory to Practice*, Oxford University Press, 1977.

Goodman, L. & Gilman, A., *The Pharmacological Basis of Therapeutics*, 6th ed., Macmillan Publishing Co., 1980.

Hafen, B. & Peterson, B., *Medicines and drugs*, 2nd ed., Lea & Febiger, 1978.

Julien, R., *A Primer of Drug Action*, W.H. Freeman & Co., 1975.

Ray, O.S., *Drugs, Society and Human Behavior*, 2nd ed., C.V. Mosby Co., 1978.

2 Symptoms of drug use and misuse

When drugs are discussed, the most frequently asked questions are: What does an addict look like? How can I tell if my client, friend, child or prospective employee drinks too much or is using marijuana, narcotics or stimulants?

A first task is to determine why the question is being asked, and some of the reasons are less than palatable. There can be no doubt that some employers want easy identification methods to sack 'undesirable' employees. Some physicians and community workers want to be able to refer 'untreatable' people away from their practices. Some public officials are looking for scapegoats; others for fame. Some parents and teachers want excuses to cover their inept handling of children.

Others genuinely want to 'help', but why? What is the problem and who has it: the user, or the observer? If a person uses or misuses drugs, what is threatened: individual health, personal development, usefulness to society, social security, morals, traditional values? The issue of individual versus community rights is critical and must be tackled in each helping relationship. Who in fact is benefiting from the exercise?

Whatever the motives for seeking to identify the drug user, the process is not simple. Short of chemical screening, few if any drugs produce definitive, objective symptoms that would permit unambiguous diagnosis. This cannot be emphasised too strongly. A surprising number of both professional and volunteer workers in the field agonise over their apparent lack of some esoteric clue that their more assured colleagues seem to possess.

Chronic, excessive use of alcohol and other drugs is often accompanied by gross pathology in almost all organ systems, but the drug can rarely be seen as the sole cause. The symptoms of drug taking are largely behavioural, with all the individual variability this implies. Some of them do not even appear in individuals but relate to their physical and social environment. To further complicate matters, almost every aspect of drug use presents a behavioural continuum. The quantity of alcohol consumed, for instance, is sometimes taken as an indicator of 'alcoholism'. However, alcohol consumption is smoothly distributed in the population. Some people do not drink; others drink excessively; most are somewhere in between, and there is no evidence of a separate peak at the excessive end to define 'alcoholics'. Because the population pattern of most symptoms of excessive drinking is similar, the best one can usually do is add up the adverse consequences to yield some kind of 'problem score'. Whether one then wishes to designate a particular score as defining the 'alcoholic' is separate issue.

Anatomy of a drug: alcohol

We are a generation of drug takers and far too many of us are drug misusers. However we assess drug problem—number of users and misusers; availability; cost in dollars; problems created for individuals and societies—alcohol is by far the most important. Incredibly, most people's knowledge of it is little more than a combination of their personal experience and the alcohol mythology of their time and culture.

Alcohol is an ancient drug. Alcoholic beverages have been and continue to be made by nearly every culture. They have a long and respectable history in medicine as sedatives and anesthetics, and in their original form contributed important vitamins and minerals as well as energy to the diet. From the earliest times, however, the chief attraction of alcohol lay in its mood-changing properties. Its use in religious ritual predates written history, and this traditional role in ceremony spread into all aspects of human life. Alcohol became mandatory not only in worship and the practice of magic but also in the rites of birth, initiation, marriage and death, political events, festivals and simpler hospitality—in other words, all important occasions—and it retains that position to this day. And, as in ancient times, the everyday use of alcohol can sometimes lead to personal and social problems.

There are four basic types of alcoholic beverage: beer, wine, fortified wine and distilled spirits. All contain alcohol and water. They differ in the quantity and type of 'congeners' (substances that add color, taste and smell) and, most obviously, they differ in strength. Strength may be defined as percentage of pure alcohol by volume. The higher the percentage of alcohol, the greater the strength, and the less the beverage tends to contain congeners. Spirits are mainly alcohol and water, with only traces of other substances. The relative average strength of common Australian beverages is shown in Table 2.1.

The considerable differences in the strength of beer and wine relative to spirits often lead people to assume that beer and wine are 'safer'. However, while these may contain less alcohol by volume, they are also drunk in greater quantities. The quantities sold as 'standard drinks' in hotels are shown in Table 2.1, and a little calculation shows that a standard glass of beer contains almost exactly the same amount of alcohol as a 'nip' of spirits: about 10 grams. A few of the physical effects of alcohol vary with the type of beverage used. For instance, beer tends to irritate to stomach less than spirits because its alcohol is less concentrated. However, all the psychological effects, most of the physiological ones and certainly all the problems arising from alcohol misuse depend on the amount of alcohol ingested, not the form in which it is taken.

Pharmacology

Alcohol requires no digestion and is absorbed unchanged from the stomach and small intestine. Its kilojoules—about 420 per standard drink—cannot be converted into fat or protein. They are used preferentially to meet the body's energy requirements, while the energy content of other foods is converted for storage. In other words, alcohol alone cannot produce obesity; it is the food taken with it that is stored as fat.

Figure 2.1 Metabolism of Alcohol

alcohol —enzyme 1→ acetaldehyde —enzyme 2→ acetic acid ——→ water + carbon dioxide + energy

Only about two per cent of the alcohol ingested is eliminated from the body unchanged. Most of it is broken down in the liver. A simplified version of the process is shown in Figure 2.1. As with all metabolic processes, each step requires the presence of a specific enzyme and it is the availability of these rather than the amount of alcohol ingested that determines the rate at which alcohol is eliminated. Enzyme 1 (alcohol dehydrogenase) is critical in this regard. In moderate drinkers, its activity permits the breakdown of roughly 12.5 ml of alcohol per hour, that is, about the alcohol content of a standard

Table 2.1 Relative average strength of common Australian alcoholic beverages

Beverage	Average alcohol content	% alcohol	Volume of 'standard drink'
Spirits (e.g., vodka)	32 g (40 ml)/100 ml	40%	30 ml (approx 1 oz)
Fortified wine (e.g., sherry, port)	16 g (20 ml)/100 ml	20%	60 ml (approx 2 oz)
Table wines	8 g (10 ml)/100 ml	10%	120 ml (approx 4 oz)
Beers	3.8 g (4.8 ml)/100 ml	5%	285 ml (approx 8 oz)
Light ('low alcohol') beers	3.1 g (3.9 ml)/100 ml	4%	285 ml (approx 8 oz)

drink. With chronic intake, the tissue of the liver proliferates somewhat and more enzymes will be available. The breakdown of alcohol (and of many other drugs) will therefore be somewhat faster and this may account for some of the tolerance shown by heavy drinkers.

The product of the first metabolic step, acetaldehyde, is a rather toxic substance and it is increasingly held responsible for some of the effects traditionally attributed to alcohol. There is some evidence that acetaldehyde levels increase with heavy drinking (Raskin, 1975) and acetaldehyde is also the basis of the Antabuse deterrent treatment. The drug Antabuse (disulfiram) blocks enzyme 2 (aldehyde dehydrogenase) in the breakdown pathway. In its presence, alcohol will still be broken down to acetaldehyde, but this will not be processed further and will accumulate. High levels of acetaldehyde produce headache, nausea, breathing difficulties and various other unpleasant symptoms. Many treatment programs urge or require their clients to take Antabuse on the theory that the prospect of an unpleasant reaction will reduce the chance of impulsively taking a drink. The validity of this approach remains controversial. By and large, though, those clients who continue to take Antabuse after completing the treatment program are the ones who usually do not return to drink anyway. They are treatment successes with or without the drug.

Physiological effects

The *immediate effects* of alcohol are relatively minor. The blood vessels dilate, especially the superficial ones in the skin. As this increases heat loss, the user will feel warm although internal body temperature actually falls. The use of alcohol in cold weather to 'keep warm' is thus obviously irrational and may be dangerous if conservation of heat is essential. There are few direct effects on the heart, but a clear diuretic effect on the kidneys has been established by many investigators and most consumers.

The effects on the stomach vary with concentration. Beverages of low strength (up to 10 per cent alcohol) stimulate gastric acid secretion. This may be helpful in debilitated or elderly people, but is clearly inadvisable in persons with peptic ulcers. Higher concentrations (20 per cent or more) tend to inhibit digestion, and strong alcoholic drinks (above 35 per cent) directly irritate the stomach lining. The simultaneous use of alcohol and aspirin is especially undesirable. Aspirin alone tends to produce gastric bleeding and damage, and these effects are much enhanced by the presence of alcohol.

The *chronic, excessive use of alcohol*, on the other hand, is associated with a number of diseases. It has been estimated that alcohol is the major causative factor in primary illness or disability in one third of patients admitted to Australian general hospitals and a significant factor in another third. Comparable figures doubtless hold in medical practices outside hospitals and in the population generally. Most body systems can be affected by excessive alcohol use, but the liver, heart and brain are especially vulnerable.

The liver. Three syndromes are relevant here. Alcohol misuse may result in *hepatitis*, an inflammatory condition accompanied by severe alterations in liver structure and function. *Fatty liver* may develop. Dietary fats are the usual fuel source for the liver, but it prefers alcohol. Under these conditions, the unused fats accumulate in liver cells, sometimes to the point of rupture. Unless cell death occurs, however, fatty liver is completely reversible once alcohol intake ceases. Prolonged excessive intake may produce *cirrhosis*, in which liver cells are replaced by non-functional fibrous tissue. Not all cirrhosis is alcohol-related but a high percentage is. The disease is not reversible, althought stopping the intake of alcohol will retard its progress and decrease the serious effects.

There is considerable controversy about the actual role of alcohol in these effects. The impoverished drinker may not be able to afford food if money is spent on drink. The stomach upsets that typically accompany misuse may cause loss of appetite, and because of the high energy content of alcohol drinkers tend to feel less hungry anyway. The result is that various dietary deficiencies are likely, and these have been blamed for the liver damage. The present position is that in most cases of human liver disease dietary deficiencies and the toxic effects of alcohol interact. However, there is no evidence that even severe protein and vitamin deficiencies can *by themselves* damage the liver.

Women seem to be generally more susceptible to alcohol-related liver disease than men (Klatzky et al, 1977). They exhibit more severe forms of disease, especially alcoholic hepatitis, with a lower daily intake and a shorter history of excessive drinking. The reasons are unclear. Certainly the liver is smaller in women, but there seem to be some real sex differences, especially in sensitivity to infection and inflammation. At the same time, women are more likely than men to be 'secret drinkers' and to conceal their true consumption, so the current findings may not be entirely trustworthy.

The heart. Myocardial infarction occurs when the coronary arteries supplying the heart become clogged and blood supply is interrupted. This is the usual 'heart attack'. The relationship of alcohol to this is complicated. Moderate drinkers (up to four standard drinks per day) appear to have fewer heart attacks than abstainers (Marmot et al, 1981). Also, cessation of moderate or heavy drinking seems to produce a sharp increase in heart attacks. Again, the reasons are not clear. The fact that alcohol dilates blood vessels may be relevant. Alcohol also appears to have some protective action against artherosclerosis.

Before this can be claimed as a 'beneficial' effect of alcohol, however, certain other factors must be considered. Heavy alcohol consumption is clearly associated with increased probability of heart attack. The threshold level is presently unknown, but consumption of more than 120 grams per day clearly puts the drinker at risk. Part of the reason may be hypertension: heavy drinkers are twice as likely to suffer from high blood pressure, an established risk factor in heart disease (Klatzky et al, 1979). It would seem, therefore, that any beneficial effects alcohol may have on blood vessels may be counter-balanced by its hypertensive effects.

The brain. *Wernicke's disease* is the result of bleeding and cell loss in certain parts of the brain. As with all brain damage, the cell loss is permanent. The disorder presents as squinting, involuntary eye movements and ocular paralysis, and because body movement depends heavily on normal vision, there is considerable disturbance of posture and gait as well. The disease is typically accompanied by *peripheral (poly-)neuritis*, a degenerative change effecting the long nerves, particularly those supplying the skin and muscles of the arms and legs. In the early stages, the sufferer complains of numbness, pins-and-needles and tenderness, usually in the feet. The disorder may progress to profound weakness, unsteadiness and inability to walk and even stand without support. A person with this disorder may appear drunk even if no recent drinking has occurred.

Wernicke's disease is often also accompanied by *Korsakoff's psychosis*. Here the dominant signs are loss of memory, inability to learn and general confusion and disorientation about time and place. The intellect is usually preserved, however, and the sufferer may 'confabulate'—make up stories to fill the gaps in memory.

The relationship of alcohol to these brain diseases is probably indirect. They can arise from a variety of pathological causes such as infection, injury, tumors and nutritional deficiencies. The B complex of vitamins, especially thiamine (vitamin B1) seems particularly important. Alcohol relates to this in several ways. As we have seen, heavy drinkers are quite likely to eat poorly. In addition, alcohol interacts directly with thiamine. It impairs the absorption of the vitamin, and because of its diuretic effects impairs the body's limited capacity to store it. To complete the vicious circle, alcohol requires thiamine for its own metabolism.

Therapy with thiamine is of variable value in alcohol-related disease. It is most effective in the early stages. Beyond this, Wernicke's disease and peripheral neuritis respond relatively well; Korsakoff's psychosis poorly if at all.

Other systems. Alcohol misuse is associated with *cancer* of body areas that come into direct contact with it, especially the mouth and throat. Most parts of the *gastrointestinal system* are affected, and one out of three heavy drinkers suffers from chronic gastritis. The lowered resistance of heavy drinkers to pneumonia and other infections is partly caused by malnutrition and liver malfunction, but alcohol also directly interferes with the *immune system*.

Behavioural effects

The behavioural effects of alcohol depend directly on the alcohol concentration in the brain. A direct estimate of this is *blood alcohol level* (BAL). This is calculated as grams of alcohol per millilitre of blood, expressed as a percentage. Thus, a BAL of 0.1 per cent means that there are 100 milligrams of alcohol in each 100 millilitres of blood. There is also a direct relationship between alcohol in breath and BAL, a fact that is put to practical use by the police. One unit of alcohol in breath is equivalent to 2100 units in the blood. The actual effects that will be seen at a particular BAL depend on two factors: the degree of tolerance developed and the rate of BAL rise.

Heavy drinkers can drink large quantities of alcohol without losing control and can perform relatively complex tasks at BALs several times those of moderate drinkers. A classic study (Goldberg, 1943) showed that visual-motor coordination was disrupted at an average BAL of 0.05 per cent in abstainers, 0.07 per cent in moderate drinkers and 0.1 per cent in heavy drinkers. The reasons are not fully understood. The rate of metabolism does increase with use, but not enough to account for such large differences. There is also evidence that some true cellular tolerance develops in brain tissue even if alcohol intake is well spaced. Nevertheless, most of the tolerance developed is probably more apparent than real. Heavy drinkers develop a number of adjustive, cover-up mechanisms to overcome the disruption caused by alcohol. Relative to moderate drinkers, they are generally better motivated to conceal these effects and they have had more practice (Gross, 1977).

In some ways, the development of such functional tolerance is beneficial. With it, the heavy drinker can keep up appearances and carry out duties. On the debit side, although such adjustive mechanisms may work well in familiar circumstances, they often fail under stress or in strange surroundings.

With increasing tolerance, consumption must be escalated to maintain the desired effects and the alcohol will cause increasing damage to liver, heart and brain. Eventually one or all of these systems becomes unable to sustain the level of tolerance, and the body becomes less and less able to cope with alcohol. This lies behind the seeming paradox that many heavy drinkers may eventually become intoxicated on quite small amounts of alcohol.

The observable effects of alcohol also vary with the speed with which BAL rises. Several factors affect this. This first is *body type*. Alcohol is not appreciably stored or eliminated prior to metabolism, and it is distributed in the body fluids. This has two implications. First, a larger person will have a lower BAL given the same intake. Second, with body weight constant, a fatter person (that is, one who has proportionally less fluid) will have a higher BAL. Both these things mean that women will be more affected by alcohol than men. They are generally smaller and carry relatively more fat per unit weight. There may also be a real sex difference in sensitivity.

Second, *stomach contents and type of beverage* make a difference. Food and water in the stomach slow alcohol absorption; the presence of carbonation increases it. Stomach emptying time also varies with its condition, and the emotional state of its owner. Some people show more gastric activity when excited or upset, some less.

Third, *previous drinking* must be taken into account. BAL falls with the rate of metabolism, approximately 12.5 millilitres of alcohol or the content of one standard drink per hour. A more personal figure may be obtained by dividing one's body weight by five times the percentage of alcohol in the beverage used. Either way, the average number of hours to sober up still equals the number of standard drinks taken. Given this relatively fixed rate, an intake of more than one drink per hour will produce a progressive BAL rise, each drink adding on to the previous one. After an evening of heavy drinking, the morning BAL may still be significant, and the addition of even a single drink may raise it beyond, for example, the legal limit for driving.

Finally, *mood, attitude and previous experience with alcohol* must be considered. BAL rise is affected by the mood of the occasion and the company present. The drinker's own ideas about what behaviour is appropriate under the circumstances, and cultural expectations of how people should behave when intoxicated, are especially important.

Intoxication and drunkenness are often used interchangeably, but strictly speaking, intoxication is any effect of alcohol on the brain that is manifested in mood or behaviour. The nature of these effects derives directly from the way alcohol affects nerve cells. It reduces their ability to generate and conduct messages, and its overall effect is depressant. All physical and mental activities are slowed.

This may be seen as good or bad, depending on the drinker and the circumstances. All alcohol users become less self-critical, more self-confident and more likely to take chances. However, there is a simultaneous decrease in alertness and the ability to think logically. This is not always obvious to the drinker at the time, or even later, when sober. Many people, for instance, feel that alcohol helps them think more clearly or drive much better. The correct interpretation is that either they have become less critical of their own performance, or have made a much greater effort than usual to compensate for the effect of alcohol. Of course, if the task in hand is making conversation or trying to impress someone or otherwise coping with some anxiety-producing social situation the deadening of self-criticism may be highly beneficial. With alcohol, the shy person may become confident, the quiet one outgoing, the anxious one more at ease. Still, if alcohol is used regularly to achieve such effects, the development of tolerance will make escalation of consumption almost inevitable.

Symptoms of alcohol misuse

There is no clear dividing line where alcohol use ends and misuse begins, or where benefits stop and problems occur. What constitutes alcohol misuse or a drinking problem has never been adequately defined although innumerable schemes of classification have been proposed. Distinctions have been drawn between alcoholics and chronic alcoholics, alcoholics and alcohol addicts, excessive and problem drinkers, excessive drinking and addiction, addiction and dependence. Some of these issues are discussed below. From the standpoint of diagnosis, however, the only thing definitely different about people for whom alcohol has become a problem is that they drink 'too much'. What this means in terms of symptoms is quite unclear.

The skid row bum stereotype fits less than five per cent of those who would currently be called alcoholics or problem drinkers. The stereotype of an alcoholic as inherently weak, hopelessly dependent, socially incompetent and irrevocably bent on self-destruction is false. So is the concept of the inevitable irreversibility of alcoholism and the presumption that sophisticated, specialist treatment is always required. There is no single set of diagnostic symptoms and several areas of functioning must be taken into account.

There may be, first, some physical signs. The heavy drinker may appear to be flushed, and, after prolonged use, a 'whiskey nose' may develop. The blood vessels in the eyes may be enlarged and the face puffy, especially about the forehead and under the eyes. Fluid accumulation in the membranes of the nose and throat may produce a chronic hoarseness. All these signs, however, are inconstant and not in themselves diagnostic. The heavy drinker, as we have seen, is susceptible to a variety of illnesses, but again none of these is diagnostic. Other causes are always possible.

In general, the most useful signs come from four areas: reaction to cessation of drinking, the actual quantity consumed, the qualitative pattern of drinking and the consequences of the behaviour.

Withdrawal from alcohol. The highly tolerant heavy drinker is likely to experience severe withdrawal on cessation of drinking. This takes the form of the usual 'rebound', both physical and psychological. The general slowing of the intoxicated person is replaced by hyperarousal and hyperactivity, the sedated mood by gross anxieties and fears, the euphoria by depression. The syndrome begins within a few hours after the last drink with tremulousness, especially in the hands, sweating, nausea and anxiety, and these symptoms are usually enough to keep the sufferer drinking if that is possible. With further abstinence, hallucinations and delusions may appear over the next day or so, proceeding to disorientation and delirium. These changes may be persistent or intermittent and amnesia for the episode usually follows. There may be one or more seizures.

Although this syndrome is designated the 'general depressant withdrawal syndrome' (sometimes also withdrawal 'of the barbiturate type', because depressants of all types produce essentially similar withdrawal patterns), it is not a clear-cut entity. There is considerable individual variation in its duration and progress and it blends imperceptibly with the milder rebound effects, colloquially called 'the hangover', that follow any alcohol intake.

As the sedative effects of normal drinking wear off, there is mild arousal, restlessness and sweating, usually accompanied by such toxic alcohol effects as headache and nausea. The rebound effects can be assuaged by the 'hair of the dog' remedy; the toxic effects are unfortunately made worse by more alcohol.

Alcohol alone will produce a hangover. However, its severity is usually exacerbated by such factors as disturbed sleep, indigestion, smoking, and guilt about previous behaviour, often compounded by a certain vagueness about what actually happened. Some beverages, notably those especially rich in congeners, do seem to produce worse hangovers, but there is no evidence that 'mixing drinks' by itself can do so. A person who has mixed some drinks has probably simply drunk too much.

As already discussed, very little can alter the rate at which alcohol is eliminated, that is, the duration of the hangover. The value of the various hangover remedies rests primarily on faith—a placebo effect.

Quantity of alcohol consumed. How much alcohol may be ingested safely is presently controversial. Most authorities agree that an intake of 60 grams per day puts the drinker at risk for physical and psycho-social problems. Many, however, feel that the safe level is considerably lower than this. Most agree that problems are almost inevitable with a daily intake of more than 120 grams per day. Daily drinking and 'binge' drinking can be equally harmful, although binge drinkers do seem somewhat more accident-prone.

Patterns of drinking. As tolerance develops, attempts to keep up BAL may become a more important reason for drinking than such earlier factors as mood, company and the social context. Drinking becomes heavier and more regular, and the drinking pattern tends to become rather contrived. Some people, for example, never drink before noon because 'only alcoholics do that', but may engage in relief drinking in the middle of the night. The day's events become oriented around acquiring and consuming alcohol and the drinker will always try to keep a supply on hand.

The tolerant drinker must consume noticeably larger than usual quantities and may be forced into various deviant behaviours to conceal this. There may be drinking before going out and between rounds, and drinks tend to be gulped rather than sipped. The drinker may lie about the amount consumed, sneak drinks and conceal supplies around the house, in the office or in the car.

Attempts to curtail drinking tend to be dramatic and sometimes bizarre, but periods of abstinence are followed by increasingly rapid reinstatement of the habitual drinking pattern.

Consequences of excessive drinking. Heavy drinkers show a gradual decline in judgement, initiative and cognition. This decline is not always obvious because the changes tend to be insidious, but the effects on memory are usually quite marked. Acute memory loss is common and may range from a vagueness about previous activities to virtually complete 'blackouts' for extended periods. The amnesias characteristically cover the immediate past. Memory for distant events usually remains relatively intact.

There are usually attempts to offset the guilt that develops about excessive drinking. There may be an undue preoccupation with the drinking behaviour of others. The drinker may begin to associate with other excessive drinkers in whose company the behaviour appears less deviant. There may be attempts to encourage others to drink more heavily.

There may be rationalisation. Previously held values may be rejected and the drinker may claim that home or job are no longer important. An alternative means of maintaining self-esteem is to blame the effects of drinking on bad luck, or more commonly on other people. The excessive drinker may rationalise losing his job because his boss 'had it in for him', or claim that his wife 'drove him to drink'. Suspicions of other people can become obsessive, and pathological jealousy, often bound up with psycho-sexual problems, is common.

These changes, and preoccupation with drink and drink-related behaviour, increasingly detach the drinker from the realities of life. Commitments to previous interests, hobbies and sports fade, and spouse, home and children are increasingly neglected. This in turn creates growing pressure within the family. The wife of an excessive drinker may be forced to work; a husband may have to take charge of housework and children in addition to his usual occupation. Chronic disharmony punctuated by violence may become the rule, and the embarrassed spouse and children may withdraw from relationships with kin, neighbours and friends. In short, the whole family can become as deviant as the drinker, and they often begin to drink excessively themselves.

Excessive drinking rarely occurs with only one type of associated harm. Beside family disruption, there will probably be trouble at work, financial problems and legal difficulties. In other words, what O'Neill (1978) has called 'grogstrife' occurs in most areas of the drinker's life, and this will form the major symptom of alcohol misuse. Assessment of grogstrife requires a searching investigation of all aspects of a person's life, from physical health through domestic and occupational matters to financial and legal considerations. This may be done in various ways. O'Neill's (1978) 'alconfrontation' procedure is especially interesting: at no stage is it suggested that the drinker's behaviour is either abnormal or excessive. Rather, the questioner implies that normality lies beyond what is apparent. The theory is that when the questioner exaggerates, the respondent will tend to pull him or her back to the real level. A similar approach may be used in determining the amount of alcohol habitually consumed.

Several cautions are in order. First, excessive drinking may be a symptom of more basic difficulties and it is unlikely to be modified while these persist. At the same time, basic problems can rarely be solved while excessive drinking continues and never while intoxication is acute.

Second, not all excessive drinkers have basic problems that antedate the drinking. For some, drinking may be an occupational hazard. Journalists, liquor industry employees, business executives and professional people are especially at risk. Their lives involve frequent occasions for appropriate social drinking and a search for psychopathological causes may be counterproductive. This of course does not alter the fact that the more alcohol a person consumes the more problems there are likely to be.

Finally, information about the role of alcohol in 'grogstrife' is rarely volunteered and the existence of stress may be vigorously denied, especially if family violence is involved. There may be a deep sense of shame, a fear of rejection or of hasty intervention and sometimes the not unrealistic possibility that attempts to alleviate the problem will make it worse. Helping professionals can treat the 'tired housewife syndrome', accident-prone people, delinquents and children with school problems for months and not know the contribution being made by serious conflicts over drinking. Alcohol misuse can occur in either sex at almost any age irrespective of social status and occupation. The truth will be forthcoming only if we are aware of the possibilities and provide the opportunity and setting for people to divulge such confidential and sensitive information.

How well can drug effects be recognised?

As the foregoing discussion suggests, even a brief consideration of the effects of a single drug is a lengthy business, and acquiring a working knowledge of the effects of all the drugs currently misused may seem almost impossible. The reality, however, is rather brighter.

First, drugs fall into relatively few chemical classes, and similarity of chemical structure usually means similarity of general physiological effects and relation to particular physical disorders. Thus except for a few specialist purposes, it is not necessary to know the detailed properties of heroin, morphine and codeine. It is sufficient to know that they are opiates, and therefore share a common spectrum of properties typical of this class of substances.

More importantly, however, we can speak of functional similarity where drugs of quite dissimilar chemical structure alter physiology and behaviour in a specific manner. For example, alcohol is a central nervous system depressant and thus shares most of its effects with the entire class of sedative-hypnotics. This includes such chemically dissimilar drugs as the barbiturates, methaqualone (Mandrax) and the various minor tranquillisers such as Serepax, Librium and Valium.

Because these drugs are chemically different their effects on the body's physiology may also be somewhat different, but the functional similarity of their effects on the brain far outweigh this. Thus, we find that cross-tolerance and cross-dependence occur throughout the group and that the drugs potentiate each other. In fact, their effects are algebraically additive, as discussed in Chapter 1. As a group they depress all body functions, dull consciousness, concentration, judgement and inhibition—in other words, all the behavioural effects of alcohol discussed above. All produce tolerance, and withdrawal in heavy users is of the same type as that from alcohol ('general depressant withdrawal syndrome') although severity and duration of withdrawal varies with duration of action. The consequences of their misuse parallel those of alcohol.

The important point is that general drug classification is made primarily on functional grounds. In the case of drugs with predominantly psychoactive effects, this refers to brain function. From the standpoint of recognizing drug effects, it is generally counterproductive to memorise catalogues of specific actions. Alteration of brain function simply isn't that specific.

For those who still feel the need for some comforting list of signs and symptoms, however, the following may help. The general appearance of the person should give some indication of the type of drug used. Restlessness or agitation suggests recent use of stimulants (cocaine, amphetamine) or psychedelics (mescaline, LSD). However, because withdrawal symptoms, if they occur, are generally the converse of the drug's effects, the same symptoms can indicate withdrawal from the opiates (heroin, morphine) or sedatives, including alcohol. If disorientation is also present, this will rule out the opiates, but none of the others.

Conversely, a quiet, withdrawn appearance may indicate stimulant withdrawal, or recent use of the opiates or sedatives. Some distinction is possible between the last two. People under the influence of opiates (short of very high doses) will be relatively easy to arouse and their motor coordination and diction will be good. The opposite will be the case with sedatives.

Certain accessible physical signs are somewhat diagnostic, again with the proviso that withdrawal symptoms are opposite to drug effects. Slow heart beat and breathing suggest use of opiates or sedatives. A rapid pulse is unspecific, but an irregular one may indicate amphetamine. A flushed dry skin suggests psychedelics. Sweating occurs with most withdrawal reactions, and chills are common in opiate withdrawal. Dilated, reactive pupils often indicate stimulants or psychedelics. Opiate use tends to produce pupil contraction although this may be masked by the simultaneous use of stimulants. Bloodshot eyes occasionally occur when marijuana is used.

Whatever the symptom, it should be bilaterally symmetrical. Changes in only one eye, or on one side of the body cannot result from the action of any drug, but they can indicate some form of brain trauma such as concussion or internal bleeding. High doses of alcohol and sedatives frequently result in falls and other accidents for which the user may have partial or complete amnesia.

For practical purposes, the most useful symptomatology comes from observing how the person interacts with others, and above all from questioning the user and significant others. Many professionals feel that by doing so they somehow lose face, but there is nothing immoral or unprofessional about asking what drug was taken, how much and what the effects were. It usually saves considerable time. If the user is actively under the influence of a drug (and this means that people with the user are also likely to be) it is essential to remember that comprehension may be slow, memory inaccurate and suspicion and anxiety high. It is necessary to be sympathetic, non-threatening, non-judgemental and patient. Above all, it is important to remember that what is said conveys both a fact and a feeling, whoever says it. If the feelings are ignored, the facts will not be forthcoming.

How well are the signs of drug use recognised in practice?

There is an enormous discrepancy between the number of people known to have drug problems and the number actually receiving some kind of treatment. This is especially noticeable in the case of social drugs such as alcohol. In 1978, official estimates (ACA, 1978) suggested that there were, as a minimum, '500,000 people in England and Wales with a serious drinking problem'. Yet when a group of general practitioners, social workers and probation officers was asked to discuss a client with a drinking problem whom they had seen within the previous three months, many were unable to think of a single one (Cartwright et al, 1975). The doctors appeared to have the greatest contact with the problem, social workers the least: only 8 out of 28 reported dealing with such people.

At the same time, a group of persons known to have drinking problems was asked about their contacts with various community agents (family doctor, clergy, psychiatrist, social worker, Alcoholics Anonymous, Samaritans and so on) for any sort of problem. Of the 16 respondents, all but three had seen their doctor during the previous year and some had made multiple visits. Five had seen psychiatrists, four social workers and one an educational psychologist. Although in most cases they had not specifically sought help for their drinking and had received none, the fact remains that they had made a considerable number of contacts with formal agents for one reason or another. In fact, those reporting the heaviest consumption of alcohol and the most problems from drinking had a rate of contact with professional helpers three times higher than the average person, yet none received help specifically for their drinking problems.

Clearly, drinkers and their problems are not hidden. They do contact professionals: three times more than the average person. Why then did they not receive direct help? Obviously, either because the subject was not brought up by the client, or was not recognised by the professional, or both.

Why do clients not present their problems as due to drugs or drinking?

This has usually been explained in terms of the personality and behaviour of drinkers. They are expected to hide and deny their problems and to be poorly motivated to seek help. Heavy drinkers do deny their problem, often quite consciously. Edwards and his colleagues (1967) for instance found that almost three-quarters of the male clients of alcohol information centers admitted trying to fool their doctors about their drinking and giving false reasons for needing medical certificates. Many are afraid of being told to cut down or stop drinking and thus lose the benefits of alcohol. Others may fear stigmatisation of themselves or of their families.

On the whole, though, a major reason for not presenting drinking problems seems to be simple ignorance. People frequently do not realise that their stomach troubles, poor sleep, depression or accidents could be related to drinking.

Morever, along with most of the general population (cf. Cartwright et al, 1975), drinkers generally feel that non-specialists do not have the knowledge or ability to deal with drinking problems. The family doctor is often considered to be a somewhat appropriate helper, but most are reluctant to approach him or her in practice. It 'isn't the doctor's job', or the problem 'isn't serious enough'. General practitioners are expected to be very busy, unable to discuss problems at length. And even those who feel that they can discuss personal matters with a general practitioner feel that a doctor could not do much to help practically.

Most people feel that social workers, probation officers and similar agents do not even have the right to bring up the topic of drinking: 'It's none of their business'; they 'haven't the same right as a doctor'. Employers were expected to be unsympathetic, clergy moralistic and in some cases hypocritical: 'They drink heavy themselves'.

The disinclination to discuss drinking problems, therefore, might not necessarily mean intentional denial of the problems. The drinker may not realise that he or she can do so, or may feel that it is pointless.

Why do professionals fail to recognise drinking and other drug problems?

It is clear that many professionals lack the necessary knowledge and skills to recognise symptoms and behaviours that indicate drug-related problems. Most of the doctors, social workers and probation officers questioned (Shaw et al, 1978) used an exceedingly narrow range of diagnostic cues. When asked what would make them suspect a drinking problem, the most frequently mentioned and sometimes the only sign was smell of alcohol on the client's breath. Unkempt appearance and family troubles were virtually the only other signs noted.

It is also clear that professionals have the same questions about role legitimacy as their clients. This takes two forms. One is uncertainty about which professional group ought to deal with drug problems. Another is doubt about invasion of their client's privacy. Both lay and professional people believe that drug use is a personal matter and discussion of drug intake seems as embarrassing to some as that of sexual topics used to be. This is particularly true of drinking habits. One survey (Cartwright et al, 1975) found that while 90 per cent of general practitioners felt they had the right to question patients about their alcohol consumption none had done so in detail and all admitted to difficulties in approaching the subject. Some were especially embarrassed about asking women and two mentioned fear of violence on the part of the patient. Social workers felt that they did not even have the right to ask in principle. Given such reticence in discussing the subject on the part of both client and professional, it is hardly surprising that recognition of drug-related problems is low.

However, overlooking drinking problems is not simply lack of awareness. As a general psychiatrist trenchantly remarked,

> The notion that the general practitioner or specialist cannot, or will not, make the correct diagnosis is absurd. Of course he can, but he has to live in the town, and if he diagnoses all his patients alcoholic and tells them this, then they will go and see someone else.
>
> In addition, and probably more important, to have to admit to himself that he cannot cure a patient is a body blow to the professional ego. This is fair enough if such a decision involves a major illness... but alcohol-related and psychological illnesses are different. Many referral notes from GPs to psychiatrists convey great hostility: they are interpreted as denigrating the patient; in fact, they are often an expression of the threat a GP feels to himself at being quite unable to offer a patient any help at all. (NADMI, 1978, pp. 136–37)

The feeling that once the problem has been discovered nothing useful can be done is highly destructive. One doctor is reported to have remarked: 'I can't handle this problem—I don't want to know how, apart from referral' (Shaw et al, 1978, p. 134). Most doctors do refer the client, typically to psychiatrists though sometimes to Alcoholics Anonymous (AA). Non-medical professionals refer to psychiatrists and AA about equally.

Although referral is the most common response to the problem, most referees are very ambivalent about the effectiveness of specialist treatment. General practitioners tend to be openly sceptical about the value of psychiatric help and their opinions about AA range from 'lay people dabbling in semi-science' to 'I am not sure what they do but it is a very good thing'. The general feeling seems to be that the specialists are little better equipped to deal with the problem than the referees themselves.

There is, moreover, the widespread complaint that specialists do not communicate or cooperate with referees. Traditional professional boundaries are partly responsible. Medical people tend to view non-medical personnel as 'not colleagues on the same level' while the non-medical professionals, with some justice, believe that the doctors belittle their professionalism and expertise. Predictably, there is little helpful communication and cooperation among community agents on the matter of drugs and alcohol. All feel that they have to 'go it alone', and, understandably, decline to tackle problems which they feel they cannot solve.

The result of all this is what Shaw and his colleagues (1978) have called 'low therapeutic commitment'. Community agents feel unprepared and unable to respond to drug-related problems both intellectually and practically, and their overt reaction is an emotional one: they do not *want* to recognise the problems let alone respond to them.

In practice, the issue is avoided wherever possible. 'People don't seem to talk about drug or drinking problems in this office'. If the problem is recognised, its seriousness tends to be minimised, with the implication that it does not require or deserve any response. When the problem is too obvious to avoid or deny, referral to a specialist maintains the veneer of having done the right thing on the grounds that only an expert could deal with such a serious case.

When treatment fails, there is a tendency to blame the client for lack of cooperation or motivation. Anxiety can also be relieved by assuming that nothing can be done because alcoholics and drug addicts are incurable, hopeless cases. Or the situation can be wearily accepted as an inevitable fact of life. Shaw and his colleagues (1978) report a classic statement by a social worker who claimed that she had no problem drinkers on her caseload: 'Every wife I have complains that her husband drinks too much'.

In sum, while ignorance and lack of necessary skills undoubtedly play a role, much of the discrepancy between the known prevalence of drug and alcohol problems and the number of people actually in treatment seems to reside in a complex series of destructive misunderstandings. Clients see lay help as inadequate and specialists as unavailable, unacceptable or unapproachable. They are not only confused about the nature of their problems but unsure whether anyone has the right or ability to deal with them. The professionals, for their part, feel pressured to respond when they feel they have neither the ability nor the right to do so, and their low therapeutic commitment seems at least partly a series of safeguards against this threat. Some openly admit their sense of failure and inadequacy to deal with a very complex and difficult problem. Others, however, rationalise their lack of commitment by blaming the character of the clients or the intractability of the problem or both. Prevailing concepts about the nature of drug misuse and drug misusers readily permit them to so.

What is recognised—is 'diagnosis' desirable?

Whether a person uses a drug is a factual question. We either drink (smoke marijuana, inject heroin) or we do not, and the level of our intake can be quantified. The goal of user identification, however, is rarely this simple. Typically, some action plan depends on the 'diagnosis', that is, the label attached to the user as a result of symptom assessment. Terms such as 'addict', 'social drinker' and 'alcoholic' carry only a spurious concreteness but an enormous emotive power. Their use greatly alters response to the drug taker and they must not be applied capriciously. The ramifications of diagnosing a person as an 'alcoholic' may be taken as an example.

The term 'alcoholism' seems to have been first used in 1849 by a Swedish doctor, Magnus Huss, and it gradually came to replace such terms as 'inebriate', 'habitual drunkard' and 'dipsomaniac'. All these terms originally described someone who could not stop drinking. Now, however, the term 'alcoholic' generally carries the additional connotation of 'sick'.

The attempt to distinguish heavy users from 'slaves to the habit' goes back to ancient times, and a concurrent notion has always been that being a slave to the habit is a form of mental or physical disease that somehow differentiates such a person from all other users. Opposition to these ideas has an equally long tradition. In modern times, AA (Alcoholics Anonymous, 1939, 1955) is widely credited with the 'discovery' that alcoholism is an illness. It was, in fact, rather a 're-discovery', but at the end of the Prohibition era in the United States people were prepared to welcome as innovative any movement that could distinguish response to drinking problems from moralistic action against alcohol. AA managed to do this without blaming the drinker. It maintained merely that the alcoholic had to accept that he had an illness, a permanent inability to handle alcohol. The progression of this illness could be arrested only by lifelong abstinence. Because alcohol was a power greater than the drinker himself, he had to seek help both from other recovered alcoholics and from God as he understood Him.

The form in which the concept of alcoholism as an illness was promulgated is largely the work of E.M. Jellinek. His theoretical position changed somewhat over time (Jellinek 1952, 1960), but his two salient points were that alcoholics experience a loss control, an irresistible compulsion to go on drinking even when they have chosen not to, and that this loss of control was due to a physiological or biochemical anomaly, an 'allergy'. The concept of loss of control is the crux of what has come to be called the 'disease theory of alcoholism'. It is because of this that the alcoholic is thought to be unable to return to normal drinking. One drink (intentional or not) = one drunk = one relapsed alcoholic.

Jellinek's work imparted scientific respectability to AA's disease concept and appeared to explain a baffling and mysterious condition. The result was general acceptance of alcoholics as sick people who had some defect that made them different from all other drinkers.

There is no good evidence to support a strict disease theory of alcoholism. Extensive research has failed to find clear biological or psychological differences between alcoholics and others that would account for loss of control, and evidence for loss of control itself is equivocal. However, our concern here is not so much with the theory's validity as with the desirability of using the term 'alcoholic' within a disease theory framework.

The benefits were initially considerable. Alcoholics who were 'ill' now elicited sympathy rather than moral censure, and social acceptance of the condition as an illness meant that they could benefit from health care and social security systems and be handled through hospitals rather than courts or prisons. There were, however, increasing disadvantages.

From a therapeutic standpoint, use of a disease theory gives the false impression that alcoholism is a clear-cut entity and that there is an accepted medical treatment. Moreover, the assumption that the causes of alcoholism lie solely in the drinker tends to divert attention from the circumstances leading to and surrounding drinking.

The drinker's reaction is also altered. On being diagnosed as alcoholics, some expect to be 'cured' by a program of medication or some other straightforward medical treatment. Others find the idea that the condition is incurable attractive because it exonerates their behaviour. A drinker who is told that he has no control over his drinking is likely to use that as an excuse to go on drinking. For still others, a diagnosis of alcoholism can become a self-fulfilling prophecy. As Shaw and his colleagues point out,

> If a drinker is repeatedly informed he will feel compelled to drink to oblivion after one drink, he is already halfway to complying with that belief. Some alcoholics identify so completely with their label that they interpret all their experiences as evidence of their alcoholism... Jellinek himself noted that when AA members were asked as to whether they experienced certain symptoms classically associated with alcoholism, a proportion gave falsely positive answers. It was almost as though they felt obliged that they should have experienced shakes, blackouts and the other traditional symptoms. (1978, p. 58)

On the other hand, a substantial number of drinkers find the idea of having an uncontrollable disease so unacceptable that they neither seek nor receive treatment. Unwillingness to assume the alcoholic identity is usually called denial—but is this surprising when it implies an abnormal physiology or personality? The label is being attached to one's essence, not merely one's experience.

For the community, defining alcoholism as an illness no longer precludes moral stigma, if indeed it ever did so on any large scale. When Cartwright and his colleagues surveyed community attitudes in 1974, 73 per cent of the respondents felt that alcoholism was a disease but 32 per cent also agreed that alcoholics were degenerate and 45 per cent believed that 'alcoholics were more dangerous than other people'. The stereotype of loss of control, obsession with drink and incurability may actually prevent the problem drinker from getting help. Behaviour must be gross and debased before the label of alcoholic can be applied or accepted, with the result that treatment becomes available only when problems are exceptionally obvious and the damage severe.

Moreover, the same stereotype distinguishes the alcoholic in the public mind from other sorts of drinkers who might get into trouble. A person convicted of drunk driving is likely to get sympathy from friends because of his or her 'bad luck', but is unlikely to be seen by them as a problem drinker. The stereotype also fosters a false sense of security:

> Those who drank heavily but considered themselves 'normal' drinkers were reassured they were not becoming alcoholics, since they were not physiologically or biochemically anomalous. They could 'give it up if they really wanted to'. To some brewers and distillers, the concept was even more attractive, since it implied that the majority of drinkers were not alcoholics and that they could drink as much as they liked without losing control. Therefore it could be argued that restrictions on alcohol sales for health reasons were unreasonable. After all, why should the pleasure of the majority be spoiled just because there were a few alcoholics whom science had shown to have an odd disease by which they could not keep control over their drinking? (Shaw et al, 1978, p. 49)

The point is that the use of labels makes it easy to dissociate scapegoats from ordinary, normal people such as ourselves. In the process, the scapegoats may acquire attributes they do not really posses and we may divest ourselves incorrectly of some that we do have.

The terms 'alcoholism' and 'alcoholic' have been officially discarded (WHO, 1976), although they obviously continue to be used by the public and by many professionals. Other labels invented to replace them—'alcohol dependence syndrome', 'problem drinking', 'dependent drinking'—have so far gained little public credence because the alcoholic stereotype is so well ingrained. In any case, their use does little to solve the problem. The fact remains that the effects of drugs lie on continua, and people experience and display them in ways that cannot be placed into neat categories. Little is gained and much may be ignored by classifying clients according to some preconceived system. Asking 'Is the client an alcoholic?' or 'Does he show loss of control?' is much less useful than questions such as 'Why does this client drink so much so regularly?', 'How are the effects of alcohol interacting with other problems he has?' and, most important, 'What does my assessment suggest would be the most appropriate response to this client?'.

References

Advisory Committee on Alcoholism, *The pattern and range of services for problem drinkers*, DHSS/Welsh Office, 1978.

Alcoholics Anonymous, *The story of how many thousands of men and women have recovered from alcoholism*, Alcoholics Anonymous World Services, 1939; second edition, 1955.

Cartwright, A., Shaw, S. & Spratley, T., *Designing a comprehensive community response to problems of alcohol abuse*, Report to the DHSS by the Maudsley Alcohol Pilot Project, 1975.

Goldberg, L., 'Quantitative studies on alcohol tolerance in man', *Acta Physiol. Scand.*, 5, 1943.

Gross, M.M., 'Psychobiological contributions to the alcohol dependence syndrome', Edwards, G. et al. (eds), *Alcohol-Related Disabilities*, WHO publication No. 32, Geneva, 1977.

Jellinek, E.M., 'Phases of alcohol addiction', *Quart. J. Stud. Alc.* 13, 1952.

Jellinek, E.M., *The Disease Concept of Alcoholism*, Hillhouse, New Jersey, 1960.

Klatzky, A.L. et al., 'Alcohol use, myocardial infarction, sudden cardiac death and hypertension', *Alcoholism: Clin. & Ex. Res.*, 3:1, 1979.

Marmot, M.G. et al., 'Alcohol and mortality: a U-shaped curve', *Lancet*, I, 1981.

NADMI, Anonymous author, *The role of a general hospital in a rural area*, National Alcohol and Drug Dependence Multidisciplinary Institute, AFADD, 1978, pp. 136–39.

O'Neill, P., *Alconfrontation*, Health Commision of NSW, 1978.

Raskin, N., 'Alcoholism or acetaldehydism', *N. Eng. J. Med.*, 292:8, 1975.

Shaw, S., Cartwright, A., Spratley, T. & Harwin, J., *Responding to Drinking Problems*, Croom Helm, London, 1978.

Edwards, G. et al., 'Clients of alcoholism information centres', *Brit, Med J.*, 4, 1967.

World Health Organization: *International Classification of Diseases*, 9th revision, Geneva, 1977.

3 Epidemiology
Assessing the problem
L.R.H. DREW

Introduction *Jara A. Krivanek*

The need to solve drug problems has been a recurrent theme for some decades. There is talk of escalating use and failure of preventive efforts, yet few ever stop to ask how we know about any of these things. An honest answer for the majority of us would be that we know this must be so because some authoritative source gave us the information.

Unfortunately, authoritative too often means authoritarian: a pronouncement is made with great conviction on what may be very flimsy grounds. The general public, and far too many 'experts' whose training and/or public position suggests that they should know better, often fail to appreciate that conclusions based on experiments or surveys are only as sound as the design and execution of those experiments or surveys, that the relationships between causes and effects are rarely simple, and that there is a difference between causation and correlation.

The study of the distribution of a phenomenon in a population and of the factors that influence it is 'epidemiology'. Epidemiology began as the study of infectious diseases. Defining what constitutes a 'case' of infection is fairly straightforward. However, 'conditions' like alcohol or drug problems typically show a behavioural rather than physical pathology, they deal with social constructs rather than identifiable bacteria or viruses, and definition of them invites moralising rather than objectivity. From the beginning, then, we have problems about what it is that should be counted. Do we want a count of addicts, or of current users, or of those who have ever used a drug? Do we want an indication of the frequency and level of use, or will we simply but the person who has used marijuana once and the individual who has used it regularly for years together in the 'ever used' category?

There is even less agreement on the terms and classifications used to present the findings. What is 'heavy use' to one investigator may be 'moderate' or even 'light' use to another. 'Current use' may mean within the last week or within the last six months. Drugs may be grouped into different classes, or meaningless categories like 'hard drugs' may be used with different referents in different studies.

Consequently, it is often impossible to compare studies done at different times or in different places.

It is also very easy to misinterpret statistical summaries of results when essential facts about response variability, the sample studied and the population from which it is drawn are forgotten or ignored. People vary on physical, psychological, social and cultural parameters, and the relationships between these are understood only imperfectly. In addition, a portion of the sample usually cannot be located, while other people refuse to be interviewed, and it is reasonable to suppose that these subgroups contain a significant proportion of the very people we wish to study. There are limits to the time respondents are willing to give to surveys, and therefore on the amount of data that can be collected. It is usually difficult and sometimes impossible to determine the truthfulness of the responses given. For these and many other reasons, charts, tables and generalized statistical inferences can at best serve as a guide or a 'guesstimate' to the situation as it really is.

Nevertheless, the epidemiology of drug-taking has recently become something of a growth industry and vast sums of money are spent on such studies. A primary reason is the belief that they can help explain the causes of the drug problem and provide useful guidelines for preventive efforts. The basic strategy is to measure the distribution of 'cases' in the population and determine the individual characteristics or environmental factors that seem to vary with the incidence of the problem. An inference of some causal relationship between them is then drawn. A rider of caution is usually added, sometimes even a disclaimer, but that is basically the model.

We may well ask whether the products of this industry have justified the faith of the investors. There have been some signal successes. Nevertheless, many feel that epidemiology increasingly discovers the same thing. It tells us that there are a lot of drug users or misusers or addicts, but we continue to be rather confused about what this means. We are told that users tend to come from deprived social backgrounds, but that this is not always true; that addicts often, though not universally, show personality disturbance; that some recover while others do not. In other words, epidemiology often seems to confirm and reconfirm the slightly obvious and its variations.

Others, however, feel more optimistic. While drug epidemiology may have got itself into something of a muddle it is still a powerful tool. Counting arrests for marijuana possession or deaths from cirrhosis may be utterly pointless or very worthwhile, depending on whether the underlying question has been formulated sufficiently rigorously, and on whether it has been translated into a procedure that actually addresses the issue at hand. This is often difficult to achieve in practical terms. Thus, we may feel that 'alienation' has something to do with drug misuse among youth. But how are we to turn the abstract concept of alienation into a questionnaire that is to be given by a hired interviewer to a group of young people who may or may not be intoxicated, who may have better things to do with their time, and who are likely to be, with some reason, rather suspicious of the whole procedure?

It is this sort of problem that makes the epidemiology of drug use so much more difficult than the epidemiology of say cholera. At the same time, it is precisely this that can make it far more exciting than the rather dessicated science it is sometimes supposed to be. To be sure, the traditional official statistics on mortality rates, consumption levels and drunk driving charges do sometimes present only 'the vision of a world seen through the holes in IBM cards'. Such statistics are often as empty of information as they are dull to read.

Increasingly, however, there is emphasis on the need to approach epidemiological questions not with tests designed by committees in remote offices but through the participant observation of people, families, neighbourhoods and cultures by epidemiologists who live and work among them. There is every reason to believe that this new 'real-life' epidemiology will provide the data we need to consider drug problems realistically and constructively.

J.A.K.

Patterns of drug use and drug-related problems in Australia

The epidemiology of drug use and drug problems has been investigated and reported on at some length recently by a number of official inquiries. Studies and reports of the South Australian Royal Commission[1] provide detailed analyses of available information and reports of original work. Much important information was reported at the First Pan-Pacific Conference on Drugs and Alcohol[2]. Drug use extends throughout society and includes a large range of drugs, and the relationships between drug use and drug problems are very complex. In most instances, data accumulated refer only to one part of the whole picture. Further, because of the limitations of available means of data collection—surveys of opinion, personal reporting of habits, anecdotes and impressions—the reliability of much of the data is open to question. Thus, even if a single aspect of the drug question is under examination—for example, adolescent drinking—only after information from a number of sources has been compared and contrasted can some reliance be placed on the conclusions reached. To obtain a useful description of the whole spectrum of drug use many sources of information need to be examined.

Much information about drug use and drug-related problems is currently available from many sources and, if looked at comprehensively, is sufficient for useful conclusions to be drawn about general trends. It is also adequate for the identification of areas which warrant special community attention, and for the overall impact of community policies and programs to be monitored. However, we lack researchers at State or national level who can bring together relevant information from a wide range of routine collections made for other purposes, and identify the changing patterns of drug use and drug-related problems in our society.

Levels of drug consumption

Routine statistical collections, whose primary purpose is usually to monitor financial transactions, are a major source of information on the overall levels of drug consumption in Australia. A growing wealth of historical material is becoming available. From this evidence, overall trends in drug use can be described.

Alcohol. The overall amounts of alcoholic beverages consumed, and the relative popularity of wine, beer and spirits, have varied greatly since 1788 (see Figure 3.1). After an all-time low of two litres alcohol per head in 1932, consumption of alcohol increased gradually to an annual rate of 6.5 litres per head by 1950. Between 1963 and 1975, consumption increased rapidly and since then (see Table 3.1) it has been about 10 litres per head per year (the equivalent of just over two standard drinks per person per day).

Tobacco. Tobacco use increased rapidly in the early decades of this century and continued to increase after World War II. Gross consumption grew until 1975, then fell by almost five per cent between 1975 and 1980 (see Table 3.1). Average consumption per head of population peaked in the late 1950s; since then it has fallen by about 15 per cent.

Legal drug use. Many psycho-active or mind affecting drugs are used legally but are subject to misuse. The drugs may be obtained on prescription or by ordinary sale. Statistical information about the overall level of legal use (for instance, sales data) of these drugs is not available. However some indication of trends in the use of these drugs can be deduced from the number of prescriptions supplied through the Commonwealth Pharmaceutical Benefits Scheme (see Table 3.2). Between 1971* and 1975 the number of prescriptions for tranquillisers rose dramatically but since then (until 1981) the number has fallen fairly steadily. The number of prescriptions for sedatives has fallen steadily over the period 1971 to 1981, whereas prescriptions for antidepressants rose quickly from 1971 until 1974, peaked at a slightly

---

* Data refers to fiscal years: e.g., 1971 means 1 July 1970 to 30 June 1971.

Epidemiology: assessing the problem 55

Figure 3.1: Average consumption per person per year of alcoholic beverages (expressed as litres of pure alcohol) in NSW (1830–1900) and Australia (1900–80) using 10-yearly averages.

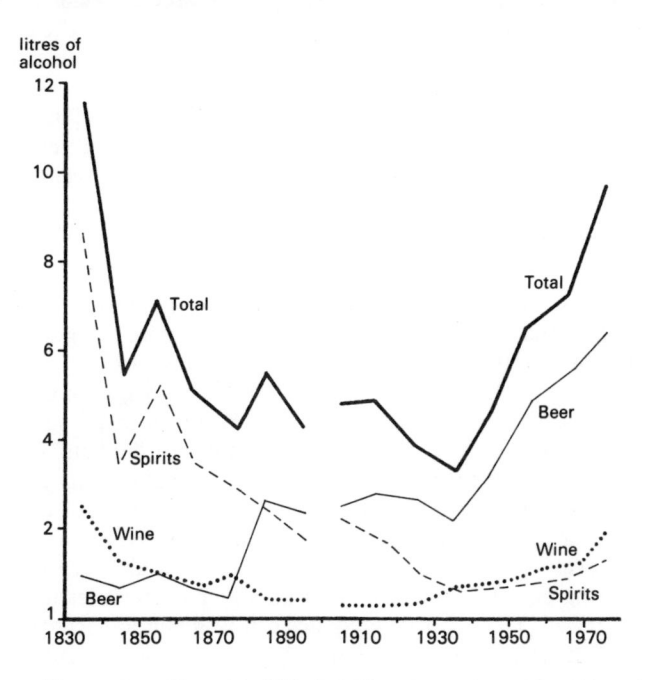

(Beer presumed to contain 4.8% alcohol by volume; wine presumed to contain 15% alcohol by volume.)
Source: Dingle and Commonwealth Department of Health

Table 3.1 Estimated consumption of alcoholic beverages person (expressed as litres of pure alcohol) and of tobacco per adult (expressed as kilograms) in Australia, 1961–70

	Alcohol (L)	Tobacco (kg)		Alcohol (L)	Tobacco (kg)
1961	6.5	3.44	1971	8.4	3.28
1962	6.5	3.31	1972	8.4	3.30
1963	6.5	3.31	1973	8.9	3.32
1964	6.8	3.30	1974	9.6	3.32
1965	7.0	3.25	1975	9.8	3.32
1966	7.0	3.24	1976	9.7	3.21
1967	7.3	3.09	1977	9.9	3.17
1968	7.7	3.21	1978	10.1	3.07
1969	7.9	3.26	1979	10.0	2.88
1970	8.3	3.24	1980	10.1	2.89

Source: Annual Reports, Director-General of Health, Commonwealth Department of Health

higher level in 1976 and fell to 1974 levels in 1980 and 1981. The number of prescriptions for analgesics (pain killers) has gradually risen from 1971 to 1981. Although these changes are, to some extent, a reflection of changes in regulations applying to the system, the trends to increases up to the early 1970s followed by a recent decrease are consistent with other evidence.

Opiates were used widely, and legally, until about 1900. Overall community consumption was far greater then than current levels (legal and illegal combined). A special Commonwealth monitoring system provides evidence that the legal trade in the substances of greatest concern to law and order has remained fairly steady in recent years[3] (see Table 3.3).

Illegal drug use. There is no reliable evidence of the overall amounts of drugs illegally used in Australia. At best any estimate is a guess, likely to be wrong by 1000 per cent in either direction. Efforts have been made to derive such figures from the amounts of drugs confiscated by authorities (see Table 3.4). Attempts have also been made to calculate overall consumption by estimating the number of 'addicts' or 'users' and multiplying this by the presumed average level of daily consumption of each addict or user. However there is no way of accurately estimating the number of addicts or users, or of estimating their average use. The terms 'addict' and 'user' are ill-defined, and refer to a diffuse and changing population whose drug-taking characteristics have never been quantified. Hence, little credence can be given to such estimates.

In the Report of the Australian Royal Commission of Inquiry into Drugs (the Williams Report) it was concluded that (in 1979) cannabis

Table 3.2 Number of national health service benefit prescriptions (million) for (i) tranquillisers, (ii) sedatives and hypnotics, (iii) analgesics and (iv) anti-depressants, Australia, 1970–81

	(i) Tranq.	(ii) Sed.	(iii) Analg.	(iv) Anti-dep.
1970	1.17	6.25	5.25	0.68
1971	1.48	5.56	6.02	1.75
1972	2.02	4.31	6.65	2.32
1973	3.57	4.68	—	2.76
1974	5.92	4.54	7.78	3.31
1975	6.21	4.64	9.39	3.45
1976	5.79	4.21	10.22	3.66
1977	4.39	2.96	9.82	3.37
1978	4.60	3.46	11.25	3.53
1979	4.31	2.87	11.45	3.40
1980	3.73	2.71	11.77	3.30
1981	3.69	2.53	12.21	3.32

Source: Annual Reports, Director-General of Health, Commwealth Department of Health

Table 3.3 Apparent consumption (licit) of the principal narcotic drugs, Australia 1965–77, and imports of principal controlled drugs of dependence 1974–80. (Apparent consumption in grams per 1000 population)

	1965	1966	1967	1968	1969	1970	1971	1972	1973	1974	1975	1976	1977
Morphine	8.7	8.7	7.0	7.7	4.7	4.8	6.0	4.7	4.7	4.0	3.7	3.9	3.9
Cocaine	1.6	1.4	1.6	1.7	1.1	1.3	1.2	1.3	1.4	1.4	1.5	1.2	1.0
Pethidine	20.7	17.9	20.1	24.7	15.8	19.8	19.2	20.4	20.2	20.3	19.9	20.1	20.3
Methadone	1.9	1.2	0.8	1.5	0.7	1.2	0.9	1.3	1.8	1.9	2.1	2.7	2.6
Codeine	283.5	262.5	283.7	307.5	336.4	320.9	301.6	316.1	259.4	281.5	238.4	229.9	227.1

Imports (kilograms, anhydrous base)

	1974	1975	1976	1977	1978	1979	1980
Morphine	77	50	40	46	72	76	106
Cocaine	17	17	13	17	15	35	18
Pethidine	307	414	333	209	406	283	385
Methadone	27	27	54	41	54	14	31

Source: Commonwealth Department of Health

58 Drug problems, people problems

Table 3.4 Quantified drug seizures, combined Australian totals (values in brackets denote number seizures)

	Opium grams	Heroin grams	Cocaine grams	Cannabis (marijuana) grams	LSD dose units
1974	6 131	6 401	46	495 827	12 548
1975	NA	NA	NA	NA	NA
1976	256 (12)	22 521 (601)	1 868 (44)	906 628 (5 074)	20 179 (130)
1977	4 691 (40)	21 741 (1 035)	556 (58)	5 286 963 (6 627)	5 376 (71)
1978	2 377 (11)	23 793 (651)	14 208 (12)	61 128 059 (4 258)	5 936 (67)
1979	28 (5)	23 558 (501)	651 (10)	793 891 (5 205)	4 781 (70)
1980	2 (10)	12 359 (585)	7 161 (27)	854 531 (7 869)	4 413 (104)

Source: Drug Abuse in Australia—Australian Federal Police

was the illegal drug most used in Australia, compared with which heroin use was small in volume but was (at that time) increasing; legal narcotic drugs were used as alternatives to heroin at times of short supply. The use of LSD was small. Cocaine was of minor importance. Methaqualone use increased and use of amphetamines and barbiturates fell considerably during the 1970s.

Over the past two years it seems that since methaqualone became a prohibited substance it has fallen from popularity but that barbiturates and Serepax (a close relative of Valium, a minor tranquilliser) have increased in popularity.

Among users of both illegal and legal drugs, multi-drug use is now common. Use of alcohol and tobacco have always coincided.

General comment. It appears that in Australia, since colonisation, major variations have occurred in the community level of consumption of drugs of various sorts. Average (per capita) consumption of alcohol was at a peak in the eighteenth century, reached its lowest level in the 1930s, but is now four times that level. Tobacco use increased markedly this century but is now falling. There was considerable legal use of opium and its derivatives (both on prescription and as a recreational activity) until a sudden reduction early this century. There is no simple, acceptable explanation of why such major variations have occurred. Rather, trends have usually reflected the confluence of a number of complex etiological factors—social, ethical and economic.[4]

Individual drug use

Drug use patterns have been the subject of increasingly detailed survey over the past ten years. A number of reviews of these studies is available[5,6]. Considerable criticism can be levelled at most of these studies. They depend on self-reports of use and rely on both honesty and

Table 3.5 Average household weekly expenditure on alcoholic beverages, Australian capital cities, compared with total household weekly expenditure, 1974–75

	Canberra	Sydney	Melbourne	Brisbane	Adelaide	Perth	Hobart	All capital cities
Weekly expenditure on alcoholic beverage (in dollars)	7.07	6.29	4.95	4.83	4.37	5.78	5.16	5.46
Total weekly expenditure (in dollars)	197.64	160.68	161.83	142.68	146.27	149.71	145.38	157.00
Percent of weekly expenditure on alcoholic beverages (in dollars)	3.6	3.9	3.1	3.4	3.0	3.9	3.5	3.5

Source: Australian Bureau of Statistics

Table 3.6 Type of drinker, with average daily consumption of alcohol in previous week, by State and sex, Australia, February 1977

Type of drinker[1]	NSW	Vic.	Qld.	SA	WA	Tas.	NT	ACT	Aust
Males %									
None	26.0	26.1	27.1	22.5	17.5	25.2	†22.8	†13.1	24.9
Light	56.0	56.5	54.6	60.9	59.1	63.8	†33.5	69.2	56.9
Medium	13.7	13.3	15.2	12.8	17.2	9.0	†29.4	†13.9	14.0
Heavy	4.3	4.1	2.3	3.7	6.2	*	*	*	4.2
Total who drank	74.0	73.9	72.9	77.5	82.5	74.8	77.2	86.9	75.1
Females%									
None	53.0	51.3	54.5	48.4	41.6	51.4	†46.1	27.9	51.0
Light	45.0	47.1	44.6	50.7	55.9	46.7	†52.3	71.0	47.4
Medium	1.7	†1.3	*	*	†1.9	*	*	*	1.3
Heavy	*	*	*	*	*	*	*	*	†0.2
Total who drank	47.0	48.7	45.5	51.6	58.4	48.6	†53.9	72.1	49.0
Total %									
None	39.8	38.9	40.9	35.7	29.4	38.4	32.9	20.7	38.2
Light	50.4	51.7	49.6	55.7	57.6	55.2	41.7	70.1	52.1
Medium	7.5	7.2	8.0	6.7	9.6	5.0	†16.7	†7.3	7.6
Heavy	2.3	2.2	1.1	1.9	3.4	*	*	*	2.2
Total who drank	60.2	61.1	59.1	64.3	70.6	61.6	67.0	79.3	61.8
Average daily alcohol consumption (grams)									
Per drinker	22.01	20.27	20.13	18.68	23.01	16.80	37.75	20.60	20.98
Per person	13.25	12.38	11.90	12.01	16.24	10.35	25.32	16.34	12.98

*Sampling variability too high for most practical purposes
†Estimates with a standard error of between 20 and 30 per cent
Note [1]Types of drinker:
   Light—Below 40 g alcohol per day;
   Medium—40 but less than 80 g per day;
   Heavy—over 80 g per day.
Source: Australian Bureau of Statistics

memory. Almost every study uses a slightly different method and so results cannot be directly compared. Studies apparently measuring the same phenomena have given such widely different results that one reviewer entitled his paper 'Drug Use Surverys—No Use to Anyone'. Recently, attempts have been made to ensure that a standard approach is used. Some studies have been repeated (by the same researchers using the same method) and these give more reliable information about trends over time than comparisons of studies conducted by separate workers in different settings.

Alcohol. Even the best surveys under-estimate alcohol consumption by 40–60 per cent. A sceptical view thus needs to be taken of reported levels of consumption (e.g., 20 per cent drinking 10–30 ml/day). Nevertheless, reported trends across age, sex, social class and geographic divisions (see Tables 3.5 and 3.6) and trends over time (see Tables 3.7 and 3.8) may reflect real differences.

Table 3.7 Drinking patterns (expressed as frequency of drinking beer) in Australia, by age groups, 1969 and 1976 (expressed in per cent)

Age group (years)	Year	Never drank (abstainers)	0–4	5–25	Over 25
15–24	1969	27.3	53.0	14.6	3.4
	1976	20.4	54.5	20.3	4.6
25–54	1969	18.5	52.8	19.5	9.3
	1976	17.9	49.5	22.5	9.9
55 or more	1969	27.4	55.1	11.0	9.1
	1976	26.5	48.2	15.2	9.1
Total sample	1969	21.4	52.8	17.7	8.0
	1976	19.5	50.2	21.2	8.7

Number of drinking occasions previous month

N (1969) = 3099   N (1976) = 2105
Source: Frank Small and Associates Pty Ltd

Table 3.8 The number of most frequent drinkers (25 or more drinking occasions in the previous month) in Australia (as a per cent) analysed by socio-economic group and educational status, Australia 1969 and 1976. Socio-economic groups A–D, in descending order, are derived from income, occupation and place of residence

		Socio-economic group				Educational status		
		A	B	C	D	Tertiary	Senior Secondary	Junior Secondary
Beer	1969	6.1	6.5	8.2	9.1	6.5	7.1	8.4
	1976	11.7	6.9	9.0	8.2	8.3	7.2	9.8
Wine	1969	8.6	4.1	4.5	2.6	5.5	5.5	3.5
	1976	14.9	13.9	5.7	1.2	9.3	6.1	3.2
Spirits	1969	5.8	1.7	1.3	1.1	3.1	3.1	1.1
	1976	6.4	5.0	1.5	0.8	3.3	2.4	0.7

Source: Drew

The elderly and the poorest changed their drinking patterns very little between 1969 and 1976, but the affluent, the well educated and the young apparently all increased at least the frequency of their drinking. Although women apparently increased their drinking, they did not catch up to the drinking levels of men.

General impressions suggest that during the past five years, although average consumption has remained unchanged, more people are drinking on more occasions, but total individual consumption is being reduced. Despite contrary impressions, available evidence (Tables 3.9, 3.10, 3.11) suggests that fewer young people may now be drinking than five years ago. Certainly not as many are drinking heavily.

Tobacco. From a national survey conducted by the Australian Bureau of Statistics, it is estimated (see Table 3.12) that in 1977, 42.9 per cent of males and 29.0 per cent of females were smokers. Of those who smoked tailor-made cigarettes, 24.6 per cent smoked more than 20 per day and

Table 3.9 Alcohol use among Form 4 (year 10) students in NSW (%)

	1971	1973	1974	1977	1980
Use at least once a week[1]	24.4	31.3	—	47.2	35.4
Feel a bit drunk more than once a week	—	—	45.0	41.0	29.0
Feel very drunk more than once a month[2]	—	—	25.0	31.0	14.0

Note [1] males and females; [2] males only
Source: Flaherty, Trebilco and Egger

Table 3.10 Prevalence of alcohol use among year 12 students in the ACT (%)

	1973	1974	1978
Boys	82.4	84.6	75.7
Girls	71.9	77.0	78.9

Source: Irwin

Table 3.11 Prevalence of alcohol use among Form 3 (year 9) and Form 5 (year 11) students in Victoria (%)

	1972[1] metropolitan	1974[2] rural city	1980[3] metropolitan
Form 3 (year 9)	N.A.	79.3	63.7
Form 5 (year 11)	84.3	84.1	81.1

Sources: [1] Krupinski & Stoller
 [2] Graves
 [3] Education Department of Victoria.

2.5 per cent smoked more than 40 per day. A total of 16.3 per cent of people surveyed saw themselves as ex-cigarette smokers. The main reason for giving up smoking was that it was believed to harm health. A total of 83 per cent of males and 67 per cent females who smoked reported smoking patterns showing a daily tar intake of 150 milligrams or higher.

Table 3.12 Estimated cigarette smoking status, and current number of tailor-made cigarettes smoked per day by current smokers, analysed by age and sex, expressed per unit, Australia, 1977

Cigarette smoking status	18–24	25–44	45–64	65 and over	Total
Males					
Never smoked cigarettes regularly	48.8	35.6	25.3	30.5	34.3
Ex-cigarette smoker	9.6	18.3	30.9	40.3	22.8
Cigarette smoker	41.7	46.1	43.8	29.3	42.9
(1–10 per day)	29.6	17.8	20.7	38.4	22.0
(11–20 per day)	52.1	45.1	39.4	39.0	44.5
(21–40 per day)	17.4	32.9	35.2	16.2	29.7
(40 + per day)	—	4.1	4.7	—	3.8
Females					
Never smoked cigarettes regularly	55.5	56.2	62.4	78.0	61.0
Ex-cigarette smoker	7.6	10.7	10.3	10.2	10.0
Cigarette smoker	36.9	33.0	27.3	11.8	29.0
(1–10 per day)	45.1	35.5	35.3	49.4	38.4
(11–20 per day)	45.9	47.3	51.0	44.1	27.8
(21–40 per day)	8.3	16.2	12.5	—	12.8
(40 + per day)	—	—	—	—	1.0

Source: Australian Bureau of Statistics.

Smoking has become less popular among mature adults, especially men. However, at least until very recently, it was becoming more common among adolescents, especially girls. The most recent surveys suggest that this trend among the young may have reversed (see Table 3.13).

Table 3.13 Tobacco use by young people in Australia (%)

	1971	1973	1977	1980
Year 10 students, using at least weekly (NSW— Flaherty, Treblico and Egger)	28.6	30.0	40.3	35.9

	1972 Metropolitan[1]	1974 Rural/city[2]	1980 Metropolitan[3]
Form 5 (year 11) Students (Victoria) currently using	46.1	51.3	45.6

[1] Krupinsky and Stoller [2] Graves [3] Education Department, Victoria

Legal use of pharmaceuticals. A national health survey which included information on medications taken in the two days before interview (undertaken in 1977–78 by the Australian Bureau of Statistics, see Table 3.14) estimated that almost half the population had used medications. 'Common pain relievers' were used by 16.6 per cent and other medicines for nervous conditions by 4.6 per cent of the population. A survey in South Australia in 1978 found that 54 per cent of people aged 13 to 16 had used prescribed psychotropic drugs at some time, including 8 per cent in the previous month. A significant proportion of this group used more than one category of psychotropic drug. A total of 52 per cent had used over-the-counter drugs within the previous month. Most of these people used drugs as medications and used them sparingly.

Table 3.14 Persons taking medication in the two days before interview, by type of medication taken, age and sex

Type of medication	0–14 ('000)	15–24 ('000)	25–64 ('000)	65 & over ('000)	Total ('000)	Per cent of all people
Males						
Common pain relievers	139.4	127.9	558.2	98.9	924.5	13.4
Medicines for nervous conditions	23.9	13.3	165.9	50.2	253.4	3.7
Sleeping pills and medicines	5.0	5.0	69.8	49.0	130.7	1.9
Females						
Common pain relievers	149.4	215.6	797.3	194.5	1356.8	19.8
Medicines for nervous conditions	12.9	21.7	277.3	97.0	408.8	6.0
Sleeping pills and medicines	2.7	8.3	136.9	104.1	252.7	3.7

Source: (A.B.S. Australian Health Survey, 1977–78)

The Williams Report noted that over-the-counter drugs currently being abused included oral analgesics and chloral hydrate preparations (by older adults) and some cough mixtures, antihistamines and weight-reducing pills (mainly by young people).

According to the ABS Household Survey, females use legal drugs more frequently than males. This is especially true of women 25–64 years of age.

Illegal drug use. It is even more difficult to obtain reliable information about individual patterns of illegal drug use than it is to obtain data on national levels of illegal use. The amount of useful information obtainable from individuals by surveys, questionnaires or by interview is very limited. Some information is available from school studies. This suggests reduced frequency of use since 1977 (see Table 3.15). Otherwise, one can only guess about what is happening among individual users from such information as the number of arrests for use and possession of illegal drugs, the number of persons appearing for treatment of drug problems, or the impressions of people in contact with the drug scene (drug users or persons working in the drug field).

Table 3.15 **Reported frequency of illegal drug use (at least weekly) among year 10 students in NSW, 1971–80 (%)**

	1971	1973	1977	1980
Cannabis	1.6	3.6	8.0	6.3
Hallucinogens	0.6	1.1	0.6	1.0
Narcotics	0.4	0.8	0.6	0.3
Stimulants	3.9	2.6	1.6	0.3

Source: Flaherty Trebilco and Egger

It would appear that more males than females are illegal drug users, and almost all are less than 30 years old. The Williams Report indicates that 'no relationship has been conclusively established between socio-economic background...and illegal drug use'. However, some studies have shown that many people who come to attention because of illegal drug use have pre-existing problems of social function (see Table 3.16). Bell and Champion conclude that 'individuals in groups which use drugs more than others have the one consistent feature in common, deviancy'.

A variety of drug users can be found in any community where illegal drug use occurs. Some experiment with drug use out of curiosity, or seek a new experience. Others use drugs occasionally as one of a range of social activities or as a means of escape or pleasure. Some dependent or addicted individuals place an unusually high value on drug use and

Table 3.16 **Criminal history of people with drug convictions, Australia 1977–78**

	\# 0	1–5	No. convictions 6–10	11 or more	Total
Before first drug conviction					
Narcotic users	53.1	34.0	6.4	6.4	100
Cannabis users	63.0	27.5	5.5	4.1	100
After first drug conviction					
Narcotic users	47.9	34.0	9.1	8.9	100
Cannabis users	66.0	29.7	2.8	1.6	100

Source: Wardlaw

use drugs to excess episodically or continuously. People move back and forth between the last two groups. If they survive, they may ultimately give up this type of drug use altogether, often gravitating to excessive use of alcohol.

Outcomes of drug use

Drug use is primarily a moral issue. If there is no demonstrable harm—as, for instance, from moderate tea-drinking—then it is a question of conscience for the user whether to indulge and whether to attempt to influence other people's behaviour. When harm occurs only to the drug taker, followers of John Stuart Mill might still say that drug problems are only a moral issue. However, most people probably see the harm to health and loss of life associated with drug use as a matter of general community interest warranting preventive action and the provision of treatment services.

It would seem reasonable that in setting priorities for action and allocating community resources attention should be paid to the degree and type of harm associated with the use of various drugs. It is convenient to deal with each type of problem in order, in each case covering the whole range of drugs together.

Drug-related death. A detailed study of drug-related death in Australia from 1969 to 1979 (based on *Causes of Death: Australia*, published by the Australian Bureau of Statistics) is awaiting publication in the *Technical Information Bulletin* (Australian Department of Health). This shows (see Table 3.17) that the ratio between the estimated number of deaths associated with the use of tobacco, alcohol and other drugs has been almost constant at 20:4:1 over the past 10 years. However, almost all deaths associated with tobacco use occurred in people over the age of 65, and almost two-thirds of alcohol-related deaths occurred in people over 35. Although almost half the deaths associated with the use of other drugs occurred among young adults, alcohol and tobacco each accounted for about 45 per cent of years of life expectancy (that is, years before age 70) lost in relation to drug use.

Table 3.17 **Estimated number of drug-related deaths, analysed by drug involved and age, Australia, 1979**

Drug involved	0–14	15–34	35–64	65 and over	Total
Alcohol	168	1 194	1 506	699	3 567
Tobacco	—	—	4 166	10 157	14 323
Other drugs	5	352	356	77	791
Total	173	1 546	6 028	10 933	18 681

Source: Commonwealth Department of Health

There were some important trends over time, especially in alcohol-related deaths (see Table 3.18). The estimated number of alcohol-related deaths from motor vehicle accidents (calculated as 50 per cent of all road deaths) fell from a peak of 1849 in 1974 to 1788 in 1979. (A peak death-rate of 15.38 deaths per 100 000 population was reached in 1970. The death-rate in 1979 was 12.40). These falls were offset by increases in deaths from alcohol dependence from 255 to 399, and in alcoholic cirrhosis from 250 to 663. The changes in numbers of deaths for road deaths, alcoholism and cirrhosis occurred across all age groups.

There were also interesting features to the statistics on deaths associated with drugs other than tobacco and alcohol. Most of these deaths were due to suicide, but this contributed a decreasing proportion of deaths (81 per cent in 1969 and 68 per cent in 1979) even though the total increased (see Table 3.19). Among young adults, the number of deaths associated with narcotic use increased dramatically between 1974 and 1978, but fell in 1979. The number of deaths associated with barbiturates increased from 1977 to 1978 and from 1978 to 1979. Most of these deaths occurred in New South Wales, with some in Queensland and Victoria; throughout the whole period, very few occurred in the other States.

Morbidity. The contribution of alcohol-related disabilities to ill-health is well documented. Recent studies show that at least 15 per cent of all general hospital admissions are for alcohol-related problems. This represents a total of 1.77 million general hospital bed-days in 1977–78, costing $242.5 million. In State psychiatric services 0.81 million bed-days costing $29.2 million were occupied by persons with specific alcohol-related disabilities in 1977–78. There are, of course, other health services provided to persons with alcohol-related disabilities. Statistics on alcohol-related hospitalisation in Queensland (see Table 3.20) show a marked general increase over the period 1969 to 1974, with little change thereafter.

Tobacco-related illnesses are more often quickly terminal than alcohol-related problems and hence only account for about 40 per cent of the general hospital use. Unlike alcohol-related disabilities, they also require no special psychiatric service provision.

There is very little useful data about hospitalisation for other drug-related disabilities. In South Australia, in each of three years, about 2000 people were admitted to hospital for the 'adverse effects of medicinal agents'. Twenty or fewer cases per year involved opiates, whereas about one-third of cases involved tranquillisers. Barbiturates, non-barbiturate sedatives and antidepressants were each implicated in about 10 per cent of cases. Similar findings were reported from a large NSW hospital.

Table 3.18 Estimated numbers of alcohol-related deaths, analysed by cause of death, Australia 1969–78

Cause of death	1969	1970	1971	1972	1973	1974	1975	1976	1977	1978
Alcoholism	255	272	298	277	331	454	476	416	469	399
Alcoholic cirrhosis	250	284	337	405	454	529	568	595	632	662
Motor vehicle accidents	1 799	1 934	1 872	1 777	1 848	1 849	1 846	1 758	1 860	1 866
Other	694	762	812	811	822	832	811	863	875	866
Total	2 998	3 252	3 319	3 270	3 455	3 664	3 701	3 632	3 836	3 793

Table 3.19 Estimated numbers of deaths related to the use of drugs other than alcohol and tobacco, analysed by cause of death, Australia, 1969–78

Cause of death	1969	1970	1971	1972	1973	1974	1975	1976	1977	1978
Drug dependence:										
opiates	32	12	54	54	67	85	47	30	43	84
barbiturates	1	—	—	3	4	6	6	14	15	19
other	35	49	74	75	92	88	100	142	121	133
Accidental poisoning by drugs and medicants:										
opiates	2	3	2	1	5	4	8	10	19	14
barbiturates	26	25	27	30	17	34	45	34	32	44
other	50	26	33	47	47	39	47	39	61	56
Suicide by solution or liquid substance	617	579	705	652	546	527	510	425	426	472
Total	763	694	895	862	778	787	763	694	717	822

Table 3.20 Hospital admissions for alcoholism, alcoholic psychosis or alcoholic cirrhosis, analysed by age and sex, general hospitals in Queensland, 1969–78

	1969	1970	1971	1972	1973	1974	1975	1976	1977	1978
All persons aged less than 30 years	195	217	243	271	341	373	391	341	400	466
All persons 30 to 60 years	2 054	2 231	2 182	2 274	3 271	2 871	3 250	2 763	3 272	2 889
All persons over 60 years	322	402	376	360	479	442	557	577	630	593
All males	2 206	2 445	2 405	2 500	3 466	3 081	3 547	3 171	3 658	3 383
All females	365	405	396	405	625	605	653	510	644	565
All persons	2 571	2 850	2 801	2 905	4 091	3 686	4 200	3 681	4 302	3 948

Table 3.21 Offences involving cannabis, Australia, 1971–80

	1971	1972	1973	1974	1975	1976	1977	1978	1979	1980
Number of offences	1 044	2 299	3 196	7 176	13 008	15 689	17 977	14 249	17 501	20 278

Source: Australian Federal Police

Available information about people attending special State government services shows that there was a steady increase in treatment for drug use between 1969 and 1976. Analgesic nephropathy (serious kidney damage associated with long-term use of mild pain killers) is one well documented drug-related problem. In Australia in 1978, it was the causative factor in 18 per cent of kidney failures. In October 1978, 1092 patients were being kept alive by renal dialysis, and 304 renal transplants were performed in that year. Thus there were probably 200 people with renal failure due to analgesic nephropathy in treatment in 1978.

Crime. There are many ways drug use may be associated with crime. For instance, drugs may activate criminal behaviour or may be taken to enable the person to commit a crime. This is often true for alcohol. Money to buy drugs (including alcohol) may be gained through crime. Possessing or using certain drugs, some types of behaviour associated with drug use (e.g., driving while impaired, public drunkenness), and unlicensed manufacture or trafficking in drugs may be defined as criminal. Crime statistics are especially difficult to interpret as measures of community harm associated with drug use, because changes in police policies and procedures are often major determinants of change in number of persons convicted.

Despite increasing community concern, the number of convictions for drunken driving offences per year has changed very little since 1974. Convictions involving cannabis increased rapidly between 1971 and 1977, but since then the increase has been less (see Table 3.21). As an index of narcotic-related problems, perhaps the most striking crime statistic is the number of robberies of chemists and doctors (see Table 3.22). These numbers have been influenced by changing policies on the storage and handling of dangerous drugs.

Other social problems. Of all the drugs used in society, alcohol is the one which seems to cause most social disruption. It is implicated in child abuse, domestic violence and marital breakdown, although all of these represent complex interactions between a number of people in complex social settings. Statistics on causes of marital breakdown show the dimensions of the problem (see Table 3.23).

Conclusion

The available evidence shows that the drugs which are causing most health, social and economic problems are alcohol, tobacco, legal pharmaceuticals and illegal drugs, in that order.

The level of drug use and of drug-related problems is apparently not increasing; rather, there are signs of a decrease in recent years. Since 1974, alcohol consumption and alcohol-related problems have been

Table 3.22 Drug thefts from chemists and doctors, Australia 1973–80

Type of offence	1973	1974	1975	1976	1977	1978	1979	1980
Chemists	180	566	575	264	243	296	378	429
Doctors	329	471	356	215	284	309	289	282

Source: Australian Federal Police

Table 3.23 Dissolution of marriage associated with drunkenness on single or dual grounds, Australia, 1963–75

	1963	1964	1965	1966	1967	1968	1969	1970	1971	1972	1973	1974	1975
Drunkenness as a single ground	75	81	103	142	128	150	135	142	165	204	225	265	295
Drunkenness with desertion or cruelty	73	82	102	118	150	134	151	174	156	248	241	251	375
Percentage of all dissolutions associated with drunkenness	1.98	2.06	2.41	2.64	2.87	2.65	2.63	2.59	2.48	2.89	2.88	2.92	2.76

Source: Australian Bureau of Statistics

steady. Tobacco consumption has decreased and tobacco-related problems have remained constant. The legal use of pharmaceutical drugs appears to have levelled out over the past few years. Even the use of illegal drugs and the incidence of associated problems seems not to have increased much since about 1978.

This is in marked contrast with the period 1965 to 1974, during which the use of all these drugs except tobacco increased dramatically. For example, the per-capita consumption of alcohol increased by almost 40 per cent and the level of drug-related problems increased at least comparably.

These trends are reassuring, but there is no cause for complacency. There has been no dramatic improvement. 20,000 or more drug-related deaths per year is too high a price for us to pay for the benefits associated with drug use, and this and other costs must be reduced. While there is no evidence that we face a drug epidemic, more research and more initiatives are required, especially as there is no simple explanation of why drug use has levelled off. Although one should not discount the effects of specific programs (such as the National Drug Education Program), social influences have problably been more important. Increasing scepticism about science as the source of all wisdom and about doctors and their drugs as miracle workers; increasing concern about self-responsibility and health and about pollution (both environmental and internal); the passing of the phase of youth revolt epitomised in reactions to Vietnam; the economic recession—all these have probably played a role in this changed community orientation.

Notes

1 Reports of the Royal Commission into the Non-Medical Use of Drugs, South Australia, State Information Centre, Adelaide.
2 Drew, L.R.H., Stolz, P. and Barclay, W.A. (eds), *Man, Drugs and Society—Current Perspectives* (Proceedings of the 1st Pan-Pacific Conference on Drugs and Alcohol), Australian Foundation on Alocholism and Drug Dependence, Canberra, 1981.
3 Report of the Australian Royal Commission of Inquiry into Drugs, Australian Government Publishing Service, Canberra, 1980.
4 Whitlock, F.A., *Drugs—drinking and recreational drug use in Australia*, Cassell, Sydney, 1980.
5 Commonwealth Department of Health, Extracts from *Technical Information Bulletin: Incidence of drug use in Australia*, National information Service on Drug Abuse, Canberra, 1979.
6 Healy, P., *Patterns of Drug Use in Australia*, Drug Education Unit, Health Commission of NSW, 1978.

4 Bases of addiction

There has been much discussion about the 'drug problem' and the fact that we live in an 'intoxicated' society. Unfortunately, these terms mean the 'illegal drug problem' to most people, and the image evoked is often some highly coloured, perhaps even horrific vignette from the psychedelic scene of the 1960s and early '70s in the United States. That scene has gone, but its impact on popular thinking has been massive. Everyone now knows that there is a drug problem. Indeed, for some it has become an everyday reality.

> ...drugs are now out of awareness for many people. They blink and don't see what would have shocked and appalled them 10 years ago. They inhale deeply and fail to appreciate that 10 years ago discovery would have meant 20 years in prison in most states. (Ray, 1978, P. 3)

The popular image reflects merely the tip of an iceberg. Illegal drugs are *a* problem, if only because we see them as such and feel strongly enough about it to insist that they be controlled by government agencies. Whether this is a legitimate concern is in some ways irrelevant. The need is felt as real; it motivates behaviour and it cannot be wished away. However, *the* drug problem facing not only professionals but society generally involves those people who have come to respond habitually to boredom, frustration, loneliness and stress with drugs that are legally manufactured and available to everyone.

Drugs have never been more available or offered in greater variety. In the mood-changing area alone there are legal drugs for anxiety, fatigue, sleep and tension relief, for a pick-up, for good social interaction and just for fun. Any four year old TV watcher could probably name a specific product for each purpose. Since infancy today's children have been taught to open their mouths and swallow whatever was popped in to cure what ailed them and they have watched their parents do the same. The average household medicine cabinet contains 30 different drugs and a significant portion of the family budget is spent on drugs, tobacco and such mood-changing beverages as alcohol, coffee and cola drinks. Why?

Why drugs?

Increasing drug use and misuse is the result of many closely interwoven developments. It is not difficult to isolate the relevant scientific and societal changes. The difficulty lies in predicting what will happen next. While the principles of societal change remain much the same, today's problems seem larger, indeed are larger, primarily because of the accelerated rate of change. In the early part of this century, the amount of scientific information was estimated to double every 50 years. Today, it doubles every five. Whether we are discussing science or societies, when rate of change is slow it is possible to hold certain truths as self-evident, make generally applicable rules for behaviour and look to the past to predict the future. These possibilities no longer hold.

Biomedical factors

Developments in medicine within the last century have come to have an increasing impact on society. Not so long ago, they merely improved the quality of living. Now they affect the whole character of culture, mores and philosophy, and it is no longer clear that all advances are beneficial. Early discoveries solved problems that most people agreed needed solution, but more recent ones permit accomplishments that do not clearly do this.

Since the turn of the century, infectious diseases that were once considered major problems have been controlled through vaccination and 'miracle drugs' of the sulfa and antibiotic classes continue to save and prolong lives. In the 1950s, mental as well as physical problems came under at least some pharmacological control with the development of tranquillisers and anti-anxiety drugs. All these medical successes were real, impressive and well publicised. So when the concept of mental health was introduced at about the same time as the tranquillisers, it is easy to see how the assumption that this could be achieved through drugs arose. And with the development of oral contraceptives there came a situation that would have been medically unthinkable even 50 years earlier and that most people today would still consider dubious were it not for the aura of respectability bestowed by medical approval. For the first time, potent drugs were being used on a large scale by perfectly healthy people for social convenience and pleasure.

Drugs that create pleasure are not yet a legal medical reality, but a great many are already being used to remove mental discomfort in otherwise healthy people. Society is clearly suffering from what Wahl (1967) has described as 'status medicamentosis': an intense belief in the power of medication. In a bizarre reversal to medieval concepts, we now use medication as a kind of magical protector. Drugs again have 'power' and we depend on them rather than on people to handle certain emotional drives and needs.

Physicians have undoubtedly contributed by permitting the traditional doctor–patient relationship to deteriorate and relying increasingly on mechanical and pharmacological means of therapy. Magical thinking about drugs is by no means restricted to patients. At the same time, physicians are not wholly to blame. They are themselves caught in a bind. First, they have to deal with increasing numbers of patients whose problems are largely non-physical and second, they are saddled with a public image of the knowledgeable and caring physician as a drug-giving one.

The role of drugs in the doctor–patient relationship has become increasingly complex. The patient can focus on drugs to avoid self-scrutiny. The physician may prescribe to dismiss a troublesome patient, a practice that is exploited by many addicts to obtain supplies. The giving and taking of medication is increasingly symbolic and, as Pfefferbaum (1977) points out, it can serve as direct or distorted communication. Prescription can be seen as a sign of care and concern or as a decision that the patient has insufficient psychological strength and needs a crutch. Patients may report unpleasant side effects as an unconscious expression of their hostility toward the physician and, in extreme cases, may attempt suicide with prescribed medication for the same reason. A physician who is reluctant to prescribe may often be manipulated into a psychological battle. If he or she then relents and prescribes, the patient may feel contempt for the defeated and the physician may feel guilty because many of the drugs requested are likely to be restricted. If drug use then escalates, as often happens, additional anger, frustration and recriminations ensue.

Commercialism and the mass media

The combined interests of the pharmaceutical and communications industries interact with all aspects of drug use. The drug companies produce and the mass media advertise drugs for every conceivable occasion. The advertising is not generally false but it can be very misleading. Cold remedies do not cure the illness but they do remove some of the symptoms. Tranquillisers do not solve problems but they will make people less concerned about them. Sometimes it is not a matter of what is said but what is left unsaid. Consider what the New York press dubbed 'the battle of the headaches' (Sloane, 1977).

In 1977, the United States Food and Drug Administration published a report on internal analgesics. It concluded that all were equally effective against pain in equivalent doses. At the time, Tylenol (paracetamol) had 21 per cent of the $US 650 million per annum analgesic market; Anacin (a buffered aspirin) had 14 per cent and Bayer aspirin 11 per cent. The three companies responded with these advertising campaigns:

> *Tylenol* claimed it was safer than products containing aspirin—it is, for those people who are allergic to aspirin.
> *Anacin* claimed to be superior to Tylenol—it is, if part of the problem is inflammation. Paracetamol has minimal anti-inflammatory effects.
> *Bayer Aspirin* pointed out that there was no basis for the claim that non-aspirin pain killers were safer than aspirin—in the context of advertisements that said: 'Makers of Tylenol Shame on You!'.

Each statement is literally true but the intent of each is thoroughly dishonest.

Apart from their association with commercial drug advertising, the mass media play a major role in the development of drug stereotypes. It is regrettable that people who have no first-hand experience of drug use are continually bombarded with the more melodramatic, news-worthy aspects of the subject. Compared with such tasty morsels, the occasional excellent presentations of the material tend to fall singularly flat.

Injudicious publicity can produce more than inaccurate social stereotypes. Both drug panics and drug epidemics can be started. The publicity given Timothy Leary and the 'flower children' doubtless did much to encourage experimentation with drugs, and the statement made by the United States Treasury Department in 1931 is still valid as a general principle:

> A great deal of public interest has been aroused by the newspaper articles appearing from time to time on the evils of the abuse of marijuana or Indian hemp . . . This publicity tends to magnify the extend of the evil and lends color to an inference that there is an alarming spread of the improper use of the drug, whereas the actual increase in such use may not have been inordinately large. (Snyder, 1970, p. 130)

Societal factors

Modern society has created two 'needs' that have a direct relevance to drug use and misuse: the need to actively produce health, and the need to escape. Whether these needs are legitimate is unimportant; they are felt to be so.

The pursuit of health. Good health has never been more acclaimed. We are so constantly exhorted to improve ourselves that it becomes difficult to believe that we could stay physically and mentally healthy without a continuing major effort on our part. The unrealistic stereotypes of health and happiness projected in most advertising do not improve matters. The modern concern over health shows up in different ways in different cultures. It has different antecedents, and, although increased use of drugs is usually an important result, different patterns of actual drug use emerge.

McCoy (1980) traces Australia's position as an 'intoxicated society' to early concerns about the unhealthy nature of the climate on the one hand and the more positive idea of racial and social improvement on the other. He presents the concept of early Australia envisioning itself as 'the last part of the world in which the higher races can live and increase freely, for the higher civilization' (p. 44), and accepting an obligation to develop its people both intellectually and physically into prime specimens of the British race. At the same time, convinced of the necessity of taking special precautions in tropical climates, colonial Australians

> swallowed a wide range of medications, both sensible and harmful, to protect every individual organ from assault. Alcohol would strengthen the constitution, pills pinken the complexion, solutions flush the liver, powders purge the bowels, opiates soothe the respiratory tract and secret remedies steady the heart. It took several generations of colonial Australians, assisted by rapid advances in medicine and changing popular attitudes toward health, to adjust to the new environment and overcome deep-seated fears for their health.
> (McCoy, 1980, p. 45)

Concerns about the climate faded early in the 20th century but faith in drugs survived, primarily because in the meantime the liquor and drug industries had made every effort to ensure that Australians equated the feeling and appearance of health with the taking of medicines and alcohol. As recently as 1933 (*Truth*, 5 February) a leading Sydney newspaper carried the slogan 'Family Physicians say "Beer is good for you". Drink More Beer. It's good for you!'.

Drug use in Australia continues to be heavy. By way of illustration, the 1979 Medicheck Survey of more than 30,000 Sydney adults (Health Commission of NSW, 1979) showed that 25 per cent of the women and 10 per cent of the men were regular users of analgesics. The great majority of these took two or more tablets a day and had been doing so for more than three years. Fully half had done so for more than 10 years. For both men and women, significantly more of the regular users were Australian-born. While there was an obvious relationship between regular use and frequent pain, especially headache, a significant number were using analgesics to 'give them a lift' or 'help them to cope'. These were mostly women. A significant number of the men, on the other hand, reported using the drugs in an attempt to prevent hangovers, and both sexes sometimes took medication to forestall anticipated pain.

The flight from reality. Drugs have been used throughout the ages to escape discomfort and misery. In our society, misery seems increasingly to be a condition not only of those who are socially or economically depressed but of many apparently in the midst of 'success'.

The world is very much with us. The explosion in information and communications technology has produced a constant barrage of knowledge, points of view, happenings and advertisements. This stimulus flooding is rather more than most brains can tolerate and they react in perfectly adaptive fashion by protectively screening out some portion of it. There are many methods: loud music, togetherness, meditation, returns to nature—and drugs.

For many, particularly the young, the present achievement conscious environment dominating, materialistically oriented society is unpalatable. There are few frontiers a person can individually challenge and identity is largely determined by externals. The rate of both technological and social change is such that the past has become largely irrelevant and the future unpredictable. One result is a need to 'drop out', 'take a holiday', at least temporarily.

Again, there are various ways. However, doing it with drugs does not require long arguments with bosses, spouses or parents, few of whom are ever persuaded that dropping out is a positive, constructive and appropriate action. For the price of his lunch money, a schoolboy can take a barbiturate and spend the day untroubled by reality.

An alternative is to emphasise only the experiences, sensations and activities of the moment—what many have called the 'credit card concept'. Drugs promise many things: opportunities to belong to a group, to bug the system (especially parents), to do something new, to obtain freedom from anxiety, gain social ease and good feelings—the Rich, Full Life the mass media have taught us we all should have. Entrepreneurs make sure that drugs are available, and the modern emphasis on activities away from such traditional moral strongholds as home and church provides the opportunity.

Which drugs?

Every society favours some form of drug use that is regarded as acceptable and useful. In general, drugs to be used in this way should be 'correct' drugs, 'good' drugs, and should be used 'for the right reason'. Each of these points bears examination.

'Correct' drugs

Only in the case of 'effective' drugs (that is, drugs that have a specific curative effect on the problem) can we speak medically, and then only when dose and duration of treatment are appropriate. Beside curative treatments, we can also speak of symptomatic ones. Here, there is no cure, but some symptoms are ameliorated. An example would be the reduction of fever, one of the symptoms of a cold, by aspirin, without any direct effect on the illness as a whole. Unfortunately, true curative effects are few, and medicine is dominated by symptomatic treatments.

In the case of symptomatic treatments, questions can be raised about whether such procedures are adequate and appropriate. Thus, we can ask whether drug therapy of ulcers, typically a psychogenic problem, is an adequate and appropriate approach. The question of appropriateness is especially troublesome because all drugs have multiple effects and in most cases a desired effect can be obtained with more than one drug. If beside analgesia morphine produces nausea and with long term use, tolerance and physical dependence, is it an appropriate pain killer? The answer typically depends not on the drug but on the patient, his or her history, circumstances and expectations.

'Good' drugs

No drug is good or bad. They merely have particular effects, and even these may vary considerably from one person to another. The use of such labels requires not so much a knowledge of the drugs' actions but the adoption of a particular set of values. We can talk about whether a drug is physically harmful, and dose and duration of use again become critical. When 'used as directed', most over-the-counter medications are probably safe; nicotine is probably not. Or we can consider the degree to which a drug disrupts a person's relation to society. In this context, nicotine is generally safe. Alcohol is less so, because at least 10 per cent of those who use it at all do so to an extent where they cannot function socially. Few intravenous stimulant or heroin users maintain a useful relationship to society; most heavy tranquilliser or barbiturate users manage to do so. Finally, we can consider whether a particular form of drug use fits compatibly with current social trends and philosophies.

The 'right reason'

There are fashions in drug use as in everything else. Some drugs are one-timers. Banana skin smoking, for instance, became popular in the late 1960s. Exhaustive experimentation (Angrist et al, 1967) failed to uncover any psychoactive effects whatever, and it appears that the craze was partly a 'put-on' staged by the hippie community in an effort to tempt a Senator to attach his name to something as ludicrous as an Anti-Banana Act. In any event, 'mellow yellow' had disappeared without a trace by the early 1970s. Other drug use—glue and solvent sniffing, for example—seems to occur in periodic waves. Of the thousands of substances that have been self-administered over the centuries, however, only a few have become staples: the opiates, the sedative–hypnotics (including alcohol), the stimulants (including caffeine) and the consciousness-altering drugs.

Western society has traditionally emphasised aggressive achievement, tight control of impulses and an outward orientation: environmental mastery through collective effort. The sedative–hypnotics and the stimulants generally alter the arousal mechanisms. As such, they can be used to cope with pressure or rise to meet it, and Western society has always accepted them with minimal restraints. Use is acceptable, with the sanction of a prescription, up to and beyond dependence levels.

The opiates have their primary action on the approach–avoidance, positive and negative emotion systems. Western culture has always been ambivalent about these drugs. Their use in reducing pain and distress is recognised and valued but the opportunity they offer for avoiding life's problems and attaining hedonistic pleasure is frowned on.

The consciousness-altering drugs offer personal, passive experiences that cannot be shared easily, and, like the opiates, remove the user from reality and prevent active contribution to the common good. Their use carries no obvious social benefit. These effects are directly opposed to traditional Western philosophies. The fact that marijuana and most hallucinogens do not produce physical dependence means that they seem to deliver pleasure without even the spiritually redeeming morning-after hangover (Smith, 1968). This probably increases their attractiveness for some, but the idea of self-indulgence without penalty has traditionally been viewed as little short of sinful.

Drug use, misuse and addiction

The first essential in discussions of drug use and misuse is to separate the legal aspects of drug use from the concept of misuse. Legal–illegal is a *dichotomy*, although what is considered illegal varies with time and place. Law and law enforcement are not absolute entities but reflections of a particular culture at a specific point in its development. Laws work as social controls only when the relevant culture wants them to, and this happens only if the law is in general agreement with the major themes and beliefs of that culture.

Drug use and misuse, on the other hand, is a *continuum* and any drug, legal or not, may be misused. Presently, four classes of psychoactive drugs are available.

Ethicals. These are available only on prescription, and about 25 per cent of all prescription drugs affect the brain in a significant way. The narcotic analgesics, sedatives, stimulants, tranquillisers and antidepressants are among the most commonly prescribed drugs. They are used to control pain, stress, anxiety, fatigue, mood and sleep. All are also used illegally, that is, without prescription. The drug so used is generally identical with those available on prescription, or is a variant that is more portable or quicker acting.

Proprietary (over-the-counter) drugs. These are designed for the self-medication of common ailments and are considered safe if used 'as directed'. The therapeutic uses of most are identical with those listed for the ethicals. By definition, they are not illegal, but many contain ingredients that by themselves would be, and all may be misused.

Social drugs. The common social drugs are nicotine, caffeine and alcohol. Use of these is so prevalent that they are often not seen as 'drugs', though they were all illegal at one time or another and continue to be so in some cultures. Their therapeutic uses are again similar to those of the psychoactive ethicals, and all may be misused.

Compounds sold for non-drug purposes. These include solvents, herbs and glues. Reasons for their use may be similar to those for the psychoactive ethicals, but a frequent purpose is some form of consciousness alteration. Illegal versions would be hallucinogenic drugs, which presently have few recognised medical applications.

The use–misuse continuum

The commonly used term 'abuse' has been deliberately avoided throughout this discussion because of its emotive overtones. The more neutral term 'misuse', however, is no easier to define. It implies use for other than the right reason, but as we have seen this depends largely on prevailing cultural attitudes. Most cultures use some drugs symbolically. Thus, the use of alcohol is not merely approved but mandatory in some religions, and is generally expected on ceremonial occasions of all kinds in Western society. At a more personal level, two additional classes of legitimate use may be distinguished: use in healing (medical use), and use for various subjective purposes (recreational use).

Again, cultural sanctions apply. Medically legitimate use might be defined as the adequate and appropriate use of medication in the treatment or prevention of diagnosed diseases or the alleveiation of physical or mental discomfort, but culture determines what will be considered disease (is alcoholism?). It also has opinions about the kind and level of discomfort that warrants medical attention (does stimulus flooding?) and which medication will be appropriate (is heroin an appropriate pain killer?).

Similarly, recreationally legitimate use of drugs might include the achievement of altered states of consciousness or mood, relief from anxiety, escape from oppressive or uncomfortable circumstances and the induction of euphoria, but culture will specify time, place and circumstances for each of these as well as the actual drugs that may be used for such purposes. As Plant (1977) pointed out, a drug *user* gets high with whatever *you* use. An *abuser* gets high with something different, and, it might be added, is a person you don't like anyway.

Beside purpose of use, a definition of misuse must deal with the quantitative aspects of the situation. When does use become misuse? Definitions in terms of actual or even the relative amount consumed do not give much information. Defining an 'alcoholic' as someone who drinks more than his doctor is clearly unsatisfactory. The most useful definitions take into account both the circumstances of the user and the consequences of the action. Julien (1975), for example, defines misuse as *'the use of drugs for medical or recreational purposes when other alternatives are available, practical or warranted, or where use endangers either the user or others'*.

In the medical area, misuse would include polypharmacy (the unnecessary use of too many drugs), the unwarranted use or non-use of any drug, the inappropriate use of drugs and the coercive use of drugs. Thus, inadequate use of the narcotic analgesics in cases of severe pain in an attempt to preclude the development of physical dependence would be misuse. So would the long-term use of tranquillisers to control anxiety without adequate attempts to uncover and deal with the cause of the problem. The prescription of drugs to exploit a patient's desire for rapid relief of psychic distress or to control behaviour that is disturbing or unacceptable to relatives and/or to the physician is obviously misuse, and so is prescription merely because the patient requests a drug.

Within Julien's definition, recreational misuse of a drug would occur when personal development outside the use of drugs became impeded, when there was preoccupation with drug use or when the physical or mental health of the user or of others became endangered. The patterns of behaviour that fall into these categories are almost infinitely variable and both individual and cultural attitudes and expectations are relevant. We all know in our bones which instances of drug use are 'misuse'. The trouble is that just as we all have our own bones we all 'know' different things and we 'learned' them for different reasons. In the end, misuse is what people categorize as such.

Still, it is generally true that a person who misuses a drug recreationally behaves as though the drug effects were necessary to produce or maintain an optimal state of well-being. In other words, there is development of psychological dependence, as earlier defined.

The intensity of this dependence can vary from a mild involvement with the use of a drug to behaviour patterns that an observer would call irrational and self-destructive. The term 'addiction' remains useful only if it is seen as describing an extreme of this continuum.

The misuse–addiction continuum

Addiction will be defined as a behaviour pattern characterised by an ongoing and overwhelming preoccupation with the use of a drug and the securing of its supply. It refers to the degree to which drug use pervades the lifestyle of the user, and in most cases it will be impossible to state with any certainty at which point misuse should be considered addiction.

It is important to note that this definition of addiction cannot be used interchangeably with the term 'physical dependence', nor does the development or degree of tolerance enter into the picture in any causal way. These are simply temporary complications of the pharmacological effects of some drugs. Addiction to tobacco, coffee or cocaine does not involve physical dependence of the kind or degree seen with opiate or alcohol use, yet the drug seeking behaviour is often extreme. Conversely, exposure to even the most 'habit-forming' drugs is not in itself sufficient to produce addiction. Most people who become physically dependent on opiates after prolonged treatment with them for medical reasons never seek the drugs. They withdraw, and the matter ends there.

A significant omission will doubtless have been noted. No mention has been made of the craving or compulsion to use drugs that is so central in most definitions of addiction. As we have seen, 'loss of control' was the critical factor in the disease theory of alcoholism. 'Alcoholism' was officially replaced by the 'alcohol dependence syndrome', but this is still 'characterised by behavioural and other responses that always include a compulsion to take alcohol' and involves an 'impaired capacity to control alcohol intake' (World Health Organisation, 1977).

The concept of loss of control actually has little clinical or scientific usefulness. In the first place, it is defined by the very behaviour it is invoked to explain. Alcoholics cannot control their drinking because they lose control. The argument is circular.

Second, and more important, compulsion and loss of control are not in themselves factual phenomena. Rather, they are interpretations of experience. What constitutes loss of control is as difficult to define and quantify, and as subject to cultural preconceptions, as drug misuse.

For one thing, loss of control cannot mean that the actual amount consumed is not under the user's control. When they start drinking, 'alcoholics' do not inevitably press on to a state of oblivion. Rather, they drink until they achieve a particular blood alcohol level and then drink only enough to maintain that level exactly (Mello and Mendelson 1978). Similarly, heavy smokers closely control their blood levels of nicotine (Jaffe 1978). The phenomenon even appears in animals: dependent rats self-administer opiates in increasing doses until a steady state is reached that nicely avoids both toxicity and withdrawal and then maintain that level. Far from indicating loss of control, these findings suggest that users can and do control intake quite precisely.

Neither can loss of control by itself explain why people who apparently sincerely resolve to abstain while in hospital immediately return to their drugs when they are discharged. At this point no physical dependence remains. We can argue that perhaps the craving is postponed by the hospital setting; or that once ex-addicts return to their usual environment the drug immediately resumes its symbolic power and triggers uncontrollable reactions; or that the social expectations, problems and motivations centered on drug use are suspended during recovery and return upon discharge. However, if the user's sense of control depends on any of these factors, it is clearly not explicable solely in terms of physiology.

Unless a person is physically constrained in some way, there is always a behavioural choice. Even if we accepted the theory that one drink would inevitably lead to further drinking, that first drink still has to be deliberately taken. Alcohol is rarely poured down our throats or heroin injected into our veins by someone else. Merely being in the presence of a drug does not produce ingestion. Two things are necessary for this to occur.

First, the person must have learned to associate certain effects with the action of the drug. The infant born to a mother addicted to heroin may die if not treated for withdrawal, but it could never be called an addict. It never learned to associate any effects with heroin.

Second, these effects must be seen as having some personally positive value for the user. The goals of drug use may be very broad. Mello and Mendelson (1978) for instance suggest that drugs may sometimes be used simply to achieve a rapid change of state without regard to the actual direction of the change—a kind of 'anywhere but here' attitude. This might help explain the simultaneous use of multipe drugs fruit-salad fashion.

Other goals may be quite specific although not necessarily always conscious. Consider the hypothetical case of a husband who feels that he must compete with the children for his wife's attention. He may try to force her to attend to him by getting drunk. If she responds by further avoidance, as is quite likely, he may begin to get drunk more often. This will increase tolerance, the amount consumed will escalate, and in time increasing withdrawal symptoms will add further motivation for drinking. At this point it might well appear to an observer that the husband has lost control over his intake. If he is not conscious of his initial reasons for getting drunk, he himself may believe that he has 'lost control'. In any case, his simultaneous awareness of the bad effects of alcohol and the suspicion that he should stop or at least reduce his drinking is itself likely to produce a subjective experience of compulsion. A feeling of being compelled to do something occurs only if there is a simultaneous feeling that one ought not to do it.

Two important points arise from this. One is that addicted persons can refrain from taking the drug if they want to or if there are sufficiently pressing reasons for doing so. There is ample evidence that opiate addicts deliberately withdraw periodically to reduce their tolerance and thus the cost of renewed drug use. Others do so to prepare for imminent court appearances or job interviews (Sapira and Cherubin, 1975). Along the same lines, Mello and Mendelson (1978) found that 'alcoholic' volunteers would work long enough to support a two- or three-day spree, then would stop drinking and resume working until enough money was accumulated for another spree even though during the abstinent working periods many showed signs of mild withdrawal. If the reason is important enough, users can abstain for long periods, perhaps for the rest of their lives. It is the fact that they do not abstain (that is, do not have a good enough reason to do so) that constitutes the addiction.

The second point is that theoretical emphasis on 'loss of control' and similar constructs confuses symptoms with causes. The subjective feeling of loss of control is taken as an explanation of why it came about, and attention is diverted from more basic problems. It must be emphasised that omitting loss of control from definitions of addiction does not imply that all or even any addicts can return to controlled drug use. It does imply, however, that whether or not they can do so depends not so much on the degree of control they can exercise over their behaviour but on their motivations for drug use and the degree to which the drug effects achieve the goals they seek.

Some characteristics of addiction

In principle, addiction can arise with the first dose of a drug if its effects exactly meet the user's needs or desires. However, both degree of addiction and the severity of its consequences are relatively independent of the drug's pharmacology, and addictive behaviour itself does not seem to be restricted to drugs. A variety of non-drug habits also produce repetitive and engrossing forms of behaviour. Over-eating, pathological under-eating ('anorexia nervosa') and gambling are clear-cut examples and a case could also be made for the intense absorption sometimes seen in sports and hobbies.

Addiction to these activities can be as obsessive, as destructive to the individual and as difficult to treat as addiction to drugs. Thus the health consequences of over-eating can be as serious as those of excessive drinking or smoking, and obese people have as much difficulty in changing their eating habits as heavy drinkers and smokers do in overcoming their addictions.

Such habits also show some of the features usually associated only with drug addiction, notably development of tolerance and extreme resistance to change, and many have obvious escapist functions. They may begin as a temporary respite from everyday pressures and end as a permanent flight from reality. Stepney (1981) illustrates these points by excerpts from a hypothetical test Miller and Marlatt (1977) proposed for 'skiism', an addictive behaviour of major proportions:

> Its adherents return in spite of the ever-increasing cost of their habit and 'seemingly oblivious to the steady stream of ambulances that carry off the casualties of intemperance and over-exposure'. Positive answers to such questions as—Has skiing ever separated you from your family?; Do you find yourself skiing instead of meeting obligations?; Do you find that it takes progressively stiffer slopes to satisfy you?—clearly demonstrate the features of escapism, development of tolerance, and personal and social dislocation, which characterise a full-blown dependence disorder. (p. 234)

It is not difficult to come up with less lighthearted examples. Whether metaphorically or literally, then, many non-pharmacological habits closely approximate more conventional drug addictions.

However, it is important to realise that addiction as defined here is also a rare phenomenon. Relative to the number of people exposed, the number who become addicts (to food, drugs, gambling or whatever) is quite small. Temporary or occasional misuse, on the other hand, is quite common. Thus,

> When heroin is available and peer group attitudes favor experimentation, most adolescents will try the drug. Many will reject it after one or a few trials; others will use it for a period of time and discontinue when circumstances change; and only a few will evolve into typical long-term addicts. In fractional terms, perhaps less than one person out of fifty exposed becomes a chronic addict. The actual frequency of addiction of course depends upon age, degree of exposure, and other conditions—but even in the most vulnerable group the incidence of persistent, life-destroying narcotics addiction appears to be surprisingly low. (Dole, 1978, p. 41)

Addiction, then, is not an inevitable consequence of exposure. Addiction also tends to be self-limiting. Many addicts 'mature out'. According to Winick (1967), typical narcotics addicts, if they live, remain addicted for only eight or nine years. This is an average; it seems that the earlier they start the longer they remain addicted, with maturing-out occurring at about 35 to 45 years of age. Heavy drinkers also tend to decrease intake with age—it is rare to meet one who is over 60 (Drew, 1980) although death and illness doubtless enter into this.

The self-limiting aspect of addiction seems to depend heavily on situational factors. Perhaps the most dramatic recent example of this comes from studies of drug use by soldiers stationed in Vietnam (Robins et al 1975). Conditions were optimal for the development of addiction. The men were of a susceptible age, removed from usual social constraints, bored, anxious and unhappy. Heroin was abundant, pure and cheap. Addiction rate in this population prior to Vietnam was estimated at less than one per cent but about half the soldiers admitted to using heroin while they were in Vietnam and 20 per cent were judged to be physically dependent on the drug. Nevertheless, within 10 months of their return to the United States use had spontaneously returned to pre-Vietnam levels. Availability was not a factor. Most could have obtained narcotics in the United States had they sought them. What did emerge clearly was the critical nature of the situation in which drugs are available. It seems that a relatively high percentage of individuals will use narcotics recreationally when particular circumstances are in force. When these alter, so does the prevalence of both use and addiction.

Determinants of addiction: who becomes an addict?

Unfortunately, the popular and often also the clinical picture of the addict is built up around those who come to the attention of 'official agencies'. These include clinics, hospitals and the police, and addicts who pass through them will either have been convicted of some drug offence or will require some treatment, usually medical, as a result of their drug use. Similarly, virtually all authoritative publications on alcohol, narcotics and most other drugs are based on populations such as AA members and inmates of hospitals or prisons. It is important to realise that such people are the casualties of the drug scene and probably not at all representative of those in the community who use or even misuse drugs. In addition, most of them come in contact with the agency because of an accident—an overdose, a bad trip, a 'bust' or some other social crisis—rather than their addiction as such. If our current concept of addiction describes only these casualties, as some suspect, it may be that some of the factors we now see as causing addiction will turn out to have quite limited predictive value.

One thing is clear: development of addiction is relatively independent of the pharmacology of drugs. Drugs are a necessary ingredient of drug addiction, but they are not a sufficient explanation. As we have seen, drugs in the opiate, sedative, stimulant and consciousness-altering classes have always dominated recreational drug use. Still, these drugs produce their typical effects in everyone, and it appears that only a very small proportion of those exposed to them becomes addicted. How does this group differ from the general population?

Genetic factors

One suggestion is that some people are especially likely to become addicted to drugs because they have some inborn, genetic predisposition. Direct study of this possibility is very difficult and present evidence is conflicting.

The greatest amount of research has been done with alcohol. Dependent drinking is strongly familial. About one quarter of the male relatives of dependent drinkers themselves drink excessively. However, beside genes relatives also share a common environment and tend to have similar experiences. The individual contribution of these factors is difficult to determine. Dependent drinking also shows strong associations with occupational and socio-economic variables, none of which is easy to fit into a strictly genetic framework.

Problems of specificity also arise. Is the genetic predisposition (if indeed it exists) specific to a particular drug or is it a more general vulnerability? Robins' Vietnam study, for instance, found that a family history of alcohol dependence predicted alcohol misuse in the returnees but seemed unrelated to their misuse of heroin, marijuana or other drugs. On the other hand, heavy drinkers almost universally smoke heavily and they tend to consume large amounts of coffee especially when they stop drinking (Jaffe, 1978). Heavy drinkers also tend to misuse other sedatives such as barbiturates and anti-anxiety agents. No definite answer is available.

One thing may be said with certainty: the relationship between any genetic factor that may be isolated and drug-taking behaviour will be rather indirect. Behaviour as such is not inherited. Gene action expresses itself as a chemical or at most a physiological change. Thus, the predisposition might take the form of changes in the rate of alcohol metabolism, or in the rate at which narcotics are absorbed. Alternatively, particular genetic configurations might result in unusually intense responses to drugs, or responses that are atypical. Most people, for instance, react to opiates with initial nausea and other unpleasant feelings. Only a few experience a 'high'. There is also some evidence that a high proportion of Oriental people are protected against alcohol misuse in the sense that they react with flushing and unpleasant subjective effects to quite small amounts of the drug. They show no equivalent protection against opiates or nicotine. Finally, a case might be made that those predisposed to drug addiction have a higher existing level of distress—a chronically over-active pain system, for example. In such cases, their drug misuse might be seen as some attempt at self-medication.

It is tempting to build theories of addiction on such apparently promising foundations, and they may well prove valid in some cases. One consideration, however, tends to argue against any generalisations: alterations in the genetic endowment of populations takes time. There is no way in which genes could change quickly enough to account for the marked and sometimes very rapid fluctuations that occur in the incidence of drug problems. Such variation is most clearly linked to socio-economic factors such as drug availability and attitudes toward drug use, and in these matters the genetic endowment of individuals is likely to be relatively unimportant.

Personality factors

Some 30 years ago, considerable effort was expended in attempting to delineate an 'addict personality'. The term was initially equated with psychopathology and the aim was to isolate the pathological trait or syndrome underlying misuse. In general, people misusing drugs were seen as having problems and conflicts (usually explained in the psychodynamic terms of Freudian theory or attributed to early childhood experiences) from which they were trying to escape.

At first, the personality portraits were rather specific. The trait cluster of depression, sexual immaturity, hostility and an acting-out mode of problem solving, for example, was seen as predisposing one to alcohol misuse. Those predisposed to narcotics misuse, while generally similar, differed from this pattern in that they preferred to solve their problems by passive avoidance (Goodman and Gilman 1970). The personality analysis was often made by inference whenever the relevant misuse pattern was observed. If there was alcohol misuse, the drinker was automatically invested with the 'alcoholic' personality. Matters have since changed considerably.

It soon became clear that the original approach was too simplistic to be fruitful. Single traits such as orality and dependency quickly proved inadequate in the face of the complexity and diversity of drug misuse. It also proved difficult to link subconscious motives and early experiences directly to later social behaviour.

The most troublesome problem, however, proved to be sampling. As already indicated, the bulk of earlier research in the area was done with drug users in clinics, prisons or counselling centres. People with personal problems are probably heavily over-represented in such populations, and the results would tend to support the assumed causal relationship between drug misuse and frustrating personal experiences. Whether drug addicts really do use drugs as a crutch to cope with the stresses of life has begun to be formally tested only recently, and the results suggest that a major reorientation is needed.

For one thing, direct tests of such a relationship would mean comparison not so much of users with non-users but of users with other users who show different levels of drug use. An interesting study along these lines was carried out by Reuband (1977) on a large sample of school children in Hamburg. A total of 416 drug users were isolated. Their typical drugs were marijuana, stimulants (predominantly amphetamine) and hallucinogens, although 20 per cent had used opiates more than a hundred times.

Contrary to what previous work would have predicted, most users had positive relationships with both parents and school, and the majority of even the heavy users had families where neither death nor divorce had separated the parents. It would seem that the significance of the broken home factor so often reported is exaggerated, probably because of the atypical character of the populations used in earlier research. The only family variable that showed a clear relationship to both level of use and willingness to continue using drugs was acceptance of the belief system and lifestyle of the parents. Most users rejected this; however, a significant though smaller number of non-users also opposed the parental lifestyle.

On a more personal level, there was little relationship between level of use and life satisfaction. Only 19 per cent of the users admitted to being dissatisfied with their life and only 10 per cent usually took drugs during depressed or otherwise negative moods. For most, use was independent of mood and flight from reality was not a dominant motive.

Results such as these suggest that it is no longer appropriate to assume that all addicts use drugs to cope with problems or to brighten a depressed mood or dreary hour. At least some of the behaviour seems to be positive in its own right.

If at least some drug effects are intrinsically positive, no psychopathological reason is needed to explain why users continue their use. However, the nature of the positive effect must still be clarified, and an explanation is needed of why use of drugs begins, particularly since the prevailing social climate often makes the act seem inexpedient, or immoral, or both.

It is not difficult to conceptualise positive drug effects and long lists have been made. In the case of those drugs that produce physical dependence, alleviation of withdrawal distress can be a powerful positive reinforcement for continued use. For some people, escape from anxiety or distressing environmental conditions undoubtedly plays a role. Various personal benefits can accrue. Heavy drinkers, for example, often say that there are many things that they can do after drinking that they cannot do otherwise. Being assertive, aggressive, affectionate and soft are perhaps the most frequent behaviours reported in this context. For some people, these behaviours seem to be possible only under the influence of alcohol. Drugs can also be blamed for various actions and the user thus freed from responsibility. However, the majority of positive effects arising from drug use have to do with social interaction. One can use drugs to assert one's autonomy or masculinity, claim adult status, express conviviality, identify with a group, manifest group solidarity and engage in a host of other actions that human beings generally regard as important and personally satisfying.

Societal factors

The role of subcultures. Culture as a whole limits our experience. It allows us only a relatively narrow range of sensations, hopes and fears. Drug effects must be selection from this possible range, and culture determines what should be experienced as positive and negative, which things are to be sought and which avoided. Actually, the societal forces that interact with drug use derive not so much from culture as a global phenomenon but from its many social subgroups. As long as these subgroups share a more or less common philosophy, essentially the same behaviours will be considered normal and deviant throughout that culture. However, if the existing or evolving subgroups develop different beliefs, norms and values it may happen that behaviour patterns that are considered normal by one group will become deviant by the standards of another. Under such conditions, it is appropriate to speak of subcultures (Arnold 1970).

Like cultures, subcultures evolve through a process of interaction and communication among their members, and contact with them can be established by adopting what Johnson (1973) has called their 'conduct norm'—an expected behaviour—without necessarily adopting the whole of their value and belief system.

People need people. The feeling of being isolated is perhaps the most distressing of human experiences. Not everyone, though, has the social competence and communication skills necessary to develop satisfactory relationships with others and some form of group identity and status remains a major need in many people's lives. Adopting the conduct norm of a subculture is one way to establish an instant identity.

The conduct norm of a drug using subculture would of course be to use drugs. There can be no doubt that much of today's drug use, both legal and illegal, is linked to various drug subcultures. In Australia, drug use is a central feature of the concept of 'mateship'. Diehm (1978) describes it this way:

> There is in this culture a subtle but compelling pressure to drink with one's mates, and it seems indeed that the intimacy implied by the term 'mateship' depends on whether one is prepared to observe the 'rule' of drinking behaviour; mateship would not last too long if one chose not to drink regularly with the group. In many instances the supposed intimacy is entirely alcohol-induced. A group of isolated individuals can acquire a group identity and cohesiveness simply by drinking together on a regular basis, the drinking situation providing perhaps the only common bond.
>
> A rigid rule of behaviour in such groups, or 'schools' is that of shouting, the practice which requires that every member of the group buys a round of drinks for the entire group, and that every member of the group should stay and drink until every other member of the group has bought a round. Should there be ten members of the group, then each has a positive obligation to buy and to drink a minimum of ten drinks. Such 'school shouting' is the rule rather than the exception in Australian society, and the daily consumption of ten or more drinks in this situation is entirely commonplace. Here the abuse of alcohol is not seen as harmful, but rather as desirable and essential to the preservation of one's position in and relationship to the group. Under these rules abuse is not merely normal, it is virtually compulsory. (p. 104–05)

A similar subculture has been described by Johnson (1973) in relation to marijuana use.

For most users, alcohol, marijuana and other drugs provide an enjoyable facet of their leisure. Most are not unduly preoccupied with these substances and have other, more pressing concerns. Plant (1977) aptly describes them as 'weekend hippies'. Those who become very involved with drugs usually lack any alternative interests. They have the least stake in job, education or family and the greatest need to create some form of social status or prestige for themselves. Most of those who become casualties either as offenders or patients are very different from the majority of users and their addiction, when it occurs, is more to the lifestyle than to the drug. For them, drug use is simply the price they must pay for admission to a group. It can also confer a certain status. A man may derive some satisfaction from the respect at least a few of his mates accord him as 'a bloody good drinker' and in the hard core of the illicit drug scene the person who uses the widest range of drugs or takes the greatest risks in skirmishes with authority often has the greatest prestige.

The security of belonging, the seemingly free and easy lifestyle and the excitement of being different may all seem worth the price. It is rarely recognised, at least initially, that conforming to the mores of deviant groups disqualifies one from acceptance by most other groups in the community. In any case, as involvement with the group deepens and consumes more and more time other recreational activities and social intercourse outside the drug-taking situation become increasingly restricted. Were a member of a hard-drinking 'school' to leave it, he 'would find himself with a vast amount of leisure time and very little experience and few resources to be able use it creatively. Similarly, he would have to remove himself from his drinking associates, with very little experience in establishing a relationship that did not revolve around drinking' (Diehm 1978, p. 101).

In other words, the pressure to remain in the deviant group or to swiftly return to it is great. Cultural attitudes toward drug users, together with the legal and medical complications of drug misuse, further increase the difficulty of obtaining realistic alternative gratification and thus foster users' return to environments where they are accepted, the drug is available and its use has been repeatedly reinforced. The ultimate tragedy is that if heavy dependence on the drug develops or major complications ensue, there may be rejection by the very group with which the user originally sought to identify.

Initiation into drug use. Contrary to the popular stereotype, initiation is not provided by a professional 'pusher' but by the peer group. The drug scene is a network of friends, not business associates. People drift in primarily because of the social pressure of friends, and drug use is seen by users as a token of intimacy and a bond between them. In any case, few users of the illicit drugs would risk buying from someone they do not know well and it is quite unlikely that anyone would begin to inject drugs without being taught by a trusted and (supposedly) experienced user.

Peer group values are probably the single most important factor influencing drug use. Recall that unless an association is made between the drug and particular symptoms, psychological dependence let alone addiction cannot occur. The peer group helps isolate particular symptoms as drug effects and interprets them for the novice. It also provides the social pressure to maintain use until tolerance develops to the unpleasant initial effects many drugs produce. While actual figures vary from study to study, it is clear that the majority of drug and alcohol users have a preponderance of current users in their friendship and acquaintance networks. In Reuband's study, 92 per cent of all drug users had current users as friends or acquaintances and the proportion went to 100 per cent with increasing frequency of use. Frequency of drug use and the number of drug-using friends one has are related: such friends can be either the cause or the consequence of one's behaviour. On the whole, though, Reuband's study suggests that friends tend to be the cause of continued drug use, not its result.

The 'contagion' of drug-using friends can be quite virulent. A recent study (Brown et al, 1976) showed that 100 heroin users who had voluntarily sought treatment had between them introduced 260 others to the drug, mainly peers and younger friends. Of these, 75 per cent became physically dependent on the drug. The novices were described as close friends in 43 per cent of the cases; 25 per cent were friends; 25 per cent acquaintances; 3 per cent strangers; 1 per cent relatives. The reason for introduction to the drug was declared in 45 per cent of the cases to be due to the novice wanting to try it; in 25 per cent because the established user wanted the novice to experience the pleasurable effects. At the time of the introduction, 94 per cent of the experienced users believed they themselves were not dependent on the drug.

Perhaps the most disturbing finding in this study was the fact that the average time between the heroin debut of the user and the time he or she initiated the first novice was only nine months, and the authors' conclusion is worth quoting:

> Clearly, then, the user's voluntary entrance into treatment an average of 4 to 5 years after the first use of heroin may have little impact on the spread of heroin through the community. However desirable for other reasons, entry into treatment occurs too late to interdict the spread process. Traditional treatment programs can make an impact on the prevalence of heroin use, but probably not on its incidence, i.e., on new use of heroin. (p. 528)

Some generalisations. Contemporary attempts to define the 'addict personality' would include few of the psychodynamic concepts that were once so fashionable. Instead, major emphasis would probably be placed on such cognitive–social factors as values, beliefs and attitudes, and on such personal controls as conformity, religiosity or tolerance for transgression. Similarly, a modern discussion of what constitutes addiction would probably place less emphasis on its traditional uniqueness and specificity. Instead, five general points would probably be made.

Drugs themselves are relatively unimportant in addiction. It is the process of using them that is significant. It has been estimated (O'Brien, 1974) that one out of five individuals who apply for treatment at narcotics addiction centres is not physically dependent on the drugs. Such needle freaks are psychologically dependent on shooting up and the symbolism and ritual associated with it, both personal and social. Places and people associated with drug use can also become powerful secondary reinforcers. There are a number of clinical anecdotes of former addicts who experience what amounts to withdrawal in environments where their former drug is available. Such conditioned abstinence probably plays a significant role in relapse.

The more different reasons there are for alcohol and drug use—including positive, social and convivial reasons—the greater is the potential for harm. This point re-introduces the importance of drugs as specific substances with specific effects. Some of these may be physiologically harmless, some not.

Drug and alcohol misuse is part of a syndrome of problem behaviour. Among young people, at least, problem drinking and drug taking was found to be associated with higher independence, lower value on and expectations of academic achievement, greater social criticism, less religiosity and more tolerance of deviance (Jessor, 1978). All of these are sometimes considered to be problem behaviours, especially if they emerge at socially unacceptable or inconvenient times or in the wrong places. These behaviours are not merely related: an explanatory account of any one of them turns out to be essentially congruent with that of any of the others. In other words, there seems to be a general proneness or susceptibility to problem behaviour as a whole rather than to drug or alcohol misuse specifically.

Similar proneness to problem behaviour can be channelled in different ways depending on differential support, opportunity and availability in the immediate social context. As part of a national sample survey of 13,000 young people in the United States, Jessor (1978) was able to isolate a group of young problem drinkers who reported no use of illicit drugs, and a group of marijuana users who were not problem drinkers and did not use other illicit drugs. The question was what accounted for their choice.

There were no differences between the groups on most psycho-social measures, but one finding was unambiguous: the drinkers reported more social support for drinking and more access to alcohol than the marijuana users, while marijuana users reported more social support for the use of that drug.

Addiction is a dynamic process involving susceptibility and exposure. Susceptibility is a complex function of individual physiology, psychology and life experiences, and as such changes constantly. Every person has a degree of susceptibility to addiction. Whether it will actually occur depends partly on current level of susceptibility and partly on exposure. Exposure in this context refers not only to the actual availability of drugs but to such factors as peer group attitude toward drug use and people's perceived need for them. Again, these all change constantly. Exposure may increase or decrease susceptibility, but in general the greater the exposure the smaller will be the critical susceptibility necessary for addiction to occur.

Some have suggested that there are several broad classes of addiction and that these can be defined in terms of risk groups showing clusters of particular susceptibility and exposure patterns. Bejerot and Bejerot (1978), for instance, distinguish what they call therapeutic, epidemic and endemic addictions.

In addiction of the *therapeutic type*, the drugs are prescribed by a legitimate healer or doctor for pain, anxiety and so on. Susceptible persons are mainly the middle-aged, both men and women, although women may dominate somewhat. As a group they show a number of personal difficulties, typically related to marriage and family in the women and occupation or career in the men. They are often more ambitious than average, but also more sensitive to criticism and reverses, and neuroses, frustration and depression are common background factors. Criminality and asocial behavior are very rare: these are in general socially responsible, anxious and hypersensitive individuals.

Exposure factors revolve around firstly the need for drugs, and this will vary with life circumstances. Conditions such as war, economic depression, urbanisation and unemployment, as well as more personal issues such as alienation and divorce will be relevant. Second, the nature of the prevailing health care system will be critical. Such matters as the structure of the system, competence of the physicians and degree of control exercised over prescribing practices would be important variables.

Therapeutic addicts as a group feel strong guilt and shame about their dependence and will try to hide their addiction as long as possible. With the exception of addicted physicians who seem to involve their spouses in their own addiction, therapeutic addicts do not spread their addiction to others. Characteristically, their addiction will involve a single drug or at most a particular drug class, and when this becomes unavailable there is little tendency to seek illicit drugs although social drugs such as alcohol may be used.

By contrast, *epidemic addiction* always involves a breach of societal norms and the drugs used are usually not accepted as legitimate in that culture. Persons at risk are mainly young, unstable, immature, adventurous or easily led individuals. Those with persistent social problems involving work, school or family are also at risk. Individual variation is large, and susceptibility changes not only with age but with incidental crises and strains. Men always predominate in this group.

Exposure factors include drug availability and above all contact between established and novice users. Ethnic, political and geographic factors are usually relevant and particular occupations may be especially vulnerable.

Epidemic addiction is characterised by the importance of group identification, and there is active proselytising. Unlike addicts of the therapeutic type, epidemic addicts are usually polydrug users. When persons therapeutically addicted to morphine cannot obtain that drug, they do not go over to say marijuana, although some may begin to use alcohol. In an abstinence situation the epidemic morphine addict willingly experiments with other drugs, both legal and illicit. The more widespread epidemic addiction becomes, the more will non-users be exposed to both drugs and drug-taking, and increasingly lower susceptibility will be necessary to draw them in. Eventually, the non-user becomes deviant, at least in a statistical sense, and epidemic addiction merges with the endemic form.

Endemic addictions arise out of more or less socially acceptable use of certain drugs for recreational purposes. Alcohol, nicotine and caffeine would be the typical drugs in Western culture, although a case could increasingly be made for marijuana. Because the drug use is socially acceptable, a more average or typical user will be at risk. Endemic addiction almost always arises out of epidemic addiction. Endemic addiction also tends to either precede or follow therapeutic addiction, and these two patterns may arise for essentially similar reasons. The major difference between them might be simply the social status of the drugs used. Interestingly, addicts of the endemic type—like those of therapeutic origin—have a strong tendency to continue exclusive use of their habitual intoxicant. They do not switch drugs.

The development of typologies such as these may have considerable value in planning general approaches to prevention, treatment and rehabilitation in particular communities. Different types of problems may need somewhat different facilities, personnel and strategies, and it is useful to know their incidence and prevalence. On an individual level, however, the spectre of stereotyping and labelling is ever-present. The danger lies not in the creation of typologies but in losing sight of the fact that they are models: they describe reality only generally and can never explain it.

Typologies have an insidious tendency to invade individuals and invest them with characteristics that may have little basis in reality. Particular people do fit the description of therapeutic addicts, while others more closely resemble the epidemic type. This information is useful. However, they are also first and foremost unique individuals capable of making their own decisions, and make them they will. When this upsets the model, it means that the model does not fit the individual and no more. Initiating a particular form of interaction, be it casual conversation or formal therapy, solely on the grounds that a person fits some model is the first step to failure.

References

Angrist, B., et al., 'Banana smoking: chromatographic analysis of baked skins', *N.Y.S. J. Med.*, 67, 1967.
Arnold, D.O. (ed.),*Sociology of Subcultures*, Berkeley, 1970.
Bejerot, C. & Bejerot, M., 'Exposure factors in drug use, abuse and addiction', In *The Bases of Addiction*, Fishman, J. (ed.) Dahlem Konferenzen, Berlin, 1978.
Brown, B., Greene, M. & Turner, N., 'The spread of addiction—the role of the "average addict"', *Am. J. Drug & Alc. Abuse*, 3, 1976.
Diehm, A.P., 'Toward a community response to alcohol abuse', in *Alcohol in Australia*, Diehm, A., Seaborn, R. & Wilson, G. (eds), McGraw-Hill, 1978.
Dole, V.P., 'A clincian's view of addiction', in *The Bases of Addiction*, Fishman, J. (ed.) Dahlem Konferenzen, Berlin, 1978.
Drew, L.R.H., 'Alcoholism as a self-limiting disease', *Quart. J. Stud. Alc*, 29, 1968.
Goodman, L. & Gilman, A., *The pharmacological basis of therapeutics*, 5th ed., Macmillan Publishing Co., 1975.
Health Commission of NSW, *Psychosocial Problems of Sydney Adults*, Sydney, 1979.
Jaffe, J.H., 'Behavioral Pharmacology of Tobacco use', in *The Bases of Addiction*, Fishman, J. (ed.), Dahlem Konferenzen, Berlin, 1978.
Jessor, R., 'Psychosocial factors in the patterning of drinking behavior', in *The Bases of Addiction*, Fishman, J. (ed.) Dahlem Konferenzen, Berlin, 1978.
Johnson, B. *Marijuana Users and Drug Subcultures*, New York, 1973.
Julien, R., *A Primer of Drug Action*, W.H.Freeman & Co., 1975.
McCoy, A.W., *Drug Traffic*, Harper & Row, Sydney, 1980.
Mello, N. & Mendelson, J., 'Behavioral pharmacology of alcohol, heroin and marijuana use', in *The Bases of Addiction*, Fishman, J.(ed.), Dahlem Konferenzen, Berlin, 1978.
Miller, W. & Marlatt, G., 'The Banff Skiism Test: An instrument for assessing degree of addiction, *Addictive Behaviours*, 2, 1977.
O'Brien, C., '"Needle Freaks": psychological dependence on shooting up', *Medical World News, Psychiatry Annual*, McGraw-Hill, New York, 1974.
Pfefferbaum, A., 'Psychotherapy and psychopharmacology', in *Psychopharmacology: from theory to practice*, Barchas, J. et al., (eds), Oxford University Press, 1977.
Plant, M.A.,'Is illegal drugtaking a problem?', in *Alcoholism and Drug Dependence*, Madden, J., Walker, R. & Kenyon, W. (eds), Plenum Press, 1977.
Ray, O.S., *Drugs, Society and Human Behavior*, 2nd ed., C.V. Mosby & Co., 1978.
Reuband, K-H., 'The pathological and subcultural model of drug use—a test of two contrasting explanations', in *Alcoholism and Drug Dependence*, Madden, J., Walker, R. & Kenyon, W. (eds), Plenum Press, 1977.
Robins, L., Helzer, J. & Davis, D., 'Narcotics use in south-east Asia and afterwards', *Arch. Gen. Psychiat.*, 32, 1975.
Sapira, J. & Cherubin, C., *Drug Abuse*, Excerpta Medica, Amsterdam, 1975.
Smith, R., 'U.S. marijuana legislation and the creation of a social problem', *J. Psychedel. Drugs*, 2, 1968.
Sloane, L., 'Pause in the battle of headaches', *New York Times*, 19 Aug. 1977.
Snyder, S. 'What we have forgotten about pot', *New York Times*, 13 Dec., 1970.
Stepney, R., 'Habits and addictions', *Bull. Brit. Psych. Soc.* 34, 1981.
Wahl, C.W. 'Diagnosis and treatment of Status Medicamentosis', *Dis. Nerv. Syst.*, 28, 1967.
Winick, C. 'Maturing out of narcotics addiction', *Bull. on Narcotics*, 14, 1962.
World Health Organization, *International Classification of Diseases*, 9th revision, Geneva, 1977.

5 Approaches to treatment

The nature and extent of the response to a problem depend on how it is conceptualised and how extensive it is thought to be. Both change with time. Available data is most complete for the opiates and alcohol, and in both cases the immediate postwar years saw the beginnings of two major shifts in emphasis.

The first was a movement away from disease concepts of addiction. In this framework, the excessive drinker was seen as suffering from an 'allergy' to alcohol that made normal drinking impossible while the opiate addict had a 'narcotics hunger' that arose from an aberrant physiology. Treatment consisted of total abstinence, or, with of the opiates, possibly maintenance on legally prescribed opiates or on other narcotics such as methadone. This strict disease concept gradually lost ground. Much less stress is now placed on physical dependence as a core problem, and both alcohol and narcotics addiction are increasingly viewed as having many causes and effects. With this change of emphasis, the treatment goal of abstinence has come to be questioned.

The second shift derived partly from the first and partly from the increasing incidence of drug-related problems. Treatment under the disease concept was seen as the concern of medical people and specialist agencies such as AA, but the modern trend is toward intervention by community services involving a variety of professional and voluntary personnel.

Neither of these shifts is complete and there is considerable controversy about whether they are even appropriate. Many continue to hold some variant of the disease theory, others continue to insist that only specialist treatment can help the addict. Some of this resistance occurs because the new trends are sometimes based on inadequate research. There is also the reasonable fear that new ideas might be used destructively to attack the work of many devoted individuals and organisations who have striven to make society's response to drug problems more compassionate. At this time, it is impossible to state categorically that this or that approach is the only correct one. New trends must be viewed constructively and the issues must be examined fully and dispassionately. What is being proposed is not necessarily an overthrow or negation of established effort... and the community support it has won. What is proposed is only that, in terms of what should be seen as a process of evolution rather than a static treatment model, there is now need for further development. And what is now put forward should itself be only a passing phase in yet further development as more is learnt about the helping process. (Edwards and Orford, 1977, p. 348)

Should abstinence or controlled drug use be the goal of treatment?

Total abstinence as a therapeutic goal in addiction has a very long history. It derives from the oldest explanations of the causes of drug addiction, which viewed it as the voluntary development of aberrant tastes by persons who lacked moral fibre. Depending on the therapist's precepts and inclinations, early withdrawal techniques were variously sympathetic. They ranged from 'cold turkey' (abrupt cessation of all drugs) at one extreme through abrupt withdrawal with some medication for abstinence symptoms to gradual reduction in the amount of the addictive substance—a kind of reducing maintenance therapy.

In the late 1930s and '40s, a number of aversion techniques were developed to help addicts stay off drugs. AA came into being at about the same time, and also emphasised total abstinence, but in addition aimed at total reform of the addict in all areas, especially moral and spiritual. As we have seen, AA's disease concept of alcoholism was given medical credibility by Jellinek who proposed that the biochemical changes resulting from drinking produced an alcohol allergy such that a single drink taken by a dry alcoholic would inevitably re-trigger uncontrollable drinking. AA was enormously influential and its demonstration that something could be done if excessive drinkers were grouped together rather than buried in jails or the wards of mental hospitals was a major factor in the development of specialised alcohol treatment units.

However, the disease concept quickly proved difficult to support empirically, especially those aspects of it that claimed the presence of some biochemical abnormality. A growing group of behavioural psychologists maintained that alcoholics were made, not born; that their bodies were not biologically different and that alcoholism represented a learned series of habits that could also be unlearned. At the same time, more socially-inclined workers argued that the disease concept placed the origin of the problem exclusively in the drinker and ignored such factors as availability and use of alcohol in the general population. AA, whose primary concern was encouraging identification among excessive drinkers irrespective of background and current circumstances, came to be criticised for failing to deal with the diverse reasons for drinking.

Not surprisingly, the treatment goal of total abstinence also came into question. The concept of the immediate, physiologically-determined loss of control when alcoholics begin to drink has aroused great scepticism and a number of studies from the 1960s on have reported no evidence that one or many drinks or even a bout of drunkenness necessarily produces such a result (Engle and Williams 1973; Sobell and Sobell, 1973). The possibility of controlled or social drinking as an alternative treatment goal is currently a very active and highly controversial issue.

Actually, the real issue is rather different. The critical question is not whether some people who are physically dependent on a drug can return to some form of controlled use but how many can do so and whether any common characteristics distinguish them from the rest of the group.

The percentage who may return to controlled drinking appears to be 'small but significant'. Data on possible distinguishing characteristics of this subgroup, however, are less encouraging (Levinson, 1977). Intake, demographic features such as sex, age, occupation, educational level, intellectual function, as well as the drinking history and pattern are all poor predictors. A greater percentage of those who achieved controlled drinking were married during the treatment and recovery phases, and more were currently employed at full-time jobs. Both these factors, though, have been shown to be general predictors of therapeutic success regardless of the specific treatment goal. In addition, major social changes—remarriage or a new job—often seem to play a part, and built-in controls are important. Levinson (1977) cites the case of a wife who at the first sign of uncontrolled drinking simply packed up and moved herself and the children into a nearby motel (charging all bills to her husband), and another of a first-generation Italian immigrant who was quite literally surrounded by a watchful wife, mother, sister-in-law and daughter. In general, though, there is little that is distinctive about the small group who manage to achieve controlled drinking.

One important point that has been largely ignored in the literature is the question of sampling. There is inadequate appreciation of the distinct likelihood that there are different kinds of excessive drinkers. The subjects of all the controlled drinking studies were identified alcoholics already in treatment programs. They may therefore represent a special group, perhaps a fairly chronic one sufficiently damaged that for them there is little clinically justifiable alternative to total abstinence.

There are currently few if any identifiable programs for individuals just beginning to develop drinking problems. When such people are identified at all, they are typically directed to treatment programs oriented toward the chronic heavy drinker. It may be that early problem drinkers might find controlled drinking both appealing and acceptable, and would do better in that framework than in more traditional treatment programs. There is some more or less anecdotal evidence to support this proposition. Levinson (1977), for instance, refers to a group of reactive alcoholics, people whose dependent drinking was precipitated by traumatic and disruptive life events. With support and psychotherapy, these are apparently able to return to social drinking.

Another likely group might be the heavy social drinkers: people whose usual lifestyle involves frequent occasions for appropriate heavy drinking. For many of these, such a 'normal' pattern marks the beginning of problem drinking and eventually dependent drinking. Perhaps intervention could be earlier and more realistic with these people if it was based on something other than total abstinence.

It does seem that the traditional view that no alcoholic can ever drink normally again must be reconsidered. Nevertheless, that is quite a different proposition from saying that controlled drinking should replace total abstinence as the general treatment goal. Total abstinence is undoubtedly the safest goal and should always be offered as the best option. In any case, at least a temporary abstinence appears to be mandatory at the start of any program. Cameron (1977), for example, has reported an interesting group therapy approach to controlled drinking in which one of the clinical pointers to success was ability to maintain a week's abstinence in the home at the beginning of the program.

Not the least reason for emphasising at least an initial goal of total abstinence is the pragmatic one of time. When first seen clinically, typical excessive drinkers have a gun at their heads: their marriage or job may hang in the balance, and spouses and employers are not prepared to let them experiment. If further difficulties arise, neither spouse nor job will remain. Abstinence in such circumstances is likely to produce at least some improvement; continued drinking is equally likely to produce trouble.

Another pragmatic reason is that many professionals in the field still require convincing that addicts deserve any sympathy or that they can be helped at all. Apart from AA, the treatment of addicts in large numbers is still a very recent phenomenon. Only a small minority of treatment agencies have controlled use as a primary treatment goal; most do not. This of course does not mean that the latter are correct, but practitioners will understandably require convincing data to show in practical terms that the experience of the last 30 years should be abandoned and treatment aims altered. In the meantime, care and diplomacy are essential.

Should addicts be treated by specialists or non-specialists?

The present shift from specialist to community-based services for drug addicts was prompted by three factors. The first was a growing realisation that specialist services had the resources to cope with only a fraction of the target population. Second, there were growing doubts that specialist services were effective with even the minority to whom they could respond. Finally, there was a shift to a more comprehensive view of addiction as a wide-ranging and varying cluster of medical, psychological and social problems.

If all people experiencing drug or alcohol problems called on existing specialist medical services, these would be completely swamped. It has been estimated (Shaw et al, 1978) that under such conditions, each of the about 1000 consultant psychiatrists in England and Wales would have to be responsible for 300 to 400 hundred persons with drinking problems, in addition to their other patients. A massive expansion in AA would be equally unrealistic and in any case contrary to its policies. AA maintains that drinkers must come to them with the sincere desire to stop drinking. It is not designed to develop this desire in the first place. Neither will it accept outside financial contributions.

Nevertheless, as the prevalence of drug-related problems rose, there would probably have been some attempt to expand specialist services as far as was feasible had it been clear that they were uniquely effective with the few who could receive their treatment. This has not proved to be the case. AA is not always an attractive organisation even for those drinkers who do want to stop. Some find it too religious, some of its concepts may seem untenable or the prescribed program for recovery may simply be unacceptable. As regards the various specialist in-patient units, the consensus of evaluative surveys has been that clients are no more likely to improve in them than in non-specialist out-patient clinics (Ritson, 1968). Each appeared to produce some degree of improvement in about 60 per cent of their clients. Given the obviously greater cost of specialist treatment, this was generally taken as an argument against expansion of such services.

However, more was involved than the relative merits of in-patient and out-patient care. The concept of what was being treated was changing; addictions were no longer clearly diseases and emphasis was increasingly placed on social functioning. In the case of alcohol, the British Department of Health and Social Security stated the situation as follows:

> Some people are excessive drinkers, they drink more than most other people, more often, or more on occasions when they drink. This may not cause much in the way of problems with either their

health or social relationships. If not, they do not concern us, but excessive drinkers with problems do. Their social functioning, work, friendships, social relationships may be affected by their drinking... The general aims of treatment are straightforward. *First*, to reverse as far as possible the damage done in the physical, mental and social life of the alcoholic and *then* to deal with such underlying addiction as is present. (1973, italics added)

Similar policy statements have been made by comparable bodies in other countries.

This new perspective completely redefined the role of non-specialist personnel. Where emphasis had been on treatment by medical staff, it was now recognised that such diverse professionals as psychologists, social workers, clergy, magistrates, police and probation officers as well as a wide variety of people engaged in voluntary work might come in contact with the problem. Earlier, their role had been seen as simply one of referral. However, it was increasingly argued that the skills required to help drug-dependent persons and their families were in fact little different from those needed to deal with other problem areas in everyday life and that most such problems do not require medical treatment. 'So long as the presence of consequential or underlying illness can be excluded they may be helped by social work support or counselling by either a professional or voluntary counsellor' (Advisory Committee on Alcoholism, 1978).

The single most important development, then, was the increasing insistence that non-specialist personnel encountering drug problems take a major responsibility for their clients' treatment. Within the new framework, professionals outside specialist institutions would use their skills to prevent further referrals, and identification, treatment and rehabilitation of clients would take place entirely within the community. Specialist treatment would be limited to clients with exceptionally severe or unusual problems.

The new policies brought response to drug-related problems within the area of responsibility of virtually every professional working in the community, and in most cases they did so rather suddenly. Reception was predictably very mixed, especially because few instructions were usually given to the newly responsible community agents about how they were to fulfill this role. Some of these issues are discussed further in later chapters. Suffice to say at this point that the situation has not helped to make treatment more available or more consistent. As already suggested in Chapter 2, many community agents feel insecure in their new role. They have doubts about their adequacy and legitimacy, and channels of inter-professional communication are poor. In sum, their therapeutic commitment is often very low, and until this improves, the success of treatment is likely to be limited.

Treatment strategies

Whatever the therapeutic goal, a broad distinction must be made between drugs that produce physical dependence and those that do not. To some extent, this is a question of definition of what constitutes a withdrawal syndrome. However, most professionals currently agree that opiates and sedative-hypnotics, including alcohol, produce physical dependence and the stimulants and mind-altering drugs do not. Drug misuse may result in an emergency of some kind, or users may come in for treatment voluntarily.

Drug emergencies

Acute toxicity. The most usual case is overdose, but some individuals are hypersensitive and show distress at doses not generally considered to be excessive. Overdose or hypersensitivity reactions with the opiates, sedatives, alcohol and to a lesser extent the stimulants can be life-threatening. Treatment is aimed primarily at maintaining the vital functions and a wide variety of pharmacological-medical procedures may be used. In the case of the mind-altering drugs, toxicity takes the form of some sort of panic reaction. This is generally self-limiting and responds well to reassurance and 'talk down' procedures. Minimal other therapy is needed.

Talk down strategies vary somewhat with the nature of the problem, and three general reactions may be encountered. The first is panic. The user feels that he or she cannot control or accept the drug-induced experience, that there is danger of losing one's mind or becoming insane. Reassurance is the key, projected both by what is done and what is said. The helper must remain warm, calm and friendly, and the user must be made to understand that the drug is causing the strange feelings. The brain has not basically changed, and when the drug goes, so will its effects. It is important to orient the user to reality as much as possible and to the control that he or she still has. For instance, the user might be encouraged to watch the strange images, not fight them, or to control the rate and depth of breathing to match those of the helper.

The second problem is the confusion and disorientation (usually compounded by panic) that may occur when phencyclidine or one of the anticholinergic hallucinogens such as Datura or atropine is misused. Since concurrent memory loss is also common, the only recourse is to repeatedly emphasize simple here-and-how reality such as the day of the week, the user's name and so on. The object is to tie the user in with real-world people and things as much as possible.

Finally, there may be an intense desire to solve problems. Because all mind-altering drugs reduce contact with reality, some psychological stability and some of the defenses built up against repressed and denied feelings will be lost. Under their influence, a user may come to realise or at least believe something about himself or herself that causes concern, anxiety or perhaps depression and will want to discuss this. The best approach here is to assume the role of friend rather than professional. The helper should emphasise that drugs often distort feelings and perceptions, and try to defer discussion of the problem. Attempts to resolve it then threaten the user further.

Medical complications. For instance, there is danger of tetanus and hepatitis infections in persons who inject drugs. Alcohol abusers are prone to acute liver or pancreatic disease. The role of drug misuse in precipitating psychosis remains controversial.

Acute withdrawal reaction. This is relevant only with those drugs that produce physical dependence. The usual treatment consists of initial control of the symptoms. This can be accomplished by giving the drug which has been misused. Many professionals, however, prefer to use one that is cross-tolerant and cross-dependent with it but has a longer duration of action, because the severity of withdrawal is generally inversely proportional to the speed with which the drug is removed from the receptors. Thus, methadone might be preferred to heroin in controlling acute withdrawal in a heroin user. Chlormethiazole (Hemineurin) is popular in the management of severe alcohol withdrawal because it not only shows both cross-tolerance and cross-dependence with alcohol but has some anticonvulsant properties as well. It has largely replaced the use of chlordiazepoxide (Librium) for this purpose.

Once withdrawal symptoms have been controlled, the patient is usually maintained at a fixed stabilisation level of the drug for a brief period. The drug is then gradually withdrawn over a period of days—the detoxification stage. There is considerable difference of opinion about all these procedures. Many, for instance, feel that abrupt withdrawal with no supportive medication has its advantages, and will give drugs only if serious problems develop.

If there are concomitant organic problems or if withdrawal symptoms are exceptionally severe, the patient will need hospitalisation or at least medical supervision, but it is increasingly realised that this will be the exception rather than the rule. The need for medical treatment is minimised when the surroundings are free from stress, and reassuring, non-judgemental people are looking after the user undergoing withdrawal. In such cases, little or no drug therapy may be necessary and withdrawal can safely occur in an entirely non-medical setting.

Detoxification units for this purpose are increasingly available in the community. These provide short-term (one to seven days) care in a non-threatening, non-clinical atmosphere. Such units usually work closely with a nearby hospital and patients are transferred there should the need arise. However, less than five per cent of the clients require hospitalisation for any immediate problem.

In the typical unit, the client is not confined to bed and meals are eaten communally. All residents are encouraged to participate in all unit activities such as housekeeping, recreation, group discussions and assisting newcomers. Because the setting is safe, supportive and comfortable, anxiety is alleviated and withdrawal symptoms are much reduced. An important secondary function is that the client is made familiar with agencies that deal with long-term therapy, and referral to them is facilitated. The ex-addict seems most ready to explore the possibility of change during the withdrawal period, and with guidance is quite likely to at least embark on some therapeutic program.

Referrals to detoxification units may be made by police, hospitals, doctors, AA and social agencies. Self-referral is also possible. In some cases, detoxification units are associated with halfway houses. These typically handle up to 20 clients whose detoxification is complete but who feel unable or unprepared to return to their previous environment. The philosophy of treatment varies from one house to another, but most seek to provide a drug-free environment, a home-like atmosphere, referrals to therapeutic programs such as AA and in some cases formal treatment and vocational counselling.

It is probably too early to judge the impact of the community detoxification systems. One of the few that have been extensively evaluated is that operating in Ontario (Smart 1977), and in terms of the recovery rates of the clientele the results have so far been disappointing. However, there are also many limitations to overcome, notably lack of effective long-term treatment centres to which clients might be referred. When these problems are resolved, a different picture may well emerge.

Self-referral

Some self-referrals are more voluntary than others. In many cases, the client has a 'choice' of going into treatment or something worse—losing a job or perhaps going to prison. Nevertheless, a significant number do go to clinics because they sincerely wish to do something about their addiction. Any drug may be involved: in the United States, for example, concern about marijuana use is the third most common reason (after alcohol and heroin misuse) why people seek help in crisis centres. In most cases, however, the drug used will be one that produces both physical and psychological dependence.

Once detoxification is achieved (if this is relevant), the type of treatment offered may be pharmacological or drug-free. In practice, it is usually some combination of the two.

Pharmacological treatments. A variety of drugs may be used adjunctively to help the client cope with anxiety, insomnia and the general distress of withdrawal. The typical drugs are sedatives and tranquillisers. Because most of these are capable of producing dependency problems, there is considerable controversy about using them in any aspect of addiction treatment. Whether they are used depends on the personal orientation of therapists and sometimes on the policies of particular clinics. However, drugs can also be an integral part of treatment, and this occurs in three general ways.

Maintenance on a drug. This may be the drug misused, as in the various morphine and heroin maintenance programs. Such programs were tried briefly in the United States in the 1920s and have recently made a come back. The British heroin maintenance system has existed since the early 1930s. The practical problems of controlling such programs are enormous and their usefulness continues to be questioned. It is partly for this reason that maintenance on substitute drugs is preferred.

At present, there is no adequate substitute for alcohol. Drugs that show cross-tolerance and cross-dependence with it are all general depressants and present much the same problems as alcohol itself.

Methadone is typically substituted for heroin and other opiates. It is a synthetic narcotic, and, taken orally, satisfies any metabolic need for opiates the user may have. It has the added advantage of a relatively mild withdrawal syndrome and it is said to block heroin-induced euphoria while producing little itself. The main object of methadone maintenance is to keep the addict off the streets and away from the illicit drug market.

The initial report (Dole and Nyswander, 1964) on the effectiveness of methadone maintenance in 750 criminal addicts claimed spectacular success. After four years in the program, 94 per cent of the subjects no longer engaged in criminal activities and most were productively employed. Methadone programs expanded steadily throughout the 1970s. In 1976, United States maintenance programs alone had a clientele of ninety thousand.

Many people objected to the programs on ethical and moral grounds because addicts maintained on methadone are still addicted. They may hold jobs and comit no crimes, but no real alternatives are developed to the drug-taking lifestyle. Some of the early optimism also proved unfounded. Dole and Nyswander (1976) themselves admitted that 'the great majority of heroin addict in our cities remain on the streets, and the programs have lost their ability to attract them to treatment'. Others (Alpern et al 1977) estimated that up to 70 per cent of those treated with methadone return to illicit drugs at one point or another.

The present consensus seems to be that the usefulness of methadone maintenance is limited to the hard-core, residual population of addicts who have persisted in daily use of opiates for four or more years. No one has ever suggested that methadone maintenance be used with young, short-term addicts. Sometimes addicts are not even admitted to a methadone program unless they have tried other forms of rehabilitation and failed.

The existing programs differ considerably in what they offer besides the methadone maintenance. Additional activities range from offers of therapy and help with occupational placement to almost total prescription of a standardised lifestyle. The majority report that their clients do well while in maintenance treatment, but addicts whose adjustment remains good after maintenance termination are rare. As a generalisation, less than 10 per cent of those who leave maintenance therapy are found to be alive, not using opiates, not alcohol-dependent, not using excessive sedatives or stimulants and not criminal on follow-up. (Nurco et al, 1978).

Interference with the reinforcement properties of the drug misused. This tactic is at present restricted to the opiates. All the pharmacological effects of these drugs can be blocked by giving a narcotic antagonist such as naloxone. While the antagonist remains in the body, the person can continue to use opiates but they will have no effects. Initially, at least, this will not decrease the addict's desire for heroin. However, if heroin continues to be used without pleasant effects, the theory is that the drug use and all behaviours associated with it will become less likely and will eventually drop out altogether. At that point, it shoud be possible to stop the regular use of the antagonist. The concept is interesting, but no clear evidence of the effectiveness of such an approach is available (Kurland et al, 1975).

Unpleasant change in the effects of the drug misused. This is limited to alcohol. Disulfiram (Antabuse) blocks the metabolism of alcohol at a specific point. If alcohol is consumed while disulfiram is in the body, asccumulation of acetaldehyde produces a highly unpleasant toxic syndrome. The theory is that the prospect of discomfort will reduce the chance of relapse.

Disulfiram therapy enjoyed considerable popularity during the 1950s and early '60s. It was seen as providing the patient with

> a simple objective act to reinforce his decision and to protect him against weakening in the next twenty-four hours. A resolution which can be given immediate objective expression is easier to keep than one which must remain a subjective hope. (Moore and Drury, 1951)

It was also claimed that use of disulfiram improved doctor–patient relationships and shortened the period of hospitalisation. However, it was early recognised that

> the patient's willingness to take disulfiram indicates, in many cases, a strong motivation to conquer his alcoholism. It is no wonder then that disulfiram-treated patients are frequently the most successful ones; they were better prospects for any treatment in the first place. (Wexberg, 1953)

Most professionals now feel that disulfiram makes little difference in the treatment outcome and that the potential severity of its effects when combined with alcohol limits its usefulness in any case. The reaction can be life-threatening and it can occur to such disguised forms of alcohol as sauces, cough syrup and even after-shave and back-rub preparations.

Drug-free treatments. Drug-free treatments are essential to the long-term rehabilitation of drug addicts. Treating only the withdrawal symptoms or the medical complications without additional therapy does no more than allow the addict to become well enough to return to previous drug-taking paterns and thus continue the destructive cycle. The basic strategy in all drug-free treatments is first an alteration of the drug-taking pattern, and second, the substitution of less harmful modes of problem-solving for the use of drugs. Beyond this, however, drug-free treatments are various, and variously effective. Broadly, they may be divided into individual and group approaches. In practice, most clients experience both. Group and individual counselling are discussed more fully in Chapter 6 and only a few general points will be made here.

Individual Counselling. It would be heartening to be able to say that there is a particular approach to drug-related problems that is clearly more effective than others, but this is unfortunately not so. In-patient programs are not demonstrably superior to out-patient treatment, although initial in-patient care may be useful with strongly dependent persons, to break the drug-taking cycle and establish rapport. Nor is there evidence that long-term institutional stay is especially curative. Emrick (1975) reviewed 384 studies of psychologically oriented treatments for alcohol problems and concluded that any treatment was likely to result in some improvement, but that there was no evidence to suggest that one program was more likely to be effective than another.

This is perhaps not entirely unexpected. Most drug misusers do not show clearly treatable psychiatric symptoms. Rather, they typically show the relatively enduring maladaptive patterns of behaviour which psychiatrists sometimes call personality or character disorders, and these are notoriously resistant to treatment even when not complicated by drug misuse. Evaluations of treatments for these sorts of problems (and indeed for all psycho-social difficulties) have shown that the theoretical perspective and the treatment strategy adopted do not predict whether or not a client is likely to improve (Armor et al, 1976). The most reasonable statement seems to be that all the various approaches work—for some clients, some of the time. Clearly, successful treatment is a very individual matter and every effort must be made to match client and therapy as closely as possible.

Group therapy. In general, the best results to date have been obtained with the various group approaches, perhaps because the development of dependence has such prominent social components.

Group therapy is more than simply working with people in groups. A degree of preselection may be necessary. Group cohesiveness is essential to success and this presupposes a degree of commonality among the group members that goes beyond sharing the same problem. The common practice of grouping people according to a diagnosis such as alcoholism, regardless of such factors as age, socio-economic and culture level, may inadvertently create group isolates: people markedly different from the rest of the group. Such people tend to terminate treatment prematurely (Yalom, 1975) and may be labelled treatment resistant as a result.

Young excessive drinkers (less than 25 years of age) may be taken as an example. Such people have traditionally been considered difficult to treat. Both physical and social damage in this group is similar and often greater than that found in their senior counterparts, but their drinking pattern differs markedly. Onset of signs of dependency, especially uncontrolled drinking, is greatly accelerated, possibly because consumption is much larger. Few of these young drinkers seem to pass through a social drinking stage, whereas most older excessive drinkers tend to have had some 10 years of non-disruptive drinking before showing signs of addiction (Gwinner, 1977). In therapy, young drinkers have been described as resistant, disruptive and hostile, and they have generally been given poor chances of recovery. However, this failure may be more apparent than real.

First, young drinkers overtly resent the time spent by their seniors in discussing difficulties with marriage, finance and career—problems that are not immediately relevant to a young person's life. They also tend to identify older drinkers with their own parents, especially fathers, who often have a history of habitual excessive drinking. The older drinkers for their part display a paternalistic but ambivalent attitude, simultaneously doubting the validity of the younger group's dependence and expressing resentment that they themselves were not treated earlier.

The young drinkers respond to this failure of group identification and cohesiveness with hostile, disruptive, acting-out behaviour.

Second, choice of staff is much more critical. Young drinkers respond poorly to both heavily authoritarian and totally permissive regimes and to both older and extremely youthful staff, however proficient and enthusiastic they may be. In other words, staff age and attitude must not be permitted to polarise. Negative responses are also generally elicited by staff seen as holding a privileged or special status—doctors, psychiatrists and psychologists.

Third, treatment requirements are different. Many young drinkers have experienced significant emotional deprivation in childhood. Many have developed few social skills and are unduly sensitive to criticism. They need education not only about alcohol and alcohol dependence but more importantly in understanding treatment as a supportive and non-judgemental learning process in which interpersonal skills can be developed.

When young drinkers are separated out as a group with special needs, the traditional therapeutic pessimism seems unfounded. There is evidence that as a group they will do 'no better and no worse than others' (Gwinner, 1977). Indeed, there are suggestions (Coyle and Fischer, 1977) that younger drinkers treated within their own special group establish and maintain contact better than older patients.

Family therapy. One aspect of group therapy deserves special mention and revolves around the issue of who is the client—or should be. Too often, attention is focused on the individual drug misuser and away from those with whom he or she interacts, especially the family. At the time of intake, many drug misusers (especially those misusing alcohol) do not have a family or do not live with one. However, the success of family substitutes like group homes and halfway houses in rehabilitating such people points to the importance of family-style support systems.

Where a family exists, the presence of drug misuse within it makes it crisis-prone. Drug misuse by one or more members of the family produces both emotional and physical problems. This has been studied most intensively in the case of alcohol. Cultural definitions of excessive drinking as evidence of weakness, inadequacy or sin, together with equally strong cultural emphasis on family self-sufficiency and solidarity, force the non-drinking members into untenable and conflicting roles of 'rescuer', 'persecutor' or 'dummy' (Albertson and Vaglum, 1973). There are successive attempts to deny, eliminate or escape the problem—or perhaps to reorganise in spite of it. In each case, home life becomes increasingly chaotic, confusing and unpredictable, and the family becomes increasingly isolated from the community.

Spouses and children of excessive drinkers may face physical abuse. As the pay packet is increasinly eroded, health and personal hygiene may deteriorate and problems such as malnutrition, debt and loss of adequate housing threaten. As guilt, resentment and hostility mount, so does the chance of domestic violence. In short, such families are caught in an accelerating downward spiral leading to disaster.

Several therapeutic approaches may be taken. The drug users may be treated independently of family, on the grounds that only they alone can resolve their problems. This at least relieves the family of painful feelings of responsibility. A more usual approach involves the family as co-therapists, and is geared to help them become more understanding and supportive of the drug user's problems. This approach has its merits, but there is a real danger that it may entrap the family in a drug-dominated system in which the user's needs become primary while those of individual family members are ignored.

The most recent approach, what Flanzer and O'Brien (1977) have called 'family focused management', in a sense combines the first two. The family's needs are placed first and emphasis is on developing each member's separate identity with the eventual goal of true family reintegration.

The underlying assumption of the family focused approach is that families, like individuals, have a hierarchy of basic needs that must be met in the proper sequence. The hierarchy is derived from the theorising of Maslow (1954) and has at its most basic level the need for physical safety. Next is the need for food and shelter, then for an adequate socio-economic environment. Finally, there are needs for rewarding social interactions both among the family members and with persons in the outside community. This level shades into the highest 'self-actualisation' level, the needs of which are never fully achieved. Essentially, at this level the family takes full charge of its own life. It not only assimilates into the activities of neighbourhood and community but begins to take the initiative in such matters according to what it perceives as its own special needs.

Following Maslow, the family focused approach maintains that each basic need cannot be truly fulfilled until the need levels upon which it is based are adequately met. As the drug user's condition worsens, he or she tends to slide to more basic needs, and, as we have seen, the family tends to follow. An important point is that although the family as a whole might be addressing needs one level higher than those of its drug-misusing member, the reverse cannot occur—although both family and misuser may of course be struggling at the same level. If both slide to the most basic level of physical safety, they cannot survive further as a family unit.

The family focused approach therefore aims first to allow the family to stabilise, not slide further to more basic needs. Once this is achieved, the next therapeutic step is to help family members reach for and meet the needs of the next higher level. Thus,

> The family will be able to grow and accept help when its basic needs show signs of being met; when the integrity of each individual family member is safeguarded; when relief from day-to-day crisis decision-making gives way to beginning realistic steps in planning for the family and family members; and when the extra-family resources permit growth and integration into the community.
>
> When this occurs, the alcoholic will be enabled to accept help; for he is released to take responsibility while his family may begin letting go emotionally. It means giving up attempts to control the drinking and providing protection from the consequences. This forces the alcoholic to decide if he wants to be part of the family and places the onus of responsibility where it belongs. (Flanzer and O'Brien, 1977, p. 245)

It also allows individual family members to work at achieving the balance between the family group and each member's self-development.

Therapeutic success

The overall success of treatment in alcohol and drug addiction is dificult to estimate. One reason is that a surprisingly large number of addicts recover spontaneously. The use of consciousness-altering drugs tends to be episodic in any case, and, as we have seen, opiate and alcohol addicts may mature out. Whatever the drug used, major changes in a person's associates, circumstances or environment can produce changes in and sometimes abandonment of drug intake. Another reason is that success seems to depend on a number of factors that are not entirely under the therapist's control.

Client-related variables

One such variable is the client's age. In general, the older the client, the better the chances of success.

Another is the client's social stability and support network. A large literature suggests that when the family of the user remains intact and supportive, the chances of a permanent reduction in problem-causing drug use are much better. Similarly, job security is positively related to the outcome of therapy. It is partly for this reason that the development of occupational drug and alcohol programs has received such enthusiastic support. A further compelling reason is of course the hope that such on-the-job intervention can offset the enormous losses in productivity incurred by industry because of illness, absenteeism, accidents and personnel difficulties related to alcohol or drugs.

Many large corporations and segments of both the military and the public service have organised programs that are generally based on these principles (*U.S. News and World Report*, 1974):

- The company makes it plain that it considers alcoholism a disease and will treat alcoholics just as it does employees with any other illness.
- Supervisors are told to report poor job performance, often the first indicator of alcoholism, to trained counsellors in medical or personnel units.
- If the problem is diagnosed as alcoholism, the employee is given the choice of entering a treatment program or losing his job for poor performance.
- A worker who enters treatment gets sick leave and medical benefits.
- Medical records on alcoholism are kept confidential.

Occupational drug and alcohol programs have unquestionably benefited industry. A program in the Oldsmobile Division of General Motors, for instance, found that participants showed an 82 per cent drop in job-related accidents, a 56 per cent reduction in absenteeism and a 30 per cent decrease in sickness and accident benefits paid. Occupational programs do not seem more effective therapeutically than voluntary programs outside the vocational setting, but they do have one advantage: they provide a powerful motivational tool, and it has long been known that therapeutic success is critically dependent on the user's motivation.

From this standpoint, the reasons use began and continued and why the user now wishes to stop are all vitally important. Users entering voluntary treatment fall into two general groups. One sees drug use as generally harmonious with their lifestyle, values and goals. Their dependence is egosyntonic. Their reasons for stopping are always contingent on temporary, situational factors: to please a friend, get a job or prepare for an imminent court case. A few may actually state that they wish to continue use, but need to stop temporarily. This is the typical pattern, and the chances of improvement are is poor. The second group views their dependence as ego-alien and they give realistic problems which use has generated over time as their reason for wishing to stop. They are 'tired of the life', too old, unable to 'hustle' any more and so on. These explanations are always delivered with a depressive affect. Recovery prospects with some form of therapy are good.

Occupational programs run along the lines described above provide a very powerful 'gun-at-the-head'. In motivating a drug misuser to seek help and stay with a treatment program, no one is in a better position than his employer, who has power—through the threat of firing or demotion—to intervene in a worker's life, as well as the right to do so once the problem begins to interfere with his work. Neither logic nor tears has the same effect on a problem drinker as the fear of losing what may be his last link to respectability—his job. (Holden, 1973)

Of course, the viability of the alternatives being offered to the client must also be considered. Total withdrawal and abstinence is often seen as an end in itself, a 'cure', but this is a difficult position to maintain if the only alternative to drug dependence is no drug dependence. The alternative being offered cannot even be a substitute. It must be something that is more effective than drugs in giving the client real satisfaction. Various lists of alternatives to drugs have been published, but so far none is particularly impressive. Almost all the alternatives require more effort than drug taking and some do not seem especially rewarding. Many are now available ('participation in discussion groups') but drug users typically do not take advantage of them. Others ('meaningful employment') are more difficult to implement. Most of the alternatives, like drugs themselves, seem to be mere palliatives.

Young illicit drug users are especially likely to have few apparent alternatives. Many have few ties outside the drug scene, and the scene itself offers many fulfilments: exciting liaisons, daily battles with the law and those who supply the drugs, schemes to manipulate doctors and the welfare system, the often generous and loyal support of fellow users. Such individuals are unlikely to relinquish their allegiance to drugs if abstinence means losing all one's friends and gaining a new and duller lifestyle. Unfortunately, few of those working in clinics can conjure up anything better.

Therapy-related variables

Some variables are very much under the therapist's control. Therapy cannot provide the good life, but it can facilitate personal development and in this the characteristics of the therapist play a major role.

Flexibility about the goals to be sought is vital. Response to therapy should be measured on a multiple scale of variables. A client with altered drug-taking patterns coupled with evidence of improved social, physical and emotional functioning is a greater therapeutic success than one who is totally abstinent but functionally incapable. Although it is reasonable to emphasise aims such as abstinence or sobriety, thinking should not be forced into such rigid categories as 'abstinence = adjustment' and 'return to drugs = maladjustment'. As Diehm points out,

> The history of voluntary welfare endeavour in health and social

welfare services is littered with the wreckage of paternalistic projects that have been designed on the principle of 'I know what is best for you. You do as I tell you and you will be all right'. Such projects, which are an expression of the good intentions of the originator, take little or no account of the needs or the resources of those the advisor quite sincerely wants to help. They frequently degenerate into attempts to manipulate clients in ways that meet the needs of the helper, with scant regard for the individuality and the autonomy of those seeking 'help'. Such manipulative programmes usually have a very short life expectancy and die through the disillusionment of the 'helper' when he discovers that his well-intentioned efforts are not well received. (1978, p. 114)

In such matters as therapeutic goals and choice of program, the client should be allowed as much autonomy as possible. If the therapist is intellectually honest, such choice will always include two alternatives. Therapy can facilitate the user becoming, in the words of one authority, 'the happiest and best adjusted dope addict possible'. Or, if in the client's opinion happiness is not compatible with continued drug use, the therapy should maximally facilitate the transition to abstinence. How this facilitation is performed is probably the most important factor in therapeutic success. The classic study by Chafetz and his colleagues (1962) still bears citing in this context.

Chafetz sought to explain why a large number of patients with drinking problems who were referred from an emergency clinic to out-patient centres never kept their appointments. Equally disturbing was the fact that very few who did keep their appointments were actually brought into treatment. Examination of the dynamics of the referral situation showed the following pattern: protracted evaluation involving delay and contact with a number of different caretakers, some of whom showed open hostility and rejection. In other words, therapeutic commitment to these clients seemed very low.

While a control group of clients continued to receive this treatment, an experimental group went through a referral procedure that emphasised

> consistent respect of the alcoholic's tenuous feelings of self-esteem and constructive utilization of his dependency needs... this means treating the alcoholic with respect and consideration, reducing the frequency of frustrating situations and gratifying his requests. (Chafetz et al, 1962)

Within the year following referral, 65 per cent of the experimental group had made an initial contact with the out-patient clinics; only five per cent of the control group had done so. Moreover, 42 per cent of the experimental clients had made five or more visits to the clinics and were defined as having established a therapeutic relationship. The comparable figure for the control clients was one per cent.

A committed therapist can markedly increase a client's motivation for treatment. The effectiveness of various therapeutic styles is taken up in Chapter 6, but a small preview seems appropriate:

> The effective counsellor is one who feels optimistic about his work, likes his clients and feels positively about his contribution to helping them... he is role secure and therapeutically commited. Clients of such therapists tend to feel that the therapist is able to relate to them as people of value and worth and that he considers them and their problems to merit his time and attention. The effective therapist understands how clients themselves feel about their problems, and he allows them their own perspective—even if he does not necessarily agree with them. (Shaw et al, 1978, pp. 161–62)

References

Advisory Committee on Alcoholism, *The pattern and Range of Services for Problem Drinkers*, D.H.S.S., Welsh Office, 1978.

Albertson, C. & Vaglum, P., 'The alcoholic's wife and her conflicting roles', *Scand. J. Soc. Med.*, 1, 1973.

Alpern, D., Sciolino, E. & Agrest, S., 'The methadone Jones', *Newsweek*, 7 Feb., 1977.

Armor, D., Polich, J. & Stanbul, H., *Alcoholism and Treatment*, Prepared for the U.S. N.I.A.A.A., Rand Corp., Calif., 1976.

Cameron, D., 'A pilot-controlled drinking out-patient group', in *Alcoholism and Drug Dependence*, Madden, J., Walker, R. & Kenyon, W. (eds), Plenum Press, 1977.

Chafetz, M. et al., 'Establishing treatment relations with alcoholics', *J. Nerv. Ment. Dis.*, 134, 1962.

Coyle, B. & Fischer, J., 'A young problem drinkers' programme as a means of establishing and maintaining contact', in *Alcoholism and Drug Dependence*, Madden, J., Walker, R. & Kenyon, W. (eds), Plenum Press, 1977.

Department of Health and Social Security, *Alcoholism: A Medical Memorandum on Alcoholism*, London, 1973.

Doles, V., Nyswander, M. & Warner, A., 'Successful treatment of 750 criminal addicts', *J.A.M.A.*, 206, 1968.

Dole, V., Nyswander, M., 'Methadone maintenance treatment, a ten-year perspective', *J.A.M.A.*, 235, 1976.

Edwards, G. & Orford, J., 'A plain treatment for alcoholism', *Proc. Roy. Soc. Med.*, 70, 1977.

Emrick, C.D., 'A review of psychologically oriented treatment of alcoholism', *J. Stud. Alc.*, 36, 1975.

Engle, K. & Williams, T., 'Effect of an ounce of vodka on alcoholics' desire for alcohol', *Quart. J. Stud. Alc.*, 33, 1973.

Flanzer, J. & O'Brien, G., 'Family-focused treatment and management', in *Alcoholism and Drug Dependence*, Madden, J., Walker, R. & Kenyon, W. (eds), Plenum Press, 1977.

Gwinner, P., 'The young alcoholic—approaches to treatment', in *Alcoholism and Drug Dependence*, Madden J., Walker, R. & Kenyon, W. (eds) Plenum Press, 1977.

Holden, C., 'Alcoholism: on-the-job referrals mean early detection', *Science*, 179, 1973
Kurland, A., McCabe, L. & Hanlon, T., 'Contingent naloxone (N-allynaroxymorphone) treatment of the paroled narcotics addict', *Int. Pharmacopsychiat.*, 10, 1975.
Levinson, T., 'Controlled drinking in the alcoholic—a search for common features', in *Alcoholism and Drug Dependence*, Madden, J., Walker, R. & Kenyon, W. (eds), Plenum Press, 1977.
Maslow, A.H., *Motivation and Personality*, Harper & Row, 1954.
Moore, J. & Drury, M., 'Antabuse in management of chronic alcoholism', *Lancet*, 261, 1951.
Nurco, D. et al., 'Group Report', in *The Bases of Addiction*, Fishman, J. (ed.) Dahlem Konferenzen Berlin, 1978.
Ritson, E., 'The prognosis of alcohol addicts treated by a specialist unit', *Brit. J. Psychiat.*, 144, 1968.
Shaw, S. et al., *Responding to Drinking Problems*, Croom Helm, London, 1978.
Smart, R.G., 'The Ontario Detoxification System', in *Alcoholism and Drug Dependence*, Madden, J., Walker, R. & Kenyon W. (eds), Plenum Press, 1977.
Sobell, M. & Sobell, L., 'Individualized behaviour therapy for alcoholics', *Beh. Ther.*, 4, 1973.
U.S. News and World Report: 'How business grapples with problem of the drinking worker', 15 June 1974.
Wexberg, L., 'Reports on government-sponsored programmes', *Quart. J. Stud. Alc.*, 14, 1953.
Yalom, I.D., *Theory and Practice of Group Psychotherapy*, 2nd ed., Basic Books, New York, 1975.

6 Individual and group counselling

J. HOWARD

Introduction *Jara A. Krivanek*

The treatment of drug and alcohol problems is a large industry. A 1976 survey by the National Institute on Drug Abuse showed that there were then 3878 treatment units in the United States, operating at a total cost of $US 605.3 million. Between them, they employed 31,000 full-time and 15,000 part-time workers as well as over 14,000 volunteers. Over half of the treatment programs were drug-free, that is, based entirely on counselling, group therapy and social service assistance. In spite of this large expenditure in money and personnel, success has not been spectacular.

Part of the problem, of course, depends on how one defines success. Many drug misusers need 'habilitation', not *re*-habilitation. Beside the actual drug problem, they often show a broad range of difficult-to-meet needs and inadequacies: no money, no home, no marketable skills and little interest or experience in ordinary living. When low motivation and low frustration tolerance are added, together with a generally low regard for professional therapy, it is hardly surprising that rehabilitation is difficult. The probability that a month or even a year in treatment can offset the experience of perhaps twenty years must surely be very small. If our goals were more realistic, the statistics on successful rehabilitation might be more encouraging. As matters now stand, we must conclude that traditional behavioural change techniques have been rather unsuccessful with drug misusers.

Two factors are important in this. One is that many drug problems do not reside solely in the user. As we have seen, the physical and social environment interacts with the user's predisposition, background and present circumstances, and available social support systems, even if fully engaged, may be inadequate to deal with particular problems. We cannot rebuild whole lives.

The second is that the client effects his or her own recovery, not the therapist. People bring the probability of their recovery into treatment with them in the form of the adequacy of their self-concept and their competency. The goal of treatment is therefore increasingly seen as the maximization of what already exists rather than an introduction of something new. This has brought about a change in concepts of what counselling should or can hope to achieve.

The Oxford English Dictionary defines 'counsel' in two ways. It can mean

1. Interchange of opinions on a matter of procedure; consultation or deliberation; or
2. Opinion as to what ought to be done given as a result of consultation; aid or instruction for directing judgement; advice, direction.

The popular concept of counselling generally assumes the second of these definitions. A counsellor is someone who tells you what to do. Clinical experience, however, suggests that this is useless, and present-day counsellors fit better with the spirit of the first definition.

Today, clients are increasingly seen as co-participants in an endeavor, not subjects to be manipulated. Counsellors, for their part, are seen as having no right of persuasion, but a duty of presenting reality as they see it, clarifying their clients' perception of their own problems, and facilitating the solution of these problems in ways that are compatible with the clients' own goals and lifestyle.

J.A.K.

Counselling adolescents with drug-related problems

The focus of this chapter is on working with adolescents and young adults who exhibit poly-drug misuse and associated anti-social behaviour. These people are the most frequent referrals to treatment facilities and are usually the most difficult to work with. The issues raised and concepts put forward about their treatment, however, have a broader applicability. The terms 'counsellor', 'therapist' and 'helper' will be used somewhat interchangeably.

Four assumptions underlie what is to follow. First, drug use and experimentation need to be separated from drug misuse. Second, drug misusers exhibit varying degrees of psychopathology. Third, drug misuse has multiple determinants. Fourth, the realistic aim of treatment of drug misusers is usually the elimination or reduction of the need for drugs—that is, cessation of the use of drugs to solve problems.

Various authors support the above assumptions. Amini et al. (1976) stated, 'The major point we wish to make...is that most of the investigators found significant evidence of psychopathology in the drug abuser, while the simple drug user shows up as being much like his 'normal' contemporaries (p. 285).

Jalali et al. (1981) have suggested: 'The majority of youngsters use drugs to relax, get high, and become part of a peer group; their use is infrequent and in small amounts. Compulsive users, on the other hand, are clearly disturbed individuals with disturbed family and individual dynamics' (p. 122).

Citron (1978) adds to this view: 'It has become clear that multiple variables tend to lead some youths from normal adolescent substance use and experimentation to substance abuse, and for some of these to progress in the addictive process. A combination of physical and psycho-social vulnerabilities appears to be a necessary ingredient for an addictive outcome' (p. 41).

The concept of vulnerability is important. Drug misuse does not have a single cause. Rather, it arises in response to a series of events that may or may not be related. These may originate before birth, at birth or during early infancy, or they may result from impaired capacities in caretakers or the social and physical environment. Poverty, inadequate schooling, the availability and status of drug misuse would be examples.

Drug users and experimenters tend to form a very heterogeneous group. Adequate upbringing, possibly supplemented with additional support and information, should suffice to avert the drift to misuse in this group.

Drug misusers also comprise a heterogeneous group, but their varying degrees of psychopathology indicate the need for treatment (Johnson 1980). This group is most difficult to cope with, both on a management and a therapeutic level. They do not resemble the more 'neurotic' self-referred client who is experiencing anxiety and dissatisfaction with life. This group, rather, tends to be hostile, to have a strong investment in keeping 'helpers' at a distance and their flimsy facades of competence intact. The approach, therefore, has to be different.

Those coming for assistance with a drug or drug-related difficulty arrive from a various sources. These may include:

(a) the voluntary referral;
(b) the parent who then convinces the son or daughter to seek assistance after first seeking it themselves, or the husband or wife who then persuades their spouse to seek assistance;
(c) the whole family referring;
(d) the apparently voluntary client who turns out to be just after a good court report;
(e) the non-voluntary client who may be hostile or conforming and who may be in the community under a court order to attend, or who is in a residential setting and ordered to attend;
(f) those in a custodial (prison or psychiatric) setting who voluntarily refer.

The source and type of referral affect the process of any counselling or therapy, and must be taken into account. All clients have expectations and these will need to be explored. For example, the parents referring their son or daughter for a minor drug use difficulty need some education and supporting reassurance and the user must not be seen as having severe difficulties. The hostile poly-drug misuser who has been involved in rather violent, anti-social behaviour differs from the one who is simply stealing, without violence, to support his or her drug misuse behaviour. However, if both are court-referred, the initial task of helping will be different from that with a keen self-referrer paying for treatment.

Assessment

The most important task before any treatment is a thorough assessment. This is sometimes completed by someone other than the therapist who will provide the treatment. However, some helpers prefer to be involved at all levels of the process and complete their own assessments, using a medical officer merely to undertake the medical examination if they are not qualified to perform this themselves.

Table 6.1 is based on the assessment procedure used by the Bourke Street Drug Advisory Service of the Health Commission of New South Wales. Any thorough assessment should include at least these areas and should also differentiate between normal age-specific use or experimentation, and misuse. Assessment of this sort may appear rather daunting, but the information outlined is essential if an adequate plan of action is to be developed.

The means of gathering the information is also important. Mere inquisition can prove fruitless, raise hostility levels and turn a prospective client away from seeking assistance. A sensitive approach that gives reasons for collecting so much information is essential. Initial distress must be dealt with, if evident. Carefully handled, it can become and integral and vital part of the treatment. Some non-voluntary clients, conversely, aim to 'con' the assesor and one must be alert to this possibility if an adequate assessment is to be obtained.

The setting may also impose constraints or encouragement. Settings can vary from private consulting rooms to an all-purpose room in the middle of a prison, and such physical–environmental variables may need to be taken into account.

Other significant variables to be considered when working with adolescent clients relate to the characteristics of the counsellor or therapist. A counsellor's decision to work in a particular area such as drug abuse may indicate individual psychopathology, and this can seriously affect the quality of his or her work. Malmquist (1978), for

Table 6.1 Data required for client assessment

Presenting problems   The clients' statement of why they are there; what they see as their main problems; and what they want from the agency, counsellor or therapist.

Family life   Type of accomodation and any problems with this; frequency of change of location; marital history; living arrangements; dependants; current relationship(s); early life (ordinal position, siblings, foster care, institutional care, separation, divorce, bereavement); family history and pattern of drug use or misuse.

Social life   Important people in client's past and present; quality of these relationships; the drug or alcohol context of these relationships; spare time interests and whether these are satisfying or not.

Education   Schools attended; reasons for leaving; highest level of schooling; difficulties with schooling (learning, relating to teachers or peers).

Employment   Current employment or unemployment; satisfaction with current occupation; previous occupation; reason for leaving and satisfaction level; current goals.

Financial   Sources of income (including illegal); income level; debts.

Legal   Criminal history and outcome; current cases pending; does criminal or anti-social behaviour pre- or post-date drug use?

Accidents and absenteeism   Sick leave in past year; accidents in past five years.

Drug use (including alcohol)
   Current use: Client's view of problem and non-problem substances used; prescribed drugs related to use/misuse difficulties; use of prescriptions; pattern of drug use; frequency of drug use, average dose; route of administration; sources; means of supporting use; use alone or with others; client's perception of reason(s) for use/misuse; client's assessment of control over use/misuse; attempts to cease use; client's view whether dependent or not.
   Past use: Age at first use for all substances used; circumstances of commencement of use of each and client's view of reasons for commencement; has there been a change from use to misuse?; if so, what client sees as contributing to this; gains seen from use/misuse; attempts to cease; treatment sought or imposed; perceived benefits from non-use and/or treatment; reasons for resumption of use.

Psychological assessment   A variety of tests may be given to assess such factors as personality, education level, indications of neurological impairment. The client's presentation, the needs of the agency and the assessor's intuition will determine the tests used.

Medical assessment   This is completed by a medical practitioner and should include individual and family medical history and a full physical examination.

Summary   This should condense the information gathered and arrive at client- and assessor-identified need areas, motivation to seek help, sources of help, degree of urgency and a treatment plan.

---

instance, warns that counsellors may use their adolescent clients to meet or relieve unfulfilled needs or unresolved conflicts.

None of us is perfect and what is being suggested is not that only 'perfect' people make good counsellors or therapists, but rather that self-awareness on the part of the worker is of the utmost importance. The worker needs to be sufficiently self-aware to be able to see where difficulties may emerge or where unresolved or unresolvable issues from the past are blocking movement. Attempting to be as 'well as possible' should be an aim of the worker, and supervision, peer appraisal and self-assessment can assist.

Supervisors need to be aware of the emotional toll this type of work takes, and of the strains placed on workers, especially those working with non-voluntary clients. Appropriate support structures must be built into any agency, or sought out and developed by the individual worker if he or she is working alone.

At times, some may use their clients to meet their own needs, or they may lean too heavily on colleagues or family. Sources of satisfaction that can keep the worker alive, awake, alert and well need to be available so that clients or other over-stressed colleagues are not drained of their limited resources.

The intense feelings of hopelessness, dependency, depression and hostility that abound in these clients can lead to similar feelings in the worker. Likewise a fear of moving into a fairly disturbed client's world of 'madness' may threaten a tenuous link with reality for some workers. Supervision, case discussion and constant self-awareness are stressed as being of the utmost importance for the worker, as well as an acceptance of limitations. The needs of some of these clients are so great and overwhelming that it may be impossible to meet them to any significant degree. Support in coping with this realisation may be needed and this involves coming to terms with one's own limitations and, often, omnipotent fantasies.

A counselling model

The model presented here relates to working individually with self-referrals who are motivated, to varying degrees, to seek assistance. Nevertheless, it is generally useful and can be easily applied to group and family work, irrespective of the therapist's theoretical orientation. The modifications necessary when working with non-voluntary or manipulative clients will be discussed separately.

Within this model (Egan 1975, a & b), the client is given three tasks or goals:

1. Explore your behaviour and examine your problem.
2. Seek action-oriented self-understanding and 'own' the consequences of self-exploration.
3. Act on these understandings.

Throughout, the helper needs training and practice in special skills to assist this process as effectively as possible. The process passes through three formal stages and an essential pre-helping stage.

The pre-helping phase requires attending on the part of the helper. This phase is possibly the most important as it may determine whether the client will stay, or see help-seeking as a waste of time. It is important to attend both physically and psychologically to the client— to indicate an interest in being with the client. Listening, rather than initiating too much conversation, is the goal so that a clearer idea of why the person is there emerges in as non-threatening an environment as possible. This will induce and encourage communication in the client.

Often clients do not initially indicate the real reasons for their being there, or, in fact, may not know them. Waiting and suspending judgement, listening to both the spoken and unspoken messages assists in determining the motives for seeking help and the issues needing attention. The question is—what is the client trying to communicate?

Stage 1: Responding/self-exploration. The goal for the client at this stage is to explore experiences, behaviour and feelings about the life issues related to current difficulties. This involves exploration of both the past and the present. The goal for the helper is to respond to the client so that the process of self-exploration is aided. This goal requires skills in accurate empathy, concreteness, genuineness and respect. An effective working alliance should emerge and form the basis for further work.

Empathy conveys that there has been an accurate understanding of the feelings, experiences and behaviours of the client, from the client's point of view—that is, they have been listened to accurately. Checking that the message being received is the message being sent is important. This may include reflecting back to the client what is heard for verification.

Concreteness assists the client to be specific and sort through the mass of often confusing and contradictory feelings, experiences and behaviours to clarify the difficulties, strengths and weaknesses present. The helper may be obliged to model specificity, and also to ask for specific instances and clarification of vague, abstract statements and evasions.

Some clients do not possess an adequate vocabulary to communicate how they feel, respond or make sense of their experience. In some cases, it may be necessary to check the client's understanding (if any) of various emotions, and to teach the client some of the words needed for a fuller understanding and communication. There are a number of ways to do this. Egan (1975 b) for example uses the following exercise. The sentence 'When I feel...' is completed from a list, of 32 words denoting, feelings such as 'angry', 'bored', 'confused', 'free', 'hopeful', 'lonely' and 'sad'. The answers are then explored. Exercises such as this do more than help the client communicate; they also aid the helper in understanding what is being conveyed so that an accurate view of the client's world can be built up.

Genuineness implies that the helper is not phoney, but is being himself. The helper, although open and spontaneous, should not overwhelm the client. The helper is communicating what he or she feels, not hiding behind jargon or techniques.

Respect implies that the helper is there for the client in a non-judgmental way, and respects the individuality of the client in a warm attentive manner.

The aim of this stage is to gain a view of the world through the eyes of the client in an accepting and genuine manner. It may be necessary to check that what is heard is what is meant, and the client may need to learn some communication skills to assist this process of exploration. It is vital to listen and check, and to remember that the initial remarks or problems presented may not relate to the real issues but may reflect a testing of the helper by the client, attempts at denial, or embarassment about the real issues.

Stage 2: Integrative understanding/dynamic self-understanding. The goal for the client during this stage is the development of self-understanding, putting together the bits and pieces so far explored into a fuller picture and accepting (owning) the pieces and the whole. During this stage, the identification of personal resources which can assist change is encouraged.

The goal for the helper is to enable the client to piece together the data produced, provide alternative points of view or perspectives, and encourage the client towards self-acceptance. This more challenging stage can only be effective if the foundations have been laid through the building of an effective working alliance based on accurate understanding of the client's world. The skills necessary are advanced empathy, self-disclosure, confrontation and immediacy.

Advanced empathy shows that the helper has not only heard the overt communication, but has read the underlying message(s). This may support the client in self-understanding at a deeper level. Inaccurate, premature, or unwarranted interpretations can damage the relationship.

Self-disclosure (by the helper) should be used wisely; only disclosures which promote client self-understanding should be made. This involves risk-taking on the part of the helper, but disclosures which relate to the client do not distract from the process of self-understanding.

Confrontation is a skill of utmost importance, especially in working with drug-misusing, manipulative clients. Discrepancies noticed should be pointed out and the client challenged with them. It must be used sensitively, however, for too-aggressive confrontation can damage the client–counsellor relationship.

Immediacy implies making overt those aspects of the relationship that are significant to the client. Styles of relating, issues evident and resistances, for example, can be pointed out and their implications for the broader interpersonal relationships of the client explored.

The aim is to help clients put together a picture of themselves, of how they relate to the world, and how the world may see them. Areas needing attention, change or development should emerge and resources possessed should be recognised. The acceptance of all of these as belonging to oneself is very important, otherwise they may be seen as only the helper's view and of no real significance or relevance to the client.

Stage 3: Facilitating action. The goal for the client during this stage is to learn the skills needed to live more effectively and put them into practice so that living may be less self-destructive and self-defeating.

The goal for the helper is to provide an environment in which the client can risk trying out new modes of coping, accept failures and encourage further growth. Specific skills may need to be taught; referrals made to resources which can provide what the helper cannot; support and follow-up in such referrals may need to the provided. The client must also recognise that this working relationship will end, and that it should do so without too many unresolved dependency issues for either the client of the helper. This represents a stage on its own, separation or termination.

Common mistakes made by helpers mainly relate to premature advice, confrontation, self-disclosure and responses which are clichéd, imply condescension or manipulation, or which are patronising. The major mistake is not to have waited and listened enough to have heard the real messages or problems, and then offering premature action plans related to this misunderstanding of the client's needs. It is tempting, at times, to ignore or deny the real issues because of their overwhelming, depressing, hostile or helplessness-inducing quality, and to apply pat answers to simple, less significant issues to safeguard one's own existence and peace of mind. This obviously doesn't assist the client and it would have been wiser to acknowledge the situation and refer the person to someone better equipped to cope. The premature removal of the chosen coping defenses of these clients may lead to increased vulnerability, flight from help, and increased acting-out, possibly of an anti-social nature.

'Real life' counselling

The model described above was developed for use with self-referring clients. For these—especially those who seem more neurotic—a warm, empathetic and rather non-directive approach is most suitable. However, most of those working in the field of drug misuse tend to be faced with a different type of client: one out to exploit the situation and resist efforts to change. This difference in motivation for seeking help changes the manner in which the helper is defined, and a different approach is needed (Korn, 1963).

Typically, the initial contact consists of the client defining all the problems in terms of grievances at the hands of unjust authorities or life in general. The world is divided into people who exploit you, and people you exploit. This is particularly so in correctional facilities and other rehabilitation units where the inmate subculture can significantly affect the attitudes and behaviour of clients and, consequently, their view of counsellors and therapists and their role.

Often the aim is to get a good court report, an early release or preferential treatment in custody. The techniques of manipulation learned by such clients are well developed, both in custody and on the streets. They range from lying through attempts to appear conforming and/or seductive, to quite sophisticated ploys. The client may, for instance, begin by being difficult and bitter, then respond to a challenge and change a little, have a minor relapse, seem to suddenly 'see the light', and throughout be extra smooth with the counsellor so that he or she feels rewarded by the apparent rehabilitation.

It is of paramount importance with such manipulative clients to expose the manipulation to begin with and to remain in control. Where the basic model presented above may be put into operation as soon as the ground rules have been established and the relationship clarified, its use with manipulative clients requires the addition of what might be called a pre-pre-helping phase. An example of how this operates is offered by Korn (1963, pp. 140–42), and involves a counsellor and client in a correctional facility.

Client:	Well, I've been talking to a few people and ... they said I should see you.
Counsellor:	Why?
Client:	(in an attempt to appear convincing, yet reticent): Well.... They said it did them good ... you need someone to talk to around here ... someone you can trust ... you can't talk to the screws ... someone like a friend.
Counsellor:	And the reason you asked to see me was that you felt I might help you—that I might be a friend? Why did you feel this?
Client:	(a little defensively): Because they told me—aren't you supposed to be a friend and help people around here?
Counsellor:	Well, let's see now. What is a friend supposed to do? (Client looks puzzled) let's take your best mate—why do you consider him to be a friend?
Client:	(puzzled and a little more aggressive): I dunno ... We help each other, I suppose ... we do things for each other.
Counsellor:	And friends are people who do things for each other?
Client:	Yes.

Counsellor:	Fine, now as my friend, what is it you feel you'd like to do for me? (Such a statement must be made confidently and in a manner that, if it provokes an aggressive response does not risk the physical well-being of the counsellor).
Client:	(visibly upset): I don't get it. Aren't you supposed to help people? Isn't that your job?
Counsellor:	Wait a minute—I'm getting lost. A little while ago you were talking about friends and you said that friends help each other. Now you're talking about my job.
Client:	(getting more annoyed) Maybe I'm thick, but I thought you people are supposed to help us, not put shit on us....
Counsellor:	I think I get it now. When you said 'friends' you weren't talking about the kind of friendship that works both ways. The kind you meant was where I help you, not where you do anything for me.
Client:	Yeh.
Counsellor:	O.K. (relaxing from previous tone of persistence) Now how do you feel I can help you?
Client:	Well, you're supposed to help people get rehabilitated aren't you?
Counsellor:	Wait. I'm lost again. You say I'm supposed to do something for people. I thought you wanted me to do something for you. Do *you* get rehabilitated?
Client:	Yes.
Counsellor:	Fine. Rehabilitated from what?
Client:	Well, so I don't get into trouble any more and don't use stuff any more.

At this point the client launched into a vehement recital of the abuses to which he had been subjected by his parents, the police, the welfare authorities and so on. His most recent offence involved stealing and smashing a car whilst under the influence of Serapax—one of the many drugs abused by him, but during the recital he never referred to any culpability on his part, just the mistreatment by others.

The counsellor heard this out, with an expression of growing puzzlement, not lost on the client. At length the counsellor broke in:

Counsellor:	Wait ... I don't understand. When you said you wanted me to help you stop getting into trouble, I thought you meant the kind of trouble that got you in here. *Your* difficulties with the law, for example. You haven't talked about what *you* did to get you in here.
Client:	(trying to control himself): But I *am* talking about that! I'm talking about all those bastards who put me here!
Counsellor:	How do you mean?

The client repeated the tirade, especially trying to get the counsellor 'on side' by saying such things as 'what about this? Do you think that's fair?' The counsellor broke in again.

Counsellor: I still don't see it. We'd better get more specific. Now your last trouble—the one that got you in here. The car you stole...

Client: But, that wasn't my fault. My mate gave me these pills and said he'd wait and give me a lift home. He pissed off and left me. I was going home and saw this car that had already been stolen. I didn't steal it.

Counsellor: But, you drove it, you knew the consequences.

At this point the client got very angry, got up and stormed around the room denouncing 'shrinks' and saying they were all like the rest—just out to get you.

Counsellor: Wait a bit. You said before you wanted me to help *you*. We've been trying to find out how. But so far you haven't been talking about anything the matter with you—just all these other people. Are we supposed to rehabilitate *you* or them?

Client: I don't give a fuck who you rehabilitate. I've had enough of this. I want to call it off.

Counsellor: I mind about that. Here you've been telling me my job is to rehabilitate you and now you want to call it off. Don't you want to get rehabilitated and out of here? (Client is silent)

Counsellor: Let's see if we can review this whole thing. You said you wanted to be rehabilitated. I asked from what, and you said from getting into trouble and drugs. I ask about your trouble and you tell me about all these people who have treated you unfairly, and haven't given you what you wanted. Now does that mean the way to keep you out of trouble is to give you what you want?

Client: That's *not* it.
Counsellor: Well, have I given you what you wanted?
Client: Shit, no!
Counsellor: You're pretty angry with me now aren't you (smiles) (Client silent, looks away).
Counsellor: (in a half-chiding, half-kidding tone): Here, not five minutes ago you were talking about what good friends we could be, and now you're acting like I'm your worst enemy.
Client: It's true, isn't it.
Counsellor: C'mon now, you're just trying to get mad. (Client softens a little)

Counsellor:	O.K. Now we've agreed to stop kidding, let's get down to cases. Why did you come to see me today?
Client:	(starts to talk about rehabilitation again). Counsellor cuts in:
Counsellor:	Come on now. I thought we agreed to stop conning. Why did you come?
Client:	Well . . . I heard you sometimes see guys . . . and . . .
Counsellor:	And what?
Client:	Help them.
Counsellor:	How?
Client:	Well, I tell you my problem . . . and . . .
Counsellor:	And then, what happens . . . (Silence)
Client:	You tell *them* about it and . . .
Counsellor:	Who do I tell?
Client:	You know . . .
Counsellor:	Should I write a report on this session?
Client:	Hell no!
Counsellor:	What do you think we should do?
Client:	Maybe I could . . . (silence)
Counsellor:	Maybe you should come back when you really have something to talk about.

This exchange shows the problems in the initial stages of working with a non-voluntary client, out to manipulate the system. Follow-up of these clients is important, so that the possibility of developing a working alliance is not lost. However, it is vital to withstand the initial attempt to 'con' the counsellor. Permissiveness, non-directiveness and unconditional acceptance have little place in the initial stages with most such clients, and none at all with some. The approach outlined above unmasks the attempt at manipulation and uncovers the true, intensely hostile feelings of the client. This has to be done with ease, an absence of moralising, and with confidence. As Korn (1963) suggests, the anger the client takes away needs to be recognised as anger at himself for not being able to 'con' the counsellor. Such attempts may 'ready' the client for work and lead to a real motivation for change.

The type of client described above will usually see 'friendship' with counsellors as a means of neutralising them and minimising the possible pain of facing themselves, accepting what is seen, recognising the need for change and putting change strategies into practice. Techniques which put responsibility back on the client are therefore essential.

Adolescents also require special techniques. Adolescence is a time when denial, projection of blame, rationalising, and acting-out are common means of coping. Premature removal of these may do great damage, so they must be worked on, within a supportive setting, so that more functional coping adaptations may emerge or be strengthened.

However, there should be little opportunity for continuing to blame others or avoid acceptance of responsibility. Vorrath and Brendtro (1974) call this 'turning it back' or reversal of responsibility.

For example, a youth who had a serious alcohol abuse difficulty saw his older brother on the weekend, got drunk and arrested for his drunken behaviours.

Client: Well, I had stopped drinking, but I only did it on the weekend because I hadn't seen my brother for ages and he wanted to have a drink with me.
Counsellor: So you're saying that you don't have a problem with grog, just a new problem of being easily misled.

The 'turning it back' technique can be very useful with some clients who are setting up a power game and who are testing the limits. For example, a new admission to a treatment facility refuses to go to the group meeting. Instead of an argument, another technique may be useful.

Client: You're not going to get me to go to group.
Counsellor: Fine, you needn't go to group now—you may not be ready. It takes a lot of guts to help others and yourself. Let us know when you are ready.

These techniques must not be used in a cold, aloof manner. Responsibility must be turned back to the clients, but they must still be assured they are valued and cared about. With some clients, however, anxiety must be increased, not alleviated.

As mentioned above, adolescence brings with it stage-specific behaviours and modes of coping. These may appear abnormal if continued into adulthood, but they are part of normal adolescent development. Often, counselling relationships presuppose some capacity for maintaining a reasonably stable relationship. Many adolescent and young adult drug misusers seen in treatment do not have this capacity, and such a deficit needs to be taken into account and some groundwork undertaken before individual work can be effective. This may be through initial placement in a group, which could be less threatening in the early stages.

Drug misusers may also be impaired in other ways. According to Amini et al (1976),

> Most of these young people have serious ego defects that need repair. They use drugs to remedy apathy, boredom, depression, and lack of capacity for intimacy; or to deal with troublesome ideation where to go crazy temporarily has less painful consequences than reality-oriented thinking.

The problem of early deprivation does not have a psychological solution. We rarely do anyone a great service by showing him how hungry he is. Therefore, the challenge which we have accepted in treating these young people forces us to provide some of the emotional putty needed to fill in the holes of prior deprivation before we can proceed with any kind of psychotherapy dealing with internal conflicts. (pp. 291–92)

Difficulties related to lack of motivation for help-seeking and the use of denial have been outlined above. Many of these clients deny any psychological discomfort and often see themselves as hypernormal ('I'm just like everyone else') and not needing any help. Most are in 'treatment' against their will and powerful peer forces are often working to undermine any assistance given. The counsellor or therapist must be sensitive to this and it is usually helpful to let the client know the counsellor recognises the dilemmas—to appear normal, yet know there are problems; to want help, yet not feel strong enough to have peers know it.

A treatment model

It may be useful to approach the treatment of these clients within the context of a four-phase model.

Phase 1: Setting limits and establishing a therapeutic/working alliance.
Adolescents are usually geared to a world of action and rapid change. The prospect of long-term work on difficulties is daunting. The approach—avoidance conflict about admitting the need for assistance needs to be worked through. At this stage there is often a lot of acting-out behaviour, much of it designed to test the capacity of the counsellor or therapist to cope. This is a very frustrating time for the worker, but only after this phase has been worked through can any worthwhile treatment goals be established. Some of the acting-out will involve arriving for appointments drunk or 'out of it', not arriving at all, arriving at the wrong time and expecting to be seen then, and attempting to make the worker feel guilty if this does not happen.

In this initial phase the counsellor or therapist will need to be more active, talkative and often more directive than usual. The work will be patchy, seeming to jump from one crisis to another. It is important for the counsellor or therapist to feel comfortable with this process, yet not adopt an unreal, phoney, all-smiling, accepting stance. When working with adolescents there must be an acceptance of this slow, rather chaotic style. The counsellor or therapist should be interested in adolescents, 'someone in easy touch with his own adolescence, and someone who manifests, but not to a clinical degree, a basically adolescent type of personality' (Anthony, 1973, p. 234).

There should also be an awareness and acceptance by the counsellor or therapist of the prevailing 'youth culture'. This does not imply an endorsement of or liking for its content, merely an appreciation of its possible worth in and significant impact on the lives of clients.

An initial aim may be to foster dependency on the counsellor or therapist so that the client may become willing to restrain some behaviour to secure a continuing relationship. However, with severely developmentally disordered adolescents, this can be a most difficult task, and should not overwhelm or swamp the client.

Testing, provocation, seduction, ridicule, taunting, and manipulation usually characterise this phase. The counsellor or therapist must surmount these. If the counsellor survives this phase, which may vary in length, a workable alliance should emerge where less confrontive and 'anti-manipulation' techniques can be employed. There should have been a shift from action to talking and expression of feeling.

Phase 2: Working through. During this phase the client is often alternatively depressed and angry. This is due to the self-exploration being undertaken and the self-understanding and acceptance emerging. Accepting unpleasant and problematic parts of oneself is not easy, especially for clients who may have little capacity to tolerate frustration, be alone or care for self or others. This is the main 'work' phase and leads through to the action component where alterantive coping strategies may be risked, within a supportive relationship.

Phase 3: Initiation of termination. During this phase the client is often anxious, fears abandonment, and as a consequence sometimes regresses in behaviour in an attempt to appear not ready to go. These unresolved dependency needs require careful attention.

Phase 4: Termination. The client may regress at this time, and the counsellor or therapist often needs to be 'quietly available' for 'boosters'.

Alternatives theory

Working through conflicts and other difficulties, especially relational, with a counsellor or therapist may only partly help the client to move away from drug abuse. Many authors have stressed the need to find alternatives to drugs for users and misusers. As Amini et al (1976) point out, 'where drugs are used to fill a void, one would do well to search for an alternative to filling the void' (p. 285).

The alternatives approach is based on the realities of drug use. Cohen (1973) has drawn up a catalogue of the types of gratification that may be sought through drugs and offers some alternatives. Some of these are shown in Table 6.2. Others not listed here include needs in the sensory, stylistic, creative–aesthetic and spiritual–mystical areas. Many of the alternatives are rather American and possibly very middle class. In fact,

Table 6.2 Types of gratification sought through drugs and some alternatives (after Cohen, 1973)

Type of gratification and some drugs use to achieve it	Examples	Alternatives
Physical Alcohol, tranquilisers, stimulants, analgesics, cannabis	Physical relaxation, relief from pain, increase in energy, avoidance of fatigue	Relaxation training; yoga; dance; preventive medicine; diet; sport (especially for fun rather than competition)
Emotional Narcotics, tranquilisers, alcohol, cannabis, barbiturates, stimulants, psychedelics	Psychological escape: reduction of tension, anxiety or conflict; emotional relaxation; mood alteration; insight seeking; avoidance of decision making; desire for privacy; rebellion; increase in self-esteem	Creation of alternative peer groups; group experiences; interpersonal skill workshops; role-playing; goal-directed activities through groups such as Scouts; assertiveness training; family life education; family therapy; premarital education; alternative families; creation of 'rap' centers
Mental–intellectual Especially stimulants and psychedelics	Reduction of boredom; curiosity; enhancement of learning; problem solving; research on self; avoiding mental fatigue	Mental–intellectual hobbies, e.g., chess; intellectual excitement through reading or discussion; challenge through education; introspection; memory training; attention exercises; training in problem solving and mind-control
Experiential Any, except tranquilisers	Desire for fun; a 'high' for its own sake; 'freaky', distorted experiences; intense involvement	Experience in 'playing'; biofeedback training; experiences of sensory deprivation; fasting and sleeplessness; 'mind-tripping'; guided fantasy; hypnosis; non-rational experiences
Social–political Cannabis and psychedelics	Identification with anti-establishment forces; rebellion; overcoming discouragement with socio-political future; induced change in mass consciousness	Involvement in politics at all levels; lobbying; involvement in social services, e.g., meals on wheels, work with aged or handicapped; involvement in ecological projects
Philosophical Most, but especially psychedelics and cannabis	Search for purpose and meaning in life; search for personal identity; creation of or change in values	Seminars, workshops on values; ethics; reading metaphysical literature; humanistic counselling; exposure to persons 'committed' to causes and beliefs; maximisation of ethnic, racial, and/or minority pride

Pigott (1975) has suggested that the options available in our society are in many ways rather limited, and that there is a need to re-think our ways of relating and transcending our experience. Nevertheless, the process of attempting to match needs and sources of satisfaction is a central issue in working with drug-misusing clients, mainly in phase two of the model presented above.

Many of the alternatives suggested by Cohen obviously require access to a wide range of community and professional resources. They are outlined to emphasise that merely sitting and chatting or even intensive psychotherapy can only go so far and that viable alternatives need to be explored with the client if any effective change is to take place. There may also be a need for fairly intensive therapy before the client is in any way ready to face or effectively practice alternative ways of satisfying needs. The needs may have been obscured for so long and the defences so well developed that premature action could be useless or counterproductive, possibly leading to flight from treatment or regression.

Family work

The family treatment of drug misuse is a growing and in many cases essential area. The contribution of family pathology to the pathology evident in drug misusers must be determined if we are to assist the client.

Because younger drug misusers are likely to be living at home or experiencing separation and individuation difficulties, a family-focused approach is appropriate. Even if the whole family is not in treatment, some family contact is still essential.

Space does not permit an adequate review of this growing area, and the interested reader is referred to Baither's (1978) and Stanton's (1979) review articles, and Kaufman and Kaufman's *The Family Therapy of Drug and Alcohol Abuse* for further information.

Group work

Group work has become a popular mode of working with adolescents and young adults. Groups are advantageous for various reasons. For instance,

- Adolescents often feel less isolated and vulnerable in group settings.
- Limited therapist time availability makes groups an economic use of scarce resources.
- There is the possibility of harnessing peer-group support for pro-social or change-oriented thinking and behaving. This may be more effective than adult pressure in the same direction.

Group work with adolescent clients can be, and usually is, a very frustrating, stressful and sometimes disappointing experience for staff. However, it can also be very beneficial. Adolescent groups are affected by the characteristics of adolescence, such as frequent mood swings, identity confusion, high activity and increasing sexual awareness. Because of these and other factors, adolescent groups tend to take on a particular style. These are typical characteristics:

- The leader(s) need to be more active than in adult groups.
- Firm limits must be set and maintained.
- Clients often take more notice of sanctions and advice from peers than from the leader(s).
- Feelings and emotions may become very intense.
- There is typically a 'here and now' focus rather than concern with past material or experiences.
- The groups may be relatively disorderly.
- There is a high sensitivity to staff changes.
- Formal interpretations are not usually useful.
- Staff survival support is essential.
- One leader is usually ineffective. Such groups place too much strain on one person, and two leaders is the norm.
- Group size tends to range between 5 and 12. A smaller number tends to thwart the development of a peer culture and larger groups become unmanageable. A group of 12, for example, means 66 possible two-person relationships!

Most authors who have used or been in adolescent group (for example, Bruce, 1975; Levine, 1978; Steinberg, Merry & Collins, 1978; Whittaker & Small, 1977) appear fairly enthusiastic about the approach even though they stress the frustration caused by the degree of acting-out present.

Groups may be 'open' or 'closed'. Closed groups meet for a set time period, with a fixed number of members, and usually specific goals determined by the group in the first session. These are useful for fairly homogeneous collections of individuals who may have similar difficulties (for example, having to cope with alcoholic parents, low self-esteem, lack of social skills, abuse of a specific drug. Such groups tend to be 'neater' and somewhat easier to manage. However, they only have a limited function.

Open groups, on the other hand, tend to be chaotic and more volatile. They are also the more usual type of approach, for a variety of reasons. It may take considerable time to gather a suitable number of members for a closed group, or continuous attendance by members may not be possible by choice or as a result of such extraneous factors as court decisions or absconding. The heterogeneity of members in open groups, plus their comings and goings over the duration of the series, may have advantages as well as disadvantages.

Whatever the approach—open or closed—groups tend to follow a series of fairly clearly defined stages irrespective of theoretical orientation. These are relatively clear in closed groups. In open groups, different members may pass through them somewhat individually.

The getting-started phase is characterised by approach–avoidance conflicts. Many of the members may not wish to be there, even though they may have agreed to or chosen group work; some of those initially keen may not be sure about whether they made the correct choice. The members are familiarising themselves with each other and the leaders. Limit setting and jointly working out the ground rules are important tasks. For closed groups this happens in the first few sessions. In open groups, this activity needs revival every so often. An essential task of the leader is to attempt to create a safe place, so that trust may develop and group members become more open and able to take risks.

The transition stage is dominated by power and control issues, and resistances strong. The leaders are often challenged for control of the group and attempts made to establish a 'pecking order'. Cliques and alliances may be developing for purposes of mutual protection. Maintaining firm limits, while permitting a wide area in which to safely challenge authority, is an important task of the leaders and may become a recurrent task in open groups. As the boundaries are maintained and weaker members supported or protected, a greater feeling of safety and trust develops. The leaders' survival is a major issue.

A *stage of intimacy* should then develop where trust is high and the major tasks can be achieved. Members are more willing to engage in greater self-disclosure. Bonds may develop within the group and to the group which can become strong and therapeutic. In positive peer culture groups (Vorrath and Brendtro, 1974), as in most adolescent groups, this stage is characterised by a positive, pro-social ethos in the group which is harnessed to bring about change in the group members. The idea is that peers can influence each other more effectively than adults, and for productive change this influence must be positive. The skills mentioned in the counselling model, above, are useful here in assisting the processes of self-exploration, self-understanding and self-acceptance.

Differentiation is the next phase: members begin to leave the group. This is essential, for dependence on the group must not become too strong. The process is akin to the normal events of mid to late adolescence, when peer groups usually break up somewhat and each member begins to form an identity that is acceptable to himself or herself, has an independent existence and does not require constant validation through peer acceptance. Leaders and group members begin to be seen as unique and separate individuals.

The stage of separation is difficult. Leaving the group, whether open or closed, may be akin to leaving home. Some can only do it by walking out or running away. Others regress to a previous level of dependency so that they can be seen as not yet ready to leave. There may be a brief recapitulation of both positive and negative behaviour before departure.

It is important for the leaders of all groups to recognise the stages individual members may be going through and to ensure that termination is completed adequately. This implies a willingness to help individual members process and piece together the experience and feel able to cope independently. The leaders must also be aware of being given, or taking, too much responsibility for the group. At all stages responsibility should be turned back to the group to deal with.

Pfeiffer and Jones (1972) outlined a number of aspects of group life leaders should be aware of. They include:

Participation: Who are the high and low participators? Are there shifts in participation? Who talks to whom? Who keeps the ball rolling?
Influence: Which members have most influence? Is there a struggle for leadership?
Styles of influence: Are some members autocratic? Are there peacemakers or democratic leaders?
Decision-making process: How are decisions arrived at? Who supports whom? Is there a majority or a clique pushing for its own way? Do some members make contributions which are ignored?
Task functions: Does anyone ask for or make suggestions about the best way to proceed? Does someone summarise? Is there any giving or asking for facts? Who keeps the group on target?
Maintenance functions: Who helps others get into the discussions? Who cuts off others? How well are members getting their ideas across? How are ideas being rejected?
Group atmosphere: Who seems to prefer a friendly, congenial atmosphere? Who tries to supress any evidence of anger, hostility, sadness? Do people seem involved and interested? Is the atmosphere one of work or play? Who provokes hostility from others?
Membership: Are there any subgroups? Do some people get scapegoated? Do members variably involve themselves?

If the answer to the 'who?' questions above is mostly 'the leader', the group is not really functioning adequately or is bogged down in the early stages of group development and attempts should be made to turn responsibility back to the group.

All the skills mentioned earlier as necessary for 'normal' counselling, as well as those needed in the 'real world' of working with drug misusers, apply to group work. There will be, however, an emphasis on the more active, confrontive skills.

Conclusion

Only a brief exposure to counselling is possible in this chapter and the brief overviews of group and family work are quite inadequate. However, no attempt has been made to teach the skills necessary for working with drug misusers. The reader requiring such skills should seek a reputable course within which to develop them. The interested lay person may wish to follow up the readings suggested in the bibliography.

The main issues raised may be summarised as follows. Traditional models of counselling need to be modified to deal with drug-misusing clients, who fit more frequently into the character or personality disorder pattern than into the neurotic one. Fairly confrontive methods may be needed initially to cut through manipulations and confused motivations for seeking assistance, or reactions to being sent for treatment. Various settings impose limits and constraints on what can be achieved. Group work is a worthwhile and economical method of assisting, and family work may be essential.

Treatment must follow thorough assessment, and it must be recognised that mere alleviation of intra-psychic conflicts may do little in behavioural terms to alter deviance. There is usually a need to assist in the exploration and implementation of alternative modes of gaining satisfaction. Staff who work in this area need a great deal of support. They must not lose their own resources, lean too heavily on similarly overworked and overstressed colleagues, or take back what has been given to their clients. If they are to keep going, a supportive network of people and resources must be developed.

Whatever happens in treatment, no matter what the setting, there should be a focus on offering hope instead of despair, hopelessness and emptiness. Tooley (1978) suggested that the unhappiness, rootlessness and fear of things to come seen in developmentally dispossessed and depressed young people was related to a lack of an inner treasury that generates hopefulness. She saw it as a 'deficiency disease'—a lack of love for their lives and a lack of hope that they might feel differently in a year or two.

Fear of change (often symbolised in the usually exaggerated fear of withdrawal) is common among drug misusers and resistances become strengthened. Staff who can cope with entering this rather frightening world and demonstrate an ability to 'get their hands dirty', who can understand their clients and who can survive this experience without being swamped and annihilated, generate hope in their clients and hence the possibility of change. It is a difficult task and not one to be taken on by the 'legions of the walking dead'—counsellors or therapists who appear to have little love of their lives, appear to have little to live for, and who appear to be living from habit.

References

Amini, F., Salasnek, S. & Burke, E., 'Adolescent drug abuse: Etiological and treatment considerations', *Adolescence*, 1976, 11, pp. 281–99.
Anthony, E.J., 'Partnership and process in the treatment of adolescents', *Aust. & N.Z. Journal of Psychiatry*, 1973, 7, pp. 233–40.
Baither, R. 'Family therapy with adolescent drug abusers: A review', *J. Drug Education*, 1978, 8, pp. 337–43.
Bruce, T., 'Adolescent groups and the adolescent process', *Brit. J. Medical Psychology*, 1975, 48, pp. 333–38.
Citron, P., 'Group work with alcoholic, poly-drug involved adolescents with deviant behaviour syndrome', *Social Work with Groups*, 1978, 1, pp. 39–52.
Cohen, A., *Alternatives to drug abuse: Steps towards prevention*, U.S. Govt. Printing Office (National Clearinghouse for Drug Abuse Information), Washington, 1973.
Cohen, S., 'Alternatives to adolescent drug abuse', *J. Amer. Medic. Assoc.*, 1977, 238, pp. 1561–62.
Egan, G., *The Skilled Helper*, Brooks Cole, Monterey, Calif., 1975 (a).
Egan, G., *Exercises in Helping Skills*, Brooks Cole, Monterey, Calif., 1975 (b).
Gazda, J., *Human relations development*, Allyn & Bacon, Boston, 1973.
Jalali, B., Jalali, M. Crocetti, G. & Turner, F., 'Adolescents and drug use: Toward a more comprehensive approach', *Amer. J. Orthopsychiatry*, 1981, 51, pp. 120–30.
Johnson, D., 'Constructive peer relationships, social development, and co-operative learning experiences: Implications for the prevention of drug abuse', *J. Drug Education*, 1980, 10, pp. 7–24.
Kaufman, E. & Kaufmann, P. (eds), *The family therapy of drug and alcohol abuse*, Gardner, N.Y., 1979.
Korn, R., 'The counselling of delinquents', in E. Harms & P. Schrebier (eds) *Handbook of counselling techniques*, Pergamon, N.Y., 1963.
Levine, B., 'Reflections on group psychotherapy with adolescents, with some implications for residential treatment', *Social Work with Groups*, 1978, 1, pp. 179–93.
Malmquist, C., *Handbook of adolescence*, Aronson, N.Y., 1978.
Pfeiffer, J. & Jones, J., *The 1972 Annual Handbook for Group Facilitators*, University Associates, La Jolla, Calif., 1972.
Pigott, R., 'The concept of altered states of consciousness and how it helps us understand the drug scene', *Med. J. Aust.*, 1975, 3, pp. 882–84.
Stanton, M., 'Family treatment approaches to drug abuse problems: A review', *Family Process*, 1979, 18, pp. 251–80.
Steinberg, D., Merry, J. & Collins, S., 'The introduction of small group work to an adolescent unit', *J. of Adolescence*, 1978, 1, pp. 331–44.
Tooley, K., 'The rememberance of things past', *Amer. J. Orthopsychiatry*, 1978, 48, pp. 174–82.
Unger, R., 'The treatment of adolescent alcoholism', *Social Casework*, 1978, 59, pp. 27–35.

Vorrath, H. & Brendtro, L., *Positive peer culture*, Aldine, Chicago, 1974.
Whittaker, J. & Small, R., 'Differential approaches to group treatment of children and adolescents', *Child and Youth Services*, 1977, 1, pp. 1–13.

7 Drug and alcohol services in Australia

P. STOLZ

Introduction *Jara A. Krivanek*

Excessive drinking has been a major political, social and personal problem in Australia from its inception. Since earliest colonial times, the dependence of many of the convicts on alcohol was exploited by the troops sent to guard them and to maintain law and order. Officers of the N.S.W. Corps—generally known as the Rum Corps—secured most of the rum sent to the colony, sold some and used the rest to pay the convicts assigned to work on their farms. Rum became the major currency. Labourers' wages were paid in rum; crops were converted into rum; farms and crops were mortgaged (and sometimes forfeited) for rum. At the time of Governor Macquarie's arrival in 1809, Sydney Town, with a total population of 6156 souls, boasted 75 pubs.

Public drunkenness then was so conspicuous as to be unremarkable. Only the most blatant symptoms of alcohol misuse were treated, and that by imprisonment, forced labor or public flogging. By the early years of the present century, the prisons could no longer accomodate the numbers committed for drunkenness and in 1912 legislation was introduced to provide treatment for intractable drunkards. An amended version of this Inebriates Act is still in force. The Act provided for the establishment of special centres for the care and control of the inebriated, and State mental hospitals were declared to be suitable venues for this.

A number of benefits was immediately apparent. A program was undertaken to rid the streets of drunks, and the mental hospitals received a bonus of continual supplies of cheap labor. Best of all, the public conscience was salved. Society had done its part by providing care and treatment for the inebriated, and there was little change in the situation until after the Second World War.

Shortly after the War AA was introduced into Australia and its members made serious efforts to develop more realistic treatment programs in State psychiatric hospitals. Special wards were set aside, and patients could be admitted voluntarily, usually under AA's sponsorship. These special services continue, and at present about one third of all admissions to psychiatric hospitals involves alcohol dependence.

Through the 1950s and 60s, a few enlightened members of AA continued to campaign for the establishment of treatment services outside psychiatric institutions. In 1956 they formed a voluntary organisation, the Foundation for Research and Treatment of Alcoholism (FRATA) of NSW, to promote the acceptance of alcoholism as a medical disability. Sydney's Langton Clinic was established through its efforts in 1960. This was the first public hospital in Australia to specialise in the treatment of alcoholism. Several private hospitals were established along these lines, and the major teaching hospitals in the capital cities also began to open special alcohol clinics. At about the same time, major social welfare agencies like the Salvation Army, the Society of St. Vincent de Paul, the Central Methodist Mission and the Sydney City Mission were co-opted. These had been providing services to the poor and disadvantaged for decades, and they now began to develop special programs and services for the rehabilitation of alcoholics, and, in some instances, for people addicted to other drugs.

By the early 1970s, quite a number of facilities were offering treatment, mostly medically oriented. Two problems, however, became pressing. First, these facilities were generally available only to chronic patients. This was partly a relic of earlier days when it was considered inappropriate to admit patients to psychiatric hospitals unless enough damage was present to justify admission on the grounds of mental illness. The prevailing concept of alcoholism as a disease and the stereotyping that tends to accompany this were also partly responsible. Consequently, there was little assistance for people whose condition had not yet become chronic, and preventive efforts were non-existent. Second, it was clear that the problem was growing. The number of chronically damaged persons was increasing at a rate much faster than available services could cope with.

The government therefore faced a dilemma: should the expensive hospital services be increased to keep up with the increased demand, or should some attempt be made to help people at risk before their condition became chronic? In the end, there were attempts to do both. The hospital services were maintained and in some cases extended, and in 1973 the Australian government provided each State with funds to develop a system of independent community health services. These were to complement existing hospital and private medical services, and concern themselves with a wide variety of public health issues including the misuse of drugs and alcohol. Present-day drug and alcohol services must be considered against this general background.

J.A.K.

Providing drug and alcohol services in Australia

Services available

Provision of drug and alcohol services in Australia is rather muddled. No single organisation deals with the problems of alcohol and drug dependence. There are agencies run by the Commonwealth and State governments, regional networks and services offered by the private sector; the whole picture is quite complicated.

Government organisations. The law enforcement approach of the nineteenth century which, in its extreme form, locked people away in isolated institutions, is still with us in the form of the Inebriates Act. It is not much used now, but it is still possible to commit people to psychiatric institutions for fairly long periods. The health departments, especially their psychiatric sections, continue to handle most of the treatment aspects of alcohol and drug dependence. This is a State matter—the Commonwealth does not provide treatment services.

The administrative requirements of the drug and alcohol field have expanded to such an extent that all States except Tasmania have created special sections or departments within government services to deal with them. States have done this in one of two ways:

1. A special section is created within the Department of Mental Health Services. This is the case in Victoria, the Australian Capital Territory and was so until recently in Queensland.

2. A statutory board is set up responsible directly to the Minister for Health rather than to the Department. This model has worked successfully in South Australia since the early 1960s and replaced an 'Inebriates Act' approach in Western Australia. New South Wales has a peculiar dual system: the NSW Drug and Alcohol Authority administers funds for all drug and alcohol agencies, and the NSW Health Commission also supports a special section dealing with drug and alcohol problems. The Northern Territory is considering a similar arrangement.

In addition to such specific drug and alcohol services, several other government departments are involved in a more peripheral way. The law courts, for example, have recently become associated with the so-called 'diversionary programs'. These allow convicted drunk drivers to work through an education or counselling course, and convicted drug offenders to undergo a period of treatment before sentencing. In implementing such programs, the courts co-operate closely with various drug and alcohol services and the State health departments. Corrective services which deal with drug or alcohol-related misdemeanors of children under 18 are provided, and these have close links with the welfare system.

Community health services are another government-sponsored network. Generally, they operate under the joint control of local community leaders and the health service. This means that, within the overall policy guiding such centres, their direction can be influenced by the needs of the local community. In theory, at least, quite specialised assistance with drug or alcohol problems could be available through these.

In the vocational area, the Commonwealth Employment Service has special sections to assist people with alcohol or drug problems in re-entering the workforce. However, their efficiency often depends on who staffs them, on job availability and the extent to which local employers have been sensitised to the needs of 'handicapped' people. Government services for special or minority groups also concern themselves with drug and alcohol problems to varying degrees.

Government involvement in the network of general hospitals around Australia is rather chaotic. Many are administered by hospital boards with very little central control from the Health Commission. Most hospitals are concerned only with detoxification and those drug or alcohol-related conditions that cause immediate concern for a person's survival. Only a very few provide special services for the treatment of alcohol or drug dependence. However, general hospitals do sometimes have access to specialised consultants.

So there are many separate treatment and rehabilitation services of government origin. This provides tremendous opportunities to 'pass the buck' and send clients on a merry-go-round from one place to another. This must be avoided if at all possible.

Non-government organisations. Drug and alcohol services offered by non-government organisations are similarly complicated. Each State except Western Australia has a 'foundation' or 'association' on alcohol and drug dependence. The original three, the Foundation for Research and Treatment of Alcoholism and Drug Dependence of NSW (FRATADD), the Victorian Foundation on Alcoholism and Drug Dependence (VFADD) and the South Australian Foundation on Alcoholism and Drug Dependence (SAFADD) were founded in 1956, 1959 and 1963 respectively. The foundations were formed by members of AA, a few sympathetic doctors and other professionals, and some lay people. Their aim was twofold: to increase public awareness of alcoholism as a treatable disease, and to give voice to AA, and organisation whose traditions preclude it from entering into public debate on any issue. The foundations provided an opportunity for AA members to speak for their principles as individuals rather than AA representatives. The original constitutions of the foundations reflect both their close association with AA and an emphasis on safeguarding AA's independence from them.

In 1967, the three original State foundations banded together to form a national body, the Foundation for Research and Treatment of Alcoholism (FRATA). This was incorporated in the Australian Capital Territory. In 1971, it became the Australian Foundation on Alcoholism and Drug Dependence (AFADD) in recognition of the increasing problems caused by other legal and illegal drugs, but emphasis has always remained on alcohol as the principal drug of misuse in Australia. The other foundations also added 'drug dependence' to their titles at this time, although FRATA of NSW had already done so in 1966.

Initially, AFADD provided an opportunity for meetings and seminars to exchange ideas between States, but increasing federal concern about alcohol and other drugs led to the establishment of the present Canberra-based, government-funded national secretariat for AFADD in 1974. Since that time, AFADD has encouraged the formation of foundations in the remaining States and territories: Queensland (1974), Tasmania (1975), the Northern Territory (1976) and the Australian Capital Territory (1977). No foundation has yet been planned for Western Australia.

By 1975, all State governments had become member organisations of AFADD, and they have played a large role in the development of various programs in each State. In general, policy is decided by all member organisations working together under the umbrella of AFADD, and the main initiative and responsibility for the development of programs is left to each State foundation.

The various State foundations differ considerably in their orientation and the services they offer. FRATADD, for example, has been more oriented towards providing services related to treatment, though it is also involved in professional training, counselling and research. This contrasts with VFADD, which has had a greater commitment to community education, law reform and counselling. In comparison, SAFADD has never been very strong although it provides some counselling through recovered AA people, education services and general information; in general, it has taken a fairly low-key approach and has played only a limited role in instituting large-scale changes. The Queensland foundation has essentially tried to make changes by stimulating interest in various community groups. The others, by and large, are very closely linked to the development of alcohol and drug dependence industry programs. The ACT foundation takes a somewhat broader role: it administers a therapeutic community-type drug dependence unit and conducts a number of education programs.

Besides the foundations network, a number of other helping organisations operate nationwide. AA and its offshoots Al-Anon and Alateen exist everywhere, and it is well worthwhile attending meetings of all three several times to learn what they can do for individuals and families. It is worth noting that the absence of a formal AA group in an area does not mean that there is no AA service. There are usually some loners who do not bother to meet any more but who can still help. The nearest AA central office will always be able to put people in touch with AA members in isolated areas. In such places, AA members are likely to be the only resource available, and, although not highly organised, AA's administrative network is more than sufficient for this.

The Salvation Army is another very influential organisation which provides many services. They usually adopt a fairly standardised approach, called the Bridge Program, and information is readily available. The St Vincent de Paul organisation also offers a variety of services, some specific for drug and alcohol problems, others of a more general nature. Their services for the homeless, for example, cater for some drug addicts and many indigent alcoholics.

Lifeline is a telephone-based crisis agency, also nationwide, and there may be comparable emergency services in some communities. Other organisations such as GROW (dealing with mental health) are also worth exploring. Then there are movements such as the Seventh Day Adventists (who provide narcotics education and programs to give up smoking), and Narcotics Anonymous, linked to WHOS (We Help Ourselves—a voluntary organisation), with only a few groups in some States. Finally, there is the national network of the temperance movement in Australia. The movement is not just a pressure group for non-alcoholic drinks; in some States they are very progressive. In Queensland, for example, they were the first to promote alcohol and drug industry programs. They also provided a theatre for the use of other agencies, premises for Al-Anon and a club for recovered alcoholics. In Victoria, they are much involved in community education and legislative reform. These groups are not funded by any government organisation but by the community. They occasionally receive government assistance, but this varies from one State to another.

Other services vary among States and capitals. In Sydney, for example, the Sydney City Mission is very active in providing detoxification services. The many other services include therapeutic communities such as Odyssey House, which caters for drug addicts and operates on a very structured, prescriptive model. The Buttery in NSW and the Moreland Hall Family Treatment Centre in Victoria take a much more flexible approach to the problem.

Finding appropriate services

One of the most important functions of agencies which provide services in the field of alcohol and drug dependence is referral. All agencies get all types of requests, reflecting the total needs of the community.

Requests may come from other agencies or directly from people seeking help, and may range through all aspects of prevention, both primary and secondary. Callers may ask for specific information, a source of help, a speaker or a training program. It is never possible to know about all the agencies available, because local ones, especially, can come and go with great speed. However, a basic knowledge of the resources in the community is essential to any helper.

First, the exact nature of the request must be established. Is it directly related to a drug or alcohol problem, or is the question more peripheral (for instance, availability of stress relief programs)? Does it concern drug education—general or specific, individual, school or community? Is therapy being requested? Of what sort—assessment, detoxification, short- or long-term care? In- or out-patient? Once these questions and others are answered, the obvious and often overlooked place to begin the search is the telephone directory. The search should cover the emergency and government sections, as well as the alphabetical index (or commercial directory) under both 'alcohol' and 'drugs'.

Beyond this, a number of very specific tools are available in the form of directories of services. AFADD publishes a revised edition each year for all of Australia. Some equivalent State foundations also occasionally publish State versions, as do government alcohol and drug agencies. This is especially true in those States where most of the services are government-sponsored.

Such directories can never be completely accurate. Getting agencies to respond, and keeping the listings up-to-date requires an enormous amount of work, and there is always the problem of the newest agencies, those established while a directory is being printed. Even if every State has only one or two in this category, the number becomes significant on an Australia-wide basis. The same problem also exists on the State level, and the only remedy is to be 'on the ball', aware of the services, and in touch with workers in the field.

Apart from the directories, a very obvious contact is the Council of Social Services (COSS) in each State. They sometimes have directories of their own for all sorts of services. Because all non-government organisations are usually members of such councils, they can be extremely valuable sources of information.

Another source of information are the AA and Al-Anon newsletters in each State. They are free, updated periodically, and very useful at a local level. These give specific information about the times and places of AA meetings in the area. In most districts, AA meets every day at various times in different locations, and because there are so many meetings, this information is not listed in any other directory in Australia. It is therefore important to have it handy, and a good trick of the trade is to have a map of the relevant district, to help explain to people how to get to the meeting most convenient for them.

Finally, many sources of help are provided at all government levels—Commonwealth, State and municipal—and lists are usually readily available. It is also worth making inquiries at all local churches. Some provide services locally; others link into Australia-wide networks such as the Salvation Army or St Vincent de Paul.

Once the agencies have been identified, the next step is to find out more about them, and this will require considerable leg-work. It is one thing to have directories at your fingertips; it is quite another to have seen the facilities, met the staff and learned how they operate. A good start is to make appointments to go and see what people do. There is nothing like face-to-face contact at all three levels: it is essential for the helper to be able to send referrals to a single key person, for the client to see or speak to a named individual, and for the people providing the service to have a contact person at the referring agency.

It is also very important to keep this personal approach up, not to do it just once for all time. Face-to-face contact should be re-established at least every six months. Without this, it is impossible to identify what is unique about the services provided and how they are perceived by clients, and a realistic evaluation cannot be made.

Certain groups may have special problems in obtaining adequate and appropriate help. Aborigines, migrants and women are examples. It is essential to find out what is available in any area, either run by such groups or by other groups for them. Unfortunately, the needs of special groups are often virtually ignored.

Services for aborigines exist all over Australia, usually with a focus on rehabilitation. Migrants, however, face a more difficult problem. There are many alcohol and drug-realted problems in migrant communities, but there are few if any resources for them in this field. We act as though they do not even exist, and there is no attempt to break down language barriers.

The drug-related needs of women are also largely ignored in our community, and services for them are especially deficient in the therapeutic area. When making referrals, remember that barriers are immediately created when female clients are given no option to being treated by male staff.

Finally, there are far too few services for professional people, managers and executives, the self-employed and those in the VIP category. The States have always developed their services on the lowest common denominator, not so much by intent but as a result of current social policies. For professional people, special contacts with private agencies or practices usually have to be established. If nothing is available locally, people in these categories are often willing to travel to another city for treatment to ensure their anonymity is maintained. The head of a department in Canberra is hardly likely to seek government-sponsored treatment there because everyone would soon know of it. Of course, the opposite could equally be true: some heads of departments would not mind at all. But those who do mind have enough hurdles to face without this one as well.

Throughout, one area that is generally underdeveloped is that of early intervention. The best programs currently available are the drug and alcohol programs in industry and the diversionary programs mentioned above. A few family programs are also being developed. In preventive education, the most obvious starting points are the drug and alcohol services in the various States, the mental health services, the health education sections of the health commissions, community health centres and school health services. A few tertiary institutions also sometimes offer relevant adult education courses.

The most important and potentially the most effective helpers in any Australian community are the general practitioners. The GP may not be doing all he ought, but he is the key person for services required in the future: a personal and better relationship between client and therapist. In my view, the GP is the best person to assist where prolonged in-patient services are not required; if they are, he can use hospitals in the same way he does when dealing with other ailments. Furthermore, he can assist the re-entry of the client into the community. Thus, the GP is the key professional in diagnosis, support, short-term treatment and re-entry. GPs are the biggest network of potential therapists available, and it will be a big challenge to involve them fully.

We are now not merely missing an opportunity to get GPs involved; we are giving them a good 'cop out' as well. Studies have shown that specialised agencies are no more effective than general ones, thus demolishing the belief that alcohol and drug dependence must be handled by a specialist. Many 'generalists' can do a very good job, and with fewer language problems.

With the trend towards earlier intervention, the GP is in an ideal position to ask about all sorts of practices that might jeopardise good health—such as smoking, drinking, under-exericisng or over-eating. These sorts of practices add tremendous costs to our national health bill: most of our costly diseases are related to our affluence. There is evidence that doctors who intervene at a low-key level and advise people to adopt a healthier way of life have considerable effect, and because doctors are the most commonly used health resource in our society, we should use them to the fullest.

In the past we have not really involved GPs in the drug and alcohol dependence field, but they must have full information if they are to treat patients adequately. I believe the onus is on us to communicate with them continually after a client has been referred. This applies to the initial referring agency, the employer and whoever else is concerned about the client.

AFADD has done some work with general practitioners in the Family Medicine Program, and, in 1978, organised a national research conference at which key representatives from the States mapped out needs around Australia. AFADD is still actively involved with the College of General Practitioners, but there is something far more important to be done at a local level: if helpers are to refer clients to doctors, they should actively sensitise them to their role in this field.

There are various ways to do this. It is probably best to start with just a handful of practitioners, a small group that will understand, and to cultivate that group. A sufficiently homogeneous group might be difficult to assemble in large cities, where the medical community is not so clearly delineated, but each locality generally has representatives of various medical organisations such as the Family Medicine Program or the Australian Medical Association, and memberships could be canvassed.

A useful and neutral discussion topic, and one which most doctors would know little about, might be the GP's function in alcohol and drug programs in industry. Someone particularly concerned with industry referrals could, for a start, identify the area with the greatest number of company programs. The audience will represent the potential GP network which will receive such referrals, and they need to learn systematically what industry programs are about.

Explaining these programs can be a vehicle to overcome their reluctance to become involved. It can be a means of communicating, getting them interested, and destigmatising drug and alcohol problems. They need to appreciate that specialisation is not required and that doctors can be very effective in this area simply by taking a low-key approach and identifying practices that affect their patients' health. Intervention of this kind is far removed from the long-term treatment some alcoholics and drug misusers require and can get from specialised agencies. Most of the people with alcohol or drug problems that a GP is likely to encounter are still functioning and still have a job.

There are many other ways to involve GPs. One example is the weekend seminar for doctors and their wives, organised by the Victorian College of General Practitioners. Over a long weekend, the participants are exposed to the whole field of alcohol and drug dependence and its management. The wives are invited to participate partly to avoid separating couples who tend to have little time to spend together, and partly because of the 'receptionist–crisis line' function they often take in the practice. This approach has proved fairly successful. Attendance at the seminars may be somewhat self-selecting, but at least they attract sizeable contingents of people with good future prospects of involvement.

Another way to involve GPs might be to develop a support system that produced cassettes with specific messages for clients. The tapes could be heard in the waiting room or taken home. We should use the technology now available to supplement the limited time doctors can give their patients.

These, however, are issues for long-term planning. For the present, we cannot blindly say 'Go and see your GP' without first ascertaining what skills the local ones possess. In other words, we need to deal with them as we would with any other agency. Nevertheless, setting up a network of informed and involved GPs is an excellent way to invest one's long-term efforts—and it has nothing to do with enforcing the 'medical model' at the cost of social workers, psychologists, nurses or anyone else.

Setting up and operating a referral service

A question that is frequently asked is 'Should there be some sort of central assessment or referral agency?'—something that matches each client to a specific service, perhaps even to a particular counsellor. An agency in Rome, for example, uses a most impressive system of this type. The personality profile and demographic information on every recovered drug addict is held in computer storage. The agency makes a similar profile of each new client, and at the press of a button can come up with three or four names in any area, who would be available with advice and support. In general, however, the most successful treatment tends to be related to informal, personal, accessible and non-bureaucratised programs rather than to the large 'collectivised' systems.

Those who provide services to people with drug and alcohol problems, or plan to do so, need to evaluate the relevance of their agency in seven critical areas: the service itself, the target group to which it is addressed, the nature of the client population; the problems encountered, the referral process, setting standards, and adequate feedback.

The service. The first decision is on what services will be provided and why people would call on them. What types of groups are aimed at? Will people be referred, or dealt with directly? Will the service concentrate on certain aspects only and refer to other agancies for additional therapy or information? Will the service be given over the telephone, by correspondence, in face-to-face interviews or in groups?

The target group. How will the target group be reached and services advertised? A telephone directory listing is an important way. Clients do not walk around with specialised directories of drug and alcohol services—they look in the 'phone book, and it is a very efficient way of letting people know of a service. Services can also be advertised in buses, trains and newspapers, in professional literature and other specific media.

Too often, advertising is just left to happen without any planning on how best to reach potential clients. In practice, the target group will determine the most suitable medium, and it is necessary to find out what each group is exposed to most. The best way to start is to ask relevant groups directly, bearing in mind that several different target groups may be involved. The person with the drug or alcohol problem may respond to something quite different than his or her spouse or employer.

In general, the most rewarding group on which to focus advertising will be the professionals: doctors, hospitals, social workers and nurses who will then pass the message on to clients. This comes back to the critical importance of individual care. The more a system individualises the attention clients receive in some sort of person-to-person relationship, the better and more lasting the results will be.

The client population. Who is the client? Do people call on services for themselves, or is most of the work with people peripheral to the problem—spouses, parents or employers? The two populations need to be handled quite differently. The first requires direct intervention; the second does not.

Follow-up also tends to produce different results in the two groups. Clients who call themselves tend to follow through with the recommended referral. Finding out what happened with those who called for others is more difficult. Intervention may fail—in the sense that the client will not follow through with the referral or will not stay with the recommended treatment agency—unless the approach is sufficiently focused.

The nature of the problem. How should the problem presented be assessed? When people call, will the helpers understand exactly what they say and what they want? What sort of questionnaire will be used, and will the information be visibly filled in or taken down in note form during the interview?

In general, it is important to develop some way to systematise assessment of the client's needs. It makes information-gathering more efficient, and also gives the client a greater sense of security that the helpers know what they are doing and will call on the right source of help.

The referral process. How will the referral be made, and will the client get there? Should the referral be made on the clients' behalf, or would it be better for them to do their own calling? This is a very important issue and could be debated at great length.

How will the referral facilities and the various alternatives clients may have be presented and described? What other services will be offered besides referral? Along with the address, should the helper ensure they know exactly where to go and who to see? Will the helper call the agency to say the client is coming, and reinforce it by asking the client to come back and report? Should pamphlets be provided? Throughout, the agency should make use of the spouse or someone like the employer who is particularly interested in the outcome of the client's referral. Such people can have a very special role in triggering a client's motivation toward treatment or whatever other assistance may be needed. Careful attention to all these issues is essential in developing a workable program of dealing with clients, and they will make the difference between clients following advice fully, half-heartedly or not at all.

Setting standards. This is an issue that will probably involve lots of politics. How to evaluate the places to which people are referred? How to gauge their standards? How to assess client satisfaction? How much time will be devoted to following-up?

Suppose that good services exist nearby. Helpers trust them implicitly and keep referring clients there, but two years later begin to hear of people who were not particularly happy with the service or whose needs were not fully met. If the service being set up is to stay operational, two things must be evaluated from the beginning and continually: clients' responses to the approach taken in referring them, and other agencies' efficiency in managing the cases sent to them. If this is not done, the referring agency will simply add to one of our biggest problems, the referral merry-go-round. Too many people refer clients to other agencies who then refer on again, and the buck never stops.

General standards and professional ethics are very important, but no national guidelines exist and no immediate solution is in sight. A large part of the problem comes from the wide range of organisations involved in drug and alcohol services. Government organisations such as hospitals and clinics are at one end, and specific standards for staff, services to be provided and ethical codes to be observed are already in operation there. At the other end of the spectrum, however, there is a whole range of voluntary organisations, some well established, others new and trying new things.

A certain amount of professionalism can be introduced through courses in welfare, but how do you do this with an organisation such as AA, which consists of recovered people dedicated to non-professionalism? Yet AA is a resource that comes into its own in problems on which the general community has turned its back. They provide a service nobody else—including governments and professionals—likes to handle, by picking up the bits and trying to do something with them. Imagine how they feel when other people start talking about standards! Who has the standards and by what right? It is a highly complex and sensitive issue.

Obtaining feedback. The ethics of most professions call for communication between different people involved with each client to ensure that he or she has adjusted well to the treatment regime and is progressing satisfactorily. Follow-up after discharge is also obviously in the client's interest. A client should not leave treatment in a worse state than on admission. Unfortunately, getting adequate feedback on clients in drug and alcohol services is not always easy.

Clients themselves are often unreliable sources of information. Many severely criticise treatment facilities, and some effort is needed to distinguish between a purely personal reaction against someone or something and a genuinely punitive or destructive element within the facility. Very often, a client's reaction changes several times throughout the course of treatment. It is almost always different at its beginning and at its end.

Some professionals for their part are loth to admit any uncertainty or need of a second opinion. Others tend to interpret what may be simple concern about a patient as a criticism of their own expertise or an interference with the treatment they have chosen.

Moreover, some agencies make a point of not releasing information. AA does not, nor do some therapeutic communities. Although there is nothing to prevent a client referred to AA from returning to the referring agency for regular visits, some therapeutic communities do not allow their patients to leave at all for some fixed period of time, and feedback becomes virtually impossible. Avoiding the use of such agencies is not the answer. Our present system of treatment contains a large number of such groups, and cutting them off means reducing your clients' options and, perhaps, their ability to recover. There is no reason to suspect that they are any less effective than organisations which do provide feedback. The only thing to do is to keep communications good, appreciate their point of view and find ways around the problem. There is usually no difficulty about the client returning to the referral agency after discharge from the community, for instance.

In general, however, routine feedback should be part of the agreed basis on which referrals are to be made between agencies, and the client should be involved in this as much as possible. It may sometimes be premature, or too much to ask, for a client in treatment to make contact with the referring agency. In such cases the treating agency can carefully suggest that the person who made the referral is interested and would welcome some contact from the client about the progress made. This is always easier if encouragement of return visits is made a normal part of the referral process. Such visits also allow opportunity for further advice or action if needed.

Throughout the whole process, personal bias must be avoided. We may prefer certain treatments to others; we may 'push our own barrow' rather than be completely fair to the client; we may believe that AA is not a very good sort of group for some, that the Salvation Army takes a religious line that is different from our own or that St. Vincent de Paul really has no relevant role.

All this has no importance at all. What is important is the way the client perceives the service. The clients must always be faced with very fair options so that they can make their own decisions. A professional must be ble to give a fair assessment of services provided, but personal biases must not show.

The science of treatment and recovery as it relates to drug and alcohol problems is not a very exact one. What works for one does not work for another. It is often difficult to tell in advance what will work because of the interaction between the client, a particular agency's staff, and many other factors. Only direct experience with an agency and feedback about whether clients received satisfactory service or not will provide the answers.

8 Preventive strategies
Primary prevention and the community

Prevention has been described as the antidote that keeps disease away, and the antidote is sometimes simple. Dr John Snow, a physician of nineteenth century London, noted during one of the frequent cholera epidemics that all the people affected in one area of Soho drew their water from a single pump. He therefore removed the handle from the Broad Street pump and the epidemic abated. With most diseases, and certainly in the case of problems associated with alcohol or drug misuse, the chain of associations between cause and effect is more complex and no single gesture can wholly eradicate the problem.

It has become customary to make a distinction between primary prevention, that is, preventing misuse from occuring in the first place, and secondary prevention, which involves recognizing that there is a problem, encouraging sufferers to seek help and supporting them while they receive it and as long as they need it. The first is presently a mixture of public education and control policies aimed at limiting the availability of and access to drugs. The second involves the development of special facilities and the training of personnel to deal with the problem, and is discussed separately in Chapter 9.

General problems in prevention

Each form of prevention has somewhat specific difficulties, but three problem areas are common to both: identification and selection of goals, development of strategies that are socially, economically and politically feasible, and adequate evaluation of the effectiveness of these strategies.

What are we trying to prevent?

Unless specific goals are made explicit, there is no basis for determining what a program has accomplished. Specification of goals is even more necessary when social attitudes toward the problem are vague, inconsistent, divergent or strongly emotional.

The goals of preventive strategies can be very diverse. A program may set out to eliminate or reduce all non-medical drug use by everyone. Or it may seek to influence use patterns only in those seriously involved. It could aim to give accurate information or a variety of views about drugs and drug users, or to assist users to make various decisions about their use. The point is that each goal presupposes a different target group, strategy and result.

Only some of the potential goals of prevention relate directly to the intrinsic properties of drugs. Thus, we can realistically seek to prevent undesirable physical effects of drug use such as overdose, or undesirable behavioural changes such as acute increases in aggression or chronic neglect of social responsibility. Many other problems, however, have little relation to drug effects. Resorting to illegal activities to obtain supplies of drugs relates not to drugs but to the legal restraints on their use and availability. Similarly, response of community agencies to drug users is often based on current social stereotypes of users rather than on actual user characteristics. Prevention of these problems has little to do with drugs as such. Even physical or behavioural problems which are clearly drug-related depend on the dose of the drug and the way it is used. Problems therefore appear in some users and not in others.

Moreover, drugs provide benefits as well as harm. They may present easy options or even the best of several possible alternatives. Thus, a case might be made that high heroin use in a black ghetto is preferable to an increase in street violence, or that overuse of Valium by socially and economically deprived housewives prevents further deterioration. Attempts to merely prevent use may address themselves to non-problems on the one hand and may create new and worse problems on the other.

Reduction of drug-related problems must aim at an optimal balance between benefit and harm rather than prevention of use as such. This is especially obvious in societies which accept the virtually unrestricted use of such social drugs as alcohol and tobacco. In terms of feasibility, impact and congruence with contemporary society, 'minimisation' rather than eradication appears to be the most viable policy. This means an improvement in people's capacity to manage the use of drugs. In the special case of alcohol, Britain's Advisory Committee on Alcoholism has formalised this philosophy as a need 'to generate strong social controls against the misuse of alcohol by encouraging moderate drinking in appropriate circumstances; by encouraging abstinence; and by strongly disapproving inebriety' (1978, p. 6). In a more general framework, the 1980 UNESCO meeting of experts on drug use and preventive education emphasised that preventive efforts 'should be concerned to minimize negative outcomes of drug use, to abolish unnecessary stigmatization and self-fulfilling prophecies: drug education should focus on promoting safe patterns of drug use'.

Which strategies are feasible?

Most existing programs have responded to criticism about lack of specified goals with prominently displayed lists of aims and objectives.

There have also been numerous statements about how the development of adequate programs is to proceed. Benjamin (1978), for example, describes the ideal process as one in which:

(a) A clear consensus of opinion in regard to the philosophy of approach, strategies and priorities and realistic goals towards minimisation of alcohol/drug problems has been reached;
(b) A solid compendium of attitudes regarding responsible decision-making as to the use of alcohol has been drawn up as guidelines for achieving these goals;
(c) Clear, appropriate and adequate legislative departmental and professional system support in the form of written policies and procedures is ensured; and
(d) The personnel to be involved in the curriculum planning, experimentation and implementation activities are adequately prepared. (p. 166)

Worthy as all these aspirations may be, the disturbing feeling persists that many of them are 'visionary and so carry within them the seeds of their own defeat in terms of viable implementation. Many proposed measures are of a "not here, not now" variety' (Blane, 1976).

Prevention strategies, even if couched in terms of minimisation, must deal with a number of harsh realities. The extent of the problem and the cost of intervention are important factors. As Benjamin has commented,

> The protagonists for prevention often claim 'an ounce of prevention is worth of pound of cure', but forget to add that prevention also costs a lot more. Or they claim that 'a fence at the top of the cliff is better than an ambulance at the bottom', and fail to realise that a warning sign placed well back will probably keep most people from entering the danger area; that perhaps a fence on top of the cliff simply becomes a challenge for some to climb, or that some people are predestined or determined to fall into danger and will always find an unfenced cliff. We cannot fence all cliffs. (1978, p. 147)

One thing is clear: minimisation of drug problems is not easy or cheap. If it were, it would have been accomplished long ago.

Moreover, increased agreement among specialists about the issue will not necessarily be reflected in the attitudes of communities and governments. Beside the practical difficulties in implementing mass preventive efforts, there is no general consensus that prevention or even minimisation of drug use is a desirable goal.

This is especially evident in the case of the social drugs, alcohol and tobacco. Here we are dealing with voluntary human behaviours which many people find beneficial and/or pleasurable and which many wish to continue for personal, ethical and economic reasons. It is not just individuals who are depentent on smoking or drinking: there are also various 'corporate dependencies'. The relevant industries are the most obvious. Growing, making and selling alcohol and nicotine is a very profitable business and a very secure one, catering as it does to a dependent market.

The pharmaceutical industries also have sound business reasons for maintaining if not increasing drug sales, and in some cases they are aided by government marketing bodies. In Australia, for instance, the Trade Practices Commission places a priority on cheapness and requires that some analgesics be readily available in supermarkets. A case could be made that restriction of their sale to pharmacies might reduce dangerous misuse. Changing their status to prescription drugs would probably effect a larger reduction still.

In all these industries there are ample funds for advertising, public relations and political lobbying when inroads into consumption seem likely, and the biggest addict is of course the Treasury. In 1978, the Commonwealth government was netting more than $500 million in excise from tobacco alone, and, as Kirby (1978) pointed out, 'in a practical world it would seem difficult for governments to rely on the tobacco and alcohol industry to supply them with huge revenue by taxation and excise, and at the same time agree that advertising, promotion and sale of these commodities is evil'.

The print media are also increasingly dependent on alcohol and tobacco advertising, especially the latter, because in many countries cigarettes cannot now be advertised on television. However, there is at present no law to prevent the use of huge signs, flags and posters at sporting events that are broadcast live. The effect of this is comparable to direct advertising, and, as Kirby has commented in his capacity as Chair of the Australian Advertising Standards Council,

> this is a problem neither my Council nor I have any authority to condemn, or do anything about; the same applies to the sponsorship of football teams and sporting competitions, such as tennis and golf, by tobacco and liquor organisations, which, it is argued, not only advertise their wares by such sponsorship but also falsely put into the minds of the young, and sports people generally, that there is something sporting and healthy about the use of these products (1978, p.14)

Other examples are easily found, and the problem has been accurately summarized by Benjamin:

preventive efforts are likely to be welcomed and tolerated by all
concerned only as long as they do not clash with substantial economic
or moral interests, this is, as long as they are not effective. The
potentially most effective measures are those most likely to be
blocked because they run against cherished beliefs and interests.
There has been a tendency accordingly, to limit preventive efforts to
directions which offer the least threat to the status quo.... In these
circumstances, the clinical and epidemiological assumption of consensus on a strong moral imperative to eradicate disease tends to
become a kind of moral entrepreneurship proposing to enforce a
standard of behaviour in people because it is good for them.... There
is one contemporary example of society where it is reported that
pre-existing alcohol problems have been eradicated and their recurr-
ence prevented, the People's Republic of China. But it seems clear
that Australian society is not prepared to pay the 'cost' in terms of
reorientation of the social and economic system, personal liberties
and daily life involved if it were to follow this example. (1978,
pp. 149–50)

Implementation of appropriate preventive stategies will depend on the outcome of careful analyses of social, economic, political and educational realities at local, State and national levels. These, for the most part, have yet to be made. It is unlikely, however, that broadly stated conceptualisations that imply total eradication of whole classes of problems will be as useful as small steps and half-measures such as the framing of modest and realistic goals.

Which strategies are effective?

The question 'Does it work?' presupposes that we know the answer to the question 'What is it meant to do?' As we have seen, specification of goals is both difficult and infrequent. Actual evaluation of programs, however, is virtually non-existent. A review of more than 100 North American drug education programs (Smart and Fejer, 1974) concluded that only six had received any evaluation at all, and this was mostly in terms of short-term attitude change. Randall and Wong (1976) similarly concluded that most programs published between 1967 and 1976 'were lacking in any meaningful evaluation'. Even today evaluation, if mentioned at all, is generally stated in terms of impressions and faith. Sound and insightful reasoning may be present, but solid evidence is conspicuously absent.

Proper evaluative efforts have been complicated by a number of factors other than lack of clearly defined goals. One is the poor quality of much of the resource material available. In 1972, for example, a three-year evaluative study of drug misuse films concluded that only 14 per cent of the 250 films reviewed were acceptable for showing; the rest were doing more harm than good (*New York Times*, 1972). Much of the effort is also misdirected: programs may be generated by highly committed people who combine serious concern with inadequate training. An Australian Service club, for instance, recently purchased 20 000 American comic books on the 'drug menace' for distribution to various children's organisations. The publication was subsequently found to be unacceptable by both the Drug and Alcohol Services and the Personal Development Divisions of the NSW Health Commission. It is not surprising that the United States National Commission on Marijuana and Drug Abuse (1973) recommended a moratorium on all new drug education programs until existing ones had been tested for effectiveness.

It must be admitted, in fairness, that effective evaluation of programs is frequently very difficult. Lack of funds, expertise and objectivity is a major problem. In addition, we measure what we can, not necessarily what we would like to measure. Thus, outcome measurements used are typically those on which information is readily available. Intrapsychic events such as changes in attitudes, values or personality are not easily measured and are therefore rarely evaluated. We concentrate instead on behavioural changes, especially fairly accessible ones like participation in illegal activities and changes in hospitalisation, accident or arrest rates. These naturally give a limited view of the situation.

If evaluations are performed by staff actually involved in the program the data produced may be very biased. This is especially so if budget cuts, staff reductions or the future of the program depend on the outcome.

The degree of control needed for the classical evaluative methods of science is rarely possible in program settings. It may be ethically indefensible, for instance, to deny certain individuals access to treatment. Or the assignment of people to treatment groups might be dictated by such non-random factors as type of facility available and its proximity to various clients' homes. Finally, it is almost never possible to generalise evaluative findings from one program to another. They tend to be specific to the population treated and the method used.

It has been argued on these and other grounds that scientific evaluation of programs costs too much time, effort and money. However, the programs themselves are also extremely costly, and unless they are objectively evaluated their effectiveness cannot be assured. A potential way out of the dilemma is to reduce the scope of evaluation. Concern with the total impact of programs is decreasing. Instead, evaluators tend to concentrate on determining the specific procedures that produce the most desirable changes. If this attack proves successful, it may be possible to measure prospective target populations on a few critical variables, and from this predict the likelihood of success of particular prevention strategies.

It must be emphasised, however, that such efforts are in their infancy. The subsequent sections of this chapter msut be read with the understanding that the small amount of research in this area has generally been exploratory, poorly conceived and executed, and of distinctly limited predictive value.

Primary prevention

The development of potentially harmful forms of drug-using behaviour can be prevented—in theory, at least—in two major ways. First, the public can be educated about drug use. Second, the environment can be structured to eliminate the factors that predispose to harmful drug use, to limit the availability of drugs, or both.

Educational approaches

Drug education is presented fairly formally in schools and rather more loosely in the general community. Each presents special problems. Several points, however, have a general relevance to both. First, society is generally ambivalent about education.

> In principle, it has great faith in education, but often, particularly in controversial areas, it is suspicious of the nature and goals of the educational process. Approval of budgets for 'reading, writing and arithmetic' and for subjects decreed by colleges to be necessary for admission is not the equivalent of endorsement of education as an important process in the solution of social problems. There is scepticism that education can help young people arrive at the 'right' decisions with respect to social problems; there often seems to be a preference to depend on increasingly punitive laws for their solution. (Nowlis, 1969, p. 54)

Education also tends to mean different things to educators and the general public. Educators generally believe that opinions, attitudes and beliefs based on all available knowledge are the soundest basis for personal and social action. By contrast, much of the general public sees education as a process of indoctrination. Educators believe that sound decisions arise out of critical examination of beliefs, and present many sides of an issue; the general public is inclined to rely on beliefs widely accepted in the past and tends to overemphasise particular aspects of issues. Education, to educators, involves a search for knowledge; the general public tends to see it as preparation for a career.

Second, education does not happen only in institutions and planned programs. Writing of drug use by American college students, Nowlis comments:

> 'Education' goes on every moment of every day, whether we choose to label it education or not. Parents are educating by example and by

precept; the mass media are educating seven days a week; schools and colleges educate both in and out of the classroom, seldom standing back to see what they have wrought. We can assume that most of what the student has learned about psychoactive drugs, for example, is based only in small part on information resulting from a formal educational effort and in large part on informal education provided by others and by his own experiences, however limited, with drugs and drug users. There is abundant evidence that the pattern of use of alcohol adopted by the college student, after perhaps a brief period of experimentation, is dependent on or a reaction to his parents' patterns of use ... Since society holds conflicting and ambivalent attitudes about drugs and since there are large discrepancies between what is said and what is done, the impact of all this education undoubtedly is to produce confusion and conflicts for the student, even when he chooses to avoid all or most drugs and to believe that he knows little or nothing about them. (1969, pp. 55–56)

The success of any educational program depends greatly on the degree to which it is consistent with the broader goals, policies and beliefs of the community.

Nowhere is this more apparent than in drug education. All sorts of people, organised and unorganised, hold all kinds of opinions and attitudes on the issue. When an education program or policy statement about drug use is announced, related issues becomes painfully apparent in a matter of days, and controversy may be expected to rage on matters ranging from philosophy of social control and academic freedom to victimless crimes and the right to privacy.

An almost inevitable issue is whether the exercise should be undertaken at all. Many people, for example, believe that drug education may simply stimulate interest where none exists, and some evidence exists for this belief. One comprehensive study (Blum et al, 1976) compared the effects of two drug education programs on drug use by grade school students. A control group received no special drug educatin and self-reports on drug use were collected before the course and over the subsequent two years. The findings were complex, but two major points emerged. First, compared with the control group, students in both education programs were more likely to move to higher levels of drug use over the next two years: in other words, drug education had increased drug use. Second, students in both education groups were less likely to show extreme increases in amount and type of drug use than control students: in other words, drug education had decreased the likelihood of irresponsible and potentially harmful drug use.

Studies such as this have led to the view that in areas where people may be pressured to do something about which they are unsure, some reliable information is better than none. Some experts also suggest that what stimulates interest is not so much facts about drugs but the opportunity to discuss needs which, rightly or wrongly appear to be satisfied by drug use. To the extent that this is true, drug education would open the door to discussion of the many more constructive ways of satisfying these needs.

Finally, what most discussions of the value of education, and especially drug education, have left out is that education can be good or bad. Good education does not simply happen; the report from the Senate Standing Committee on Social Welfare (1977) states this succintly:

> The aims of drug education are to reduce ignorance, to modify behaviour, and to uphold the mores of society. The committee is aware that information alone can be counterproductive and may even contribute to an increase in the incidence of drug use. There is considerable variability in the type, content and quality of educational programmes and it is likely that they have differing effects on behaviour. It is wrong to assume that every educational intervention is in itself desirable. All education programmes should be evaluated and those which cannot demonstrate a positive effect should be abandonned.

Drug education in schools. Primary prevention almost inevitably raises the issue of drug education in schools. School children are conveniently accessible. Everyone has to go to school, and for a few years each succeeding generation is a captive audience. For practical and apparently logical reasons, the temptation to invest a substantial part of the drug education dollar in schools is enormous. However, neither the real value of the exercise nor its cost-effectiveness has been fully evaluated.

Education is not a new concept in the prevention of drug misuse. Its roots go back to the temperance movements that developed in the United States in the 1840s. These fostered moral righteousness and the belief that legislation could solve social problems. All States were urged to require teaching about the 'evils of alcohol' in schools and this became reality by the 1880s. The 'evils' approach dominated until the 1930s, then gradually gave way to the 'scientific–objective' approach. By the 1960s, this was firmly established and alcohol education was a defined role of the school. At about this time, rising levels of illegal drug use by youth produced a crisis in the public mind. Other drugs were added to alcohol in school curricula, and a mass of poorly planned and hastily executed programs appeared.

In this framework, the earliest guise of the 'scientific–objective' approach was what has come to be known as the 'scare' technique. Students and sometimes interested parents were exposed to a presentation by a police officer or some other drug expert that emphasised various horrible consequences of drug use. The scare technique continues to be used, particularly in community-operated programs on drugs. In educational circles, however, it soon became apparent that the technique is at best ineffective and often actively counterproductive. It was therefore replaced in school curricula by a variety of 'substance focused' approaches. The theory behind these was that if one simply presented the facts about drugs and alcohol such knowledge would be sufficient to discourage use. Again, substance focused approaches continue to be used. From an educational standpoint, however, they presented major problems.

First, there was no general agreement on what should be taught. In the case of illegal drugs, many felt that education should consist simply of saying 'Don't do it because it's against the law'. Many questions produced conflicting answers. Should one concentrate on drug effects, or on psychological and social factors, or on the consequences of drug use? Should the issues society is ambivalent about be spelled out? What should the goals be—abstinence, or more responsible use? When should drug education start and how is it to be presented? Should teachers do it, or outside experts?

It is hardly surprising that when reports began to suggest that substance focused approaches might increase drug use the harassed educational community quickly adopted what has been dubbed the 'affective' approach. Many would doubtless have gladly dropped all drug education from school curricula forthwith had there not been pressure from parents and the public that such education be given, no matter what its form.

The affective approach evolved out of the 'psychosocial' drug use model of Nowlis, who emphasised the 'need to relate information, attitudes and values regarding socially unacceptable drug use to the development needs of the individual, and to place them in the broader context of risk-taking, of decision-making, of clarifying values' (1975, p. 15). The approach is non-drug-specific: emphasis is on talking about people rather than drugs. Unfortunately, program designers have tended to lose sight of the original objective and in some programs drugs are not mentioned at all!

Other countries have generally followed the pattern set by the United States, though the timing naturally differs. At present, teaching about at least alcohol is a prescribed part of the primary school curriculum in all Australian States, but in practice there is no overall plan of action and no set of accepted aims. Drug education in Australian schools, according to Benjamin,

> tends to be inadequate, unplanned, uncoordinated and unevaluated. It also tends to be sparse and fragmentary, consisting of occasional visits from individuals who often represent a particular point of view (usually abstinence or concern with alcoholism). Representatives of churches sometimes provide viewpoints about alcohol use, and

occasionally the subject may be broached more or less accidentally in English or Religious Instruction lessons. Even more rare is the incorporation of content about alcohol wherever it seems natural and relevant in the curriculum, whether in Social Studies, Citizenship Education, Biology, Chemistry, Home Sciences, etc... In practice, alcohol is often treated in 'one-shot' school-wide meetings, arranged by the school administration, that consist of a lecture or other presentation by an outside 'expert'. One-shot presentation, or the isolated short-term unit, fails to engage students, is arbitrary and neglects individual student readiness and interest. (1978, p. 156)

Evaluation of drug education in schools is problematic. As we have seen, program evaluation is difficult under the best conditions. Moreover, the present theoretical perspective on drug education is at variance with actual practice. The affective approach exerts considerable theoretical influence, but old-style preventive education continues alongside it or in combination with it. Typically, curriculum projects are based on the affective approach but use project materials which rely on traditional substance-focussed information giving. In the classroom, this mixture tends to be translated into substance-focussed discussion because both students and teachers are attracted by the subject of drugs and their effects. On the whole, the newer curricula are rarely well executed. The affective approach requires educational methods that stimulate the students' interest and involve them actively in the learning experience; panel discussions, role-playing and committee work would be examples. Such techniques are labor-intensive and require a degree of curricular flexibility and teacher expertise not always available. Similarly, resource materials available are sometimes excellent and comprehensive, but more often scanty and inadequate. To date, only a few countries have made any effort to prepare general guidelines for the production and distribution of such resource material (cf. UNESCO, 1980).

The policy muddle is being reproduced in the classroom. It may well be that the undercurrent of dissatisfaction with the affective approach to education that is beginning to surface partly reflects this state of affairs. As one educator remarked, rather cynically, 'the narrower the focus, the more effective the affective education'. It would be unfortunate if a reversal to the earlier approaches occurred in response to such inadequate trials of the newer programs.

When formal evaluation has been carried out, some thought-provoking results have emerged. Perhaps the largest controlled study included about 5000, 14–18-year old school children in England and Wales (Dorn and Thompson, 1974; 1976). Questionnaires were given before, immediately after, two months after and one year after several types of lessons on drugs given by the students' regular teachers. The lessons were short—about two hours each—so the results may not be applicable to longer term programs.

There were three essential conclusions. First, the immediate effect of drug education is not a reliable indicator of long-term effects. The students' responses two months later were substantially different from their immediate reactions.

Second, drug education neither 'turns off' nor 'turns on' in an overall sense. The lessons had some preventive effects and some counter-preventive ones. In general, two months after the initial lesson there were no significant decreases in intention to accept any drug, and some increases in the intention to accept marijuana. The effect on attitude was mixed. There was a general decrease in the tendency to see drug-takers as like oneself and a slight leaning to an anti-drug position. There was no clear link between intention change and attitude change, and the one-year follow-up failed to demonstrate any behavioural change. This discrepancy between information, attitude and behaviour has been noted elsewhere. Jahoda and Crammond (1972) studied Glasgow school children, and they showed that although most eight years olds appeared to accept the conventional morality about the dangers of drink, this did not seem to influence their behaviour as they grew older. Clearly, children can be aware of the facts but this need not alter their attitude, which in turn may not correlate particularly closely with behavioural change.

Third, 'prevention' is too broad and abstract a concept to be useful in practice. The authors concluded that more useful aims were changes in behaviour, or intention, or attitudes to drugs, or attitudes to users. In other words, teachers must define the purpose or goal of their teaching more accurately if they wish to develop more effective methods.

Many goals are possible. We can aim to minimise the use of certain drugs, or the consequences of existing experimentation; we can seek to promote particular attitudes toward individual drugs; to increase knowledge, decision-making skills, teacher-pupil communication and much else. Realistically, however, only a small number of these goals can be implemented at any one time and the choice among them must take into account the special needs of each locality, school, syllabus and class.

It is also realistic to assume that acceptance of such specific measures and goals will be resisted. There is great comfort in such abstract concepts as 'prevention' and 'educating the whole person'. Their vagueness permits only token coverage of the field, and, as we have seen, many people—educators among them—are not convinced that the field should be covered to begin with.

What role then can we expect schools to take in drug and alcohol education? Such a question must ge placed in proper perspective. First, *is it realistic to require teachers to undertake this task?* Because drug education in schools is normally nested in other subjects, responsibility for it falls on teachers in charge of biology, social studies and similar courses. Such teachers are rarely expert in preventive education and many must rely on the sometimes very limited information supplied in some school texts, and such documentation as may reach them from other sources. This lack of specialisation at least partly accounts for the widespread recourse to outside 'specialists' such as medical and paramedical personnel, psychologists, social workers and police officers. This practice, while often useful and sometimes necessary, is regarded by many with considerable reservation. Outside specialists tend to isolate and spotlight the issue, and many feel that it is better dealt with as a normal part of the course into which it is integrated. Finally, outside specialists are seldom skilled teachers accustomed to contact with young people and able to inspire their confidence. However, it is clear that if teachers are to be trained to act as drug educators, most of them will need to be trained in more facts about drugs.

In addition, the current emphasis on affective education implies that the teacher's task is to help students develop alternative strategies and goals that are personally satisfying and socially acceptable without ignoring any of the realities involved and with the understanding that people have differing concepts of what constitutes reality. This means that students must be taught skills in decision-making, communication, values clarification, coping, problem solving and constructive use of leisure, among other things. That this is a truly formidable task is not generally appreciated.

Teacher preparation for the small group method is also time-consuming, exacting and costly. Unterberger and DiCicco (1976) recommend eight to ten sessions in which group dynamics are learned by participation. In their opinion, 'this amount of time is required for adults to clarify their feelings about their own drinking and about teenage drinking, and to determine goals and methods in their approach to young people'.

The extent of the drug education teacher's responsibility must also be defined. Such specialist educators, even if not specifically asked to do so, will counsel students in the normal course of events. In many cases, they are encouraged to set up regualr schedules of consulting hours for students and parents, and they will be asked to intervene in drug problems as they arise. The principle is a sound one, but the degree to which such teachers possess counselling skills is highly variable. There is in general a real need to define roles more clearly and to ensure either that appropriate avenues of referral exist and are used, or that adequate training is undertaken.

Second, *is drug education a realistic part of the school curriculum?* The decision-making process is not simple and cannot be taught neatly in the confines of a class period or even of a semester. The mere presentation of facts about drugs is time-consuming. Universities and colleges which train teachers are constantly being bombarded by requests from special-interest groups to include this or that program in their curriculum. It has been claimed that if training institutions responded to these requests there would soon be no time in teacher preparation programs to train teachers to be teachers, or for teachers in schools to devote their time to the teaching of academic subjects. There is little actual logic in this argument, because the addition of one new program does not mean that all requests must be granted. In general, when a program is turned down it means that it is not wanted, for various reasons. In practice, however, the rationale is difficult to overthrow. A limited amount of time must be divided between many subjects. Introduction of drug education requires a thorough examination of all priorities, including the educational goals of each institution, and these are rarely stated clearly.

Third, *is the school a suitable place for drug education?* Much teaching fails because it focuses on what the older generation thinks young people should be told rather than finding out what their needs are. The elements of control and compulsion that exist in most school systems tend to inhibit genuine decision-making by students. Much of the relationship between students and teachers is essentially adversary, and compliance is far more usual than true learning. Since young people who misuse drugs tend to have negative or hostile attitudes towards authority in general, teachers may not be the ideal people to undertake drug education. They tend to have low credibility in the eyes of their students, and 'when teachers speak of the necessity to control behaviours that have strong elements of attraction to young people, or where discrepancies exist between teacher description and student observation, credibility decreases along with message effectiveness' (Benjamin, 1978, pp. 159–60).

Whoever is responsible for drug education should be a 'detached neutral'. Teachers must not have an official attitude, and students must be motivated to reveal and examine their beliefs. Neither of these goals can be realised unless the school administration publicly supports them. Teachers must not be made to feel that they should publicly deplore all student drug use lest parents or principals interpret a neutral stance as a pro-drug orientation and reprisals follow.

Perhaps the most crucial point is that school education programs can have only limited success without reinforcement from other and more powerful socialising influences in the community. The impact of the school as a socialising force is relatively small. The family continues to be the major factor; peers and sometimes Churches occupy an intermediate position; schools come last. The soundest policy would seem to be to allocate resources in such ways as to take full advantage of this hierarchy. However, attempts continue to be made to solve drug problems through isolated school efforts or curriculum development programs without actively soliciting the participation of the community.

None of the foregoing should be taken to imply that drug education in schools is inappropriate or that it should be discontinued. However, a plea is being made on the one hand that schools recognise the full extent of the commitment drug education implies and act accordingly, limiting their goals and responsibility as appropriate, and on the other that the family and the community shoulder their share of the burden.

Community education. Community education about drugs and alcohol comes under the heading of mental health. Besides psychosis and neurosis, mental health problems include what Cawte (1978) calls 'problems in living'—crises sufficiently overwhelming to require at least temporary intervention by a professional helper—and what he calls 'inadequacy'. For many reasons, people may not be socially, intellectually or educationally adequate to meet the demands of a particular lifestyle. Problems related to drugs or alcohol may cross over any or all of these categories.

Community drug education, that is, providing the public with relevant and factual material on drug issues, is a very fragmented area. It shares all the problems discussed earlier in the context of school drug education, but it lacks the long-established structures and communication networks the school system can rely on. Projects and activities are heterogeneous and dispersed, and many organisations and individuals spanning every level of competence are involved. As with school drug education, 'encouragement of moderation and the acceptance of abstinence' is currently the main message, and drug education programs are usually nested in more general health education programs. The approach favored by most policy-making bodies is the affective one described earlier, and in general it suffers the same difficulties. Its effectiveness in promoting the rational use of drugs is taken utterly on faith, and it co-exists with equally common and equally unevaluated substance focused approaches and scare techniques.

This generally uncoordinated effort is further hampered by fragmentation of effort at the policy-making level and chronic shortage of resources, especially personnel. For example, community drug and alcohol education in New South Wales is the joint responsibility of the Department of Education, the Health Commission, and the Drug and Alcohol Authority. Their policies are generally similar in intent, but the fact remains that three large statutory bodies are involved, two regionalised and concerned with a wide variety of other programs and projects, while the third interfaces with all non-governmental as well as government-sponsored drug and alcohol agencies. Even with ideal cooperation, development of coherent statewide or regional programs would be slow and complex. Moreover, all three bodies lack sufficient adequately qualified staff, and those who are available have been generally reluctant to delegate responsibility to community volunteers or to train them.

The result is that the drug or alcohol education now available is the product of self-starters in the community, who design and implement the best programs they can with little real support from State or regional bodies. Practically, this means that the materials and teachers used are often inappropriate, and the problem is compounded by the entry of various commercial interests into the field.

Lack of information, support and resources often results in education programs that consist of a series of disjointed 'one-night stands'. A concerned group gets together and obtains a speaker supposedly knowledgeable about drugs but actually likely to give a biased if not erroneous viewpoint. The situation is not improved by the fact that all three statutory organisations generally refuse to conduct 'one-night stands' if requested to do so, for the excellent reason that research has shown this technique to be useless if not counter-productive. Unfortunately, the public does not know this, and on refusal by the 'experts' will do the best they can elsewhere. Consequently, well-developed programs are not available, and the public is constantly exposed to a bewildering range of competing projects of extremely variable quality. Guidelines for what might constitute an effective program are not difficult to draw up on the basis of available research. The following points might be made about program content, target groups, method of delivery and the personnel to be involved.

The program. There is general agreement that drug education should be part of a total education for living in which positive and enriching alternatives are promoted, and that it should be integrated into a person's development from an early age. Attempts should be made to keep what is seen as drug misuse in perspective. Consideration of currently illegal drug use should not dominate the discussion and adequate attention should be given to the statistically much greater problems that result from the misuse of social drugs and legally obtained medicines.

The target group. Blanket campaigns are usually not successful, although increasing social awareness of the problems has some value. It must be recognised that different groups will be concerned with different drugs, and that within each group there will be those with little information or interest; those with some information and no interest; those with considerable knowledge who have tried drugs once or twice; those who use one or more drugs occasionally; and those for whom drug use has become an exclusive or dominant concern, at least for the moment. In terms of both content and approach, educational efforts must vary according to the number of people in each of these categories expected to participate in each program.

The method of delivery. Misuse of drugs should never be described or demonstrated. Scare tactics should be avoided, and short-term programs are generally successful only if they draw attention to relevant issues and indicate further sources of information and help. Throughout, it is important to realise that information alone, especially if presented to an 'at risk' audience in a 'one-night stand' format, is likely to be counterproductive.

Debate on a single statement is generally not as effective as the presentation of the merits and shortcomings of a variety of positions. Outcomes of debates tend to depend too much on the personality, charisma and verbal skills of the debaters.

Beyond this, basic facts about drugs are best presented to a relatively uninformed audience without any emotional appeals and without much commentary on social issues. A more knowledgeable audience responds better to minimal factual information with ample opportunity to discuss relevant non-drug issues and some mention of alternatives to drug use. Heavy drug users are typically extremely difficult to reach and are probably not suited to group approaches. They respond best to information about the availability of individuals, who can guarantee confidentiality, with whom they might wish to talk about their views.

Personnel. Ideally, the teacher should come from the same ethnic group as the audience; cultural, socio-economic and educational differences should be minimised. The use of ex-addicts and an emphasis on legal issues generally tends to be counterproductive, especially with young audiences. Ex-addicts may occasionally be of value in lecturing to special target groups.

In general, a lecturer already identified through the media or other sources as a crusader with strong biases about drug use, whether for or against, will be less effective than one who wins respect because of his or her objectivity and respect for the audience.

Lecturers and discussion leaders must demonstrate that they are accurate and authoritative (not authoritarian!): that is, they should be thoroughly familiar with the source and context of the facts they present to substantiate their conclusions. Throughout, there is need to emphasise personal, parental and community responsibility. Parents need to be made aware that the extent to which their own drug use influences the behaviour of their children, and that ease of access to drugs in the home and community activates drug misuse. It is also essential that educators be aware of the available community resources, and be able to refer people who need information, guidance and perhaps counselling or other treatment.

Guidelines are easy enough to establish, but implementing such programs is harder. Increasingly, the trend is to draw the educators from the community. Cawte (1978) has outlined a procedure for selecting mental health workers that should be equally applicable to drug educators:

> You don't appoint a person to do a job; you go to the community and find out who the leaders are, and you ask what they know about the people creating the problems in the community... Once you have the support of the leaders, you can then ask who, amongst your people, do you think would be a good mental health worker? It is usually an older person who is trusted and respected—it is not a bright, young person with a shiny new Higher School Certificate. They might be good health workers, but they are not likely to be good mental health workers, because it demands other qualities, such as maturity and acceptance... it isn't education that matters, it's being a member of the community ... Being able to listen to, and talk to people, and to work on a solution according to the available means—these are the qualities that are needed in a mental health worker. You then set up some kind of program... Finally, ensure there is on-going supervision... For this you need to appoint your community psychiatrist, social worker, psychologist or whoever is best, to meet with your little group as many times a week as can be managed, not to treat the cases but to hear them and work out what is needed. This creates a mental health situation in the community, and, before long, they are working on getting their alcohol rehabilitation centre. (pp. 25–26)

Before all this can occur, there must be a 'key person', or, preferrably, a team, who can make the initial contact with the community, help analyse their feelings, needs and resources, train the workers and assist in the development of a strategy suitable to the area. This is where State and regional statutory bodies fit most appropriately. In general, State levels are best adapted to the development of general guidelines, coordination and provision of back up resources. Regional authority personnel are best used to develop the network of key people needed, train them and continue to work with them in a supportive capacity through the life of the program.

This long-term commitment is critical. Drug and alcohol problems can be minimised, but it is naive to believe that they can be eradicated. Adequate drug and alcohol education must be continuing, sustained process, not just a once-and-for-all effort.

Environmental manipulation

There has been increasing debate on whether individual education is the most useful venue for the limited funds available for prevention programs. Hawk (1974), for instance, has urged a distinction between 'education that has as its objective the persuasion of the individual, and education whose goal is the rearrangement of the environmental contingencies which affect individuals'. He has argued that rather than focusing on individuals and attempting to help them cope with the environment, it might be equally valid to direct health education efforts toward those who have most control over the environment and can effect changes in it. The availability of drugs, dispersal of information about them and public attitudes towards their use are three major areas where environmental controls might profitably be exercised. It is impossible to separate these factors; they interact in complex and subtle ways, and considering them under spearate headings is a matter of convenience only.

Control of availability. It is fatuous to state that there is no significant problem in obtaining the support of all key Government, business and community groups and the community at large when the objective is to restrict the availability of even illegal drugs. McCoy (1981) has ably demonstrated that corruption at all these levels is prerequisite for illegal drug traffic. When it comes to social drugs such as alcohol or tobacco, however, there is no question that any proposal for effective controls on their availability brings the forces concerned with health into conflict with those who benefit economically and otherwise from the production, supply and sales of these substances.

The variety of control policies that have been enacted or proposed for alcohol alone is well beyond the scope of this discussion, but some general consideration of the arguments for and against restrictive controls seems worthwhile. The production of social drugs and their distribution is of considerable economic and political importance in most countries, and the drugs are widely used for recreational purposes. Because government policies on their use will affect large numbers of consumers and significant sectors of the economy, it is essential that evidence in support of restrictive controls is both relevant and valid. Regrettably, the quality of the arguments could be much improved.

Arguments for and against controls centre on three main issues: the relationship between consumption and the incidence of problems, the concept of special vulnerabilities to drug misuse, and the position that restrictive controls foster an unhealthy ambivalence towards drug use. Because the control controversy is perhaps greatest in the case of alcohol, examples will be taken from that area.

Where arguments for control have considered the effects of levels of consumption, selection of data has been remarkably inept. In general, proponents of control have emphasized the long-term consequences of excessive drinking on physical health. However, death and disease in excessive drinkers are largely attributable to their deviant lifestyle, lack of proper nutrition and general unhappiness, and not to excessive alcohol use as such. At the same time, the social problems caused by acute and chronic intoxication (on which a much better case for implementation of legal controls can be based) have been largely ignored. Also ignored is the fact that while the evidence to date is not sufficient to infer the exact nature of the relationship between average consumption and excessive use (De lint, 1977), there is sound evidence that overall levels of consumption and rates of excessive use rise and fall together. There is no recorded instance of a population in which high overall consumption prevails in the absence of a high rate of excessive drinking, however that population is selected.

The special vulnerability issue may be illustrated by the disease concept of alcoholism. Arguments against restrictive measures often maintain that heavy drinking by 'alcoholics' is a symptom of their peculiar physiology, and that the same patterns would not occur in 'normal' people. Those speaking for the alcohol industry have a special fondness for this line of reasoning. The argument against this view has been clearly stated by De Lint:

> 'There are indeed significant differences in the likelihood of becoming an alcoholic but it is also well known that in exceedingly wet environments, where beverage alcohol is readily available and frequently consumed, excessive drinking is a much more prevalent behaviour. Restricting alcohol availability cannot prevent a very vulnerable person from becoming a heavy drinker, but it can prevent less vulnerable persons from indulging. (1977, p. 438)

Unfortunately, that argument has had little currency.

An especially popular argument is that restrictive controls prevent the adoption of 'healthy' drinking. In particular, it is argued that young people should be introduced to drinking at an early age so that they can learn to drink moderately and come to regard drinking as a normal part of their lives. In fact, age is irrelevant and the environment in which the introduction takes place is critical. There is ample evidence that young people learn to drink, and that the pattern of their drinking depends on the source of their instruction. To emphasise age alone is simply irresponsible.

An especially problematic related area is that of 'civilised drinking'. The issue is presented more fully below, but essentially the idea is that if moderate, appropriate drinking is encouraged, undesirable heavy consumption patterns will drop out. In this context, it must be pointed out that there exists no evidence to support this theory, and there is some that suggests that it may not work as expected. In Finland, the State Alcohol Monopoly, acting on scientific advice, active promoted so-called 'desirable practices' in drinking for a number of years. It was believed that the integration of these practices into social custom would gradually replace the traditional weekend benders and thus reduce the incidence of alcohol problems. Regrettably, these expectations were not fulfilled. Within a relatively short time, this change in policy led to quite dramatic increases in both alcohol consumption and alcohol-related problems (Bruun et al, 1975).

It is to be hoped that the many programs and advertising campaigns currently extolling the virtues of civilised drinking will be subjected to thorough evaluation. Previous experience suggests that continuous proliferation of alcohol use and rapid increases in overall consumption are unlikely to benefit public health.

One fact must be borne in mind throughout. No matter how much evidence is marshalled in support of legal restraints on drug availability, most of the studies have methodological shortcomings. As we have seen, this is almost unavoidable. However, because legal control of drugs is a controversial issue, these weaknesses tend to be exploited by the adversaries of control. At the same time, the degree of consistency in the truly vast amount of evidence linking availability, overall level of consumption and the incidence of drug-related problems tends to be ignored. One must try to keep a perspective on the forest while examining the individual trees.

Advertising: the role of the media in misuse and prevention. The amount of money available for preventive efforts is relatively small. For example, the largest public health organisation in Britain, the Health Education Council, spent £2,775,000 of its £4,600,000 budget for 1978–79 on various health campaigns conducted through the press and other media. Of this, £407,030 was spent on its anti-smoking campaigns. When it is realised that the entire anti-smoking campaign cost less than the advertising budget for a single brand of cigarette, the extent of the problem begins to be apparent. The 'enormity and remorseless nature of the counter curriculum' (Health Education Council, 1978–79) is not generally appreciated.

Most countries now have some sort of advertising standards code that relates to drugs. In Australia, for example, the code for alcoholic beverages requires that:

- advertisements are to be directed only to adults;
- children are not to be portrayed, except in a scene where it would be natural for them to be present, and even then it must be clear that they are not drinking alcoholic beverages;

- anyone drinking in an advertisement shall be obviously above the legal drinking age;
- advertisements should aim at a change in the share of the total liquor market, and not at increased consumption;
- advertiscments should do no more than reflect people drinking responsibly in natural situations;
- advertisements should not imply that success or social distinction or sexual success, accompany drinking alcohol;
- advertisements will not show people drinking at work;
- except in advertisements designed to educate consumers, characters may never be portrayed as both drinkers and drivers;
- advertisements should not 'dare' people to try a particular drink, to imply they will 'prove' themselves in some way if they accept the 'challenge' offered by the drink;
- inducements to prefer specific brands because of high alcoholic content are forbidden; and
- no liquor advertising should encourage over-indulgence. (Kirby, 1978, pp. 11–12)

The degree of pressure placed on the relevant industries varies considerably from one country to another. In the United States, legislation has recently been proposed to raise liquor taxes and the minimum drinking age, restrict the nature and content of spirits advertising, outlaw deductions for liquor at business lunches, impose ingredient labels and special warnings to pregnant women and much more. The industry responded in two ways. First, they voluntarily restricted the style of their own advertising. Second, they embarked on massive education programs to show consumers how to enjoy their products responsibly.

Cynics might argue that encouragement of moderation in people who might otherwise remain abstainers still represents a substantial contribution to the industry's coffers, and probably offsets any slight losses in trade that the campaigns might produce. And the sobering results of the Finnish experiment cited above must be borne in mind. Nevertheless, United States practices seem to be an improvement on current policies in Australia. Farmer describes the Australian position as follows:

> It seems to me the Australian liquor industry has not yet faced up to its social responsibilities, despite the moves towards voluntary advertising codes. In California we would not be watching John Newcombe telling us about the drink for today. Nor would Penfold's Wines be able to sponsor a football team, even if they are Saints. These Australian companies apparently do not see any conflict between their advertising and their social responsibilities. Nor has the Australian press raised any doubt the propriety of Parramatta having famous Grouse 'Eels'.

In Australia, the association between alcohol and sport is a strong one. The NSW cricket team is sponsored by a brewery, and the team drinks Tooheys beer in exactly the 'ocker' way, so that it dribbles down the shirt. KB sponsor amateur athletics, North Melbourne have Courage, and Carlton United back the 'Blues'.

On television, advertising of alcohol is banned before 7pm with one exception: liquor ads can be shown during live sporting broadcasts. I myself was approached to sponsor a local television station's live transmission of the Bathurst motor racing. Alcohol and motor cars?

I believe it is right and proper that the liquor industry, and the media who run their advertisements, should be called to account for their actions... If we don't do so voluntarily, then pressures will build here, as they have in the United States, for it to be done compulsorily by government. And that holds dangers not only for the liquor industry, and the revenues of the media, but, I believe, for the community as well. (1978, pp. 18–19)

Most lay and professional thinking is dominated by the propaganda methods of the media. Not all of these are being used inappropriately; but many are, and there is considerable agitation that some steps be taken. Farmer, for example, has castigated the Australian press for ignoring its social responsibilities:

Basically, the Australian press steers away from complex stories. Alcoholism is a complex subject—the reasons for it, the best ways of curing it. True to form, the Australian press has treated it by ignoring it. Sure, it has reported the findings of parliamentary committees on drug abuse—but in a dull way that encourages no one to read them. It has not dug and probed into stories for itself.

The attitudes of the Australian press can best be shown, I think, by reference to the current NSW Royal Commission into Drugs. The press—including radio and television—has seized on every reference to organized crime; headlined every reference to the millions of dollars of profits; traipsed with glee with their television cameras to ceremonial burnings of marijuana plantations. But their enthusiasm wanes whenever the evidence before the Commission becomes what I would call serious: whenever anyone tries to analyse why people in Australia are taking marijuana and narcotics in greater number than ever before. Not from the Australian press are we getting established ideas challenged. A political party with the platform for legalising marijuana can provide a light-hearted divertisement to dull election coverage, but an analysis of its platform, and the effects that would follow legislation, is beyond the Australian press.

Even by its own standards as entertainers, the Australian press wants to entertain or frighten without actually doing any work. It revelled in the story of the recent capture of a huge haul of marijuana being imported by a fishing trawler, but it has not stopped to question why the major drug hauls in Australia tend to be marijuana, and not heroin. Why is it that police and Customs drug squads in this country devote so much of their time and effort to the least dangerous illegal drug? Is it true that cutting off supplies of marijuana by such spectacular raids makes it easier for heroin pushers to peddle their poisonous wares? Are our drug squads making more heroin addicts by their very action of curbing marijuana imports and cultivation, so highly publicised? Don't bother reading an Australian newspaper to find out. It would be entertaining, good crime reporting to have an answer, but it would also require hard work by intelligent and well-paid journalists with a lot of time at their disposal. That, I'm afraid, is too hard for the Australian press. (1978, p. 16)

Increased responsibility in the media when dealing with drug issues is clearly necessary. There is also a need for a more balanced presentation of drug effects. Both positive and negative consequences should have 'equal time'. Britain's Advisory Council on Alcoholism, for instance, said:

It is not inconsistent for advertising to reinforce social controls against alcohol misuse... Advertising, and the media in general portray alcohol in a one-sided way. The media hardly ever show that alcohol impairs; and that it often contributes to accidents at work, at home, or on the road. The attention of those responsible for the media should be drawn to the need to give a balanced view of alcohol—both the good and bad effects. It would be useful if the media gave more prominence to the need for greater public awareness that drinking can lead to problems. (ACA, 1978, p. 7)

Alternative ways of using drugs also need to have equal time, and these include abstinence. Moderate, appropriate and responsible use are all relevant and valid in the context of reducing consumption, but non-use typically gets brief and even condescending mention as an option:

While our knowledge about the drug age increases every day, much less is really known about those for whom chemicals, whatever the substance and circumstances, have little or no relevance. There are people who do not drink alcohol. There are kids who are not into drugs. More needs to be known about, and heard from those whose lives are founded on convictions rather than chemicals. There is a place for a viable and articulate position which could be called in short responsible abstinence. (Editorial, *Addictions*, 1973)

The public image of drug use and misuse. The community is very much at the mercy of the media. In the absence of programs which deal realistically with drugs and drug misusers, the media determine how the public conceptualises these matters and how it reacts to them, and it must be remembered that politicians, law-makers and educators are all members of the public. The stereotypes developed in this way may have no bearing on real events, and can panic the community into quite inappropriate responses to its perceived drug problem.

In Australia, for example, stereotyping of this sort has produced an essentially negative perspective on drug and alcohol problems. Emphasis has been on the prevalence of drug and alcohol misuse, the rising incidence of related problems and the pressure such forces as the tobacco and liquor industries can bring to bear against any initiatives designed to stem the tide of addiction. Public authorities and the media have combined to perpetuate the image of the 'ocker' beer-swilling Australian as the norm, and drunkenness as a socially-approved and circumscribed excess. Over time, repetitions of variations on the theme that heavy drinking is the rule have created a self-fulfilling prophecy. People who do not conform to the image are now reluctant to admit it, and many are attempting to live up to it.

The assumption that heavy drinking is an integral part of social life has also aborted most initiatives calculated to reduce alcohol-related problems. In such a climate, it is easy to conclude that any government interference with the drinking habits of the community or restrictions on the production and availability of alcohol would amount to political suicide. Because the stereotype is assumed to fit all drinkers, it is assumed that restrictive measures would also inconvenience all drinkers equally.

So, despite concern expressed about the alcohol problem, new programs remain unsupported and there is a general absence of any change. Drew (1978) sums up the problem this way:

> If authoritative statements are to be believed, then more people are drinking more, problems are getting worse in spite of our best efforts to control them, most people are against changes which could reduce problems, if those changes interfere with their own freedom, and even health personnel avoid confronting patients with the need for a change in drinking habits when the current pattern is life-threatening. Governments will not act, because the alcohol beverage industry is a significant element in the economy in general, and provides a major income in excise and licensing fees.

If such is the case, then only two positions seem tenable. One can believe the community wants things to stay as they are. Increasing affluence, a threatened economy, changing life-styles and the mounting stress of modern life, all mean that increasing consumption of alcoholic beverages is inevitable for the future, and a whole range of other factors are against a reduction of problems becoming a reality. The problems are so large that there is no place one could confidently start. The opposition to change is so strong, why try? Why should governments take risks? Why should we waste more money on useless endeavours? We may as well go on as we are and stop worrying. (p. 158)

In 1976, the Minister for the Australian Capital Territory assessed the direct costs of alcohol misuse in Australia at $1000 million, of which $400 million was in costs and losses to industry. In 1976–77, about one in five adult admissions to general hospitals in New South Wales alone was related to alcohol, at a total cost of $81 million. In the same period, one in three admissions to State psychiatric hospitals was directly related to alcohol: estimated cost, $26 million. In the area of human costs, there is, for example, one chance in two that during a normal driving lifetime of 50 years each non-drinking driver will be involved in some kind of accident with a drinking driver. There is one chance in ten that during the same period such an accident will result in a fatality. The danger to the drinking driver is of course much higher (Farquhar, 1978).

Because something clearly has to be done, the other alternative, according to Drew, 'is to abandon recourse to reason and the development of balanced policies, to seek a scapegoat and advocate *drastic* action be taken, regardless of other considerations' (1978, p. 158).

Various drastic actions have indeed been proposed. They range from total bans on all liquor advertising through dramatic price increases to suggestions that all beer should contain less than 3.5 per cent alcohol by volume. Each of these approaches could have a positive effect but would be counterproductive if applied indiscriminately. For instance, there is some evidence that increased tax on alcohol can bring about a reduction in consumption (Nyberg, 1967). However, such increases need to be very large to produce a lasting change, and they bring with them such 'unexpected' consequences as a shift to home brewing, smuggling, illicit distillation and consumption of various alcohol substitutes. Most important, other parts of the family budget are usually restricted so that drinking may continue. Thus, when the tax on liquor was increased in Britain in 1975, the proportion of average weekly income spent on food, clothing, heat, light and fuel dropped by 10–17 per cent and the proportion spent on alcohol rose by 17 per cent (Central Statistical Office, 1975). Such fiscal controls of course hit the poorest people hardest. It is clear that implementation of drastic measures is effective only when it reflects or at least is closely followed by significant changes in public opinion.

A new approach is needed to counter the confusion, ambivalence, fear and sense of impotence that the current stereotype of the alcohol problem in Australia has created. What Drew (1978) has called a 'positive approach' emphasises the need to break up the stereotype of uniform heavy drinking into a more realistic national drinking profile.

He proposes a classification that includes *non-drinkers and light drinkers* (less than four standard drinks a day) who are almost immune to the negative effects of alcohol; *hazardous drinkers*, who run an increased risk of alcohol-related harm, with degree of risk depending on various factors; and *dangerous, heavy drinkers* (more than 12 drinks a day) who are very likely to experience or cause alcohol-related harm.

Statistics for 1977 show that in that year only five per cent of each age group fell into the heavy drinker category. Hazardous drinkers made up another 15 per cent, and 80 per cent of males and more than 95 per cent of females were either non-drinkers or light drinkers (Australian Bureau of Statistics, 1977). In other words, more than four out of every five adult Australians is a non-drinker or a relatively safe, light drinker, and this majority needs to be given a sense of identity and encouragement to use their numerical strength in initiating action to reduce the threat less responsible drinkers pose to themselves and to society.

Alternative images of drinkers are needed. Ambivalence about alcohol use must be removed and a positive feeling of security must be attached to light drinking. There have been many fervent (and valid and necessary) campaigns to destigmatise the alcoholic, but the same has yet to be done for the wowser. The decision not to drink, or to drink to a fixed limit, should need no explanation.

The environment should also be altered to give more real choice to light drinkers and non-drinkers. In many public bars, for instance, coffee or tea is available only with full meals. Selection of non-alcoholic beverages in most restaurants is distinctly limited and their availability is poorly advertised. In fact, it is difficult to find places of entertainment that are not intimately connected with alcohol. As Ritson (1977) has pointed out, 'if the leisure time of the young is inevitably linked with alcohol through lack of alternatives, it is tempting to hypothesize that alcohol and happy occasions will become linked so that the one comes to stand for the other, and the individual becomes conditioned to associate alcohol and fun or a good time to such an extent that one cannot exist without the other' (p. 460). Once the need for change is recognised, it is not difficult to envisage where changes might be made. Many of them are modest and would require little alteration of law or custom.

People who drink responsibly also need to be assured that activism on their part is appropriate, and that 'they are not being hypocritical in demanding action to reduce alcohol problems, or in personally intervening to protect individuals from alcohol misuse: there is a world of difference between relatively safe (responsible) and dangerous drinking patterns. Individuals have the right to protect themselves and the responsibility to protect others from themselves, when addictive substances, such as alcohol, impair judgement' (Drew, 1978, p. 159).

As far as legal controls are concerned, it needs to be made clear that most people, including politicians, have nothing to lose by the introduction of reasonable measures directed at reducing misuse and limiting alcohol-related damage. Thus, increased and properly directed enforcement of drink-driving legislation (for instance, concentrating breathalyser test on drivers outside hotels and in drinking localities) would hardly affect most drinkers at all except to make the roads safer.

In any case, policies directed at reducing problems need not be punitive. If detection of the problem occurs early enough, there is every reason to believe that rehabilitation is possible. This includes the resumption of more normal drinking in at least some cases. If legal provisions are seen as avenues for coercing excessive drinkers into recognising their problem and accepting treatment rather than simply as a system of punishments for offenders, some progress might be made.

That essentially coercive measures can be used constructively is shown by the increasing success of industrial drug and alcohol programs. In Australia, these enjoy the support of both management and trade unions, and their philosophy is well summarised by Polites:

> Employers, and employer organisations are in a unique position of advantage to encourage and, if necessary, to coerce (using that term in its broadest sense) people into thinking seriously about the issues confronting them. It is possible for employers and unions together to explain to people that they cannot continue to be employed if their work performance continues to be poor. What we are concerned to do is to promote programmes in such a way that a person needing help may be persuaded to accept it, preserve his place in the workforce and continue to make a valuable contribution to society.
>
> In my view the essence of an effective attack on addictions in the workplace is for management to proclaim, and for all employees to understand, that in the plant, in the office, in the factory, in the warehouse, alcoholism and drug addiction are not in themselves employment offences.
>
> The real offence is poor work performance which, if it continues, must merit dismissal. The addictions themselves are no more than treatable illnesses which cause unsatisfactory work. Employees must understand that they need to face up to this disability and seek a positive and effective treatment which will enable them to return to positive work performance. If that is done, then the whole matter is finished. On the other hand it should also be made quite clear that if he will not do this then ultimately the sanction of dismissal must follow, for not only is he a danger to himself and a problem to his associates, but he may well become a serious danger to all his fellows in the workplace. It is important for him to understand that he has a responsibility to them, as well as they have to him. (1978, p. 194–95)

In the larger social arena, policy measures framed along similar lines can only improve a situation in which there is ample evidence that prohibition does not work and that legal deterrents such as fines and prison sentences are generally ineffective.

References

Advisory Committee on Alcoholism, *Report on Prevention*, DHSS/Welsh Office, 1978.
Australian Bureau of Statistics, *Alcohol and Tobacco Consumption Patterns*, (Feb. 1977, Cat. No. 43120) AGPS, Canberra, 1978.
Benjamin, M.L., 'Alcohol education in schools', in *Alcohol in Australia*, Diehm, A., Seaborn, R. & Wilson, G. (eds), McGraw-Hill, 1978.
Blane, H.T., 'Education and the prevention of alcoholism', in *The Biology of Alcoholism*, Kissin, B. & Beglieter, H. (eds) vol. 4, Plenum Press, 1976.
Blum, R.H., Blum, E. & Garfield, E., *Drug education: Results and Recommendations*, D.C. Heath & Co., 1976.
Brun K. et al., 'Alcohol control policies in public health perspective', The Finnish Foundation for Alcohol Studies, 25, 1975.
Cawte, J., *Training Aboriginal Health Workers*, National Alcohol and Drug Dependence Multidisciplinary Institute, A.F.A.D.D., 1978, pp. 20–26.
Central Statistical Office, *Annual Reviwe of Statitics*, H.M.S.O., 1973.
De Lint, J., 'Alcohol control policy as a strategy of prevention: a critical examination of the evidence', in *Alcoholism and Drug Dependence*, Madden, J. Walker, R. & Kenyon, W. (eds), Plenum Press, 1977.
Drew, L.R.H., *Alcohol problems: can we do better?*, National Alcohol and Drug Dependence Multidisciplinary Institute, A.F.A.D.D., 1978, pp. 156–61.
Editorial, *Addictions*, Addiction Research Foundation, Toronto, Summer, 1973.
Farmer, R., *The responsibilities of the Australian press and liquor industry vis-a-vis alcohol*, National Alcohol and Drug Dependence Multi-disciplinary Institute, A.F.A.D.D., 1978, pp. 15–19.
Farquhar, M.F., 'The drinking driver', in *Alcohol in Australia*, Diehm, A., Seaborn, R. & Wilson, G. (eds), McGraw-Hill, 1978.
Hawk, D., *Research on methods and programmes of drug education*, Addiction Research Foundation, Ontario, 1974.
Health Education Council, *Annual Report*, 1978–79.
Jahoda, G. & Crammond, J., *Children and alcohol*, H.M.S.O., 1972.
Kirby, Sir R., *Advertising and the Role of Australian Advertising Council*, National Alcohol and Drug Dependence Multidisciplinary Institute, A.F.A.D.D., 1978, pp. 9–14.
McCoy, A.W., *Drug Traffic*, Harper & Row, Sydney 1980.
New York Times, 'Drug abuse films termed harmful', 13 Dec. 1972.
Nowlis, H.H., *Drugs on the College Campus*, Anchor Books, 1969.
Nowlis, H.H., *Drugs demystified*, UNESCO, Paris, 1975.
Nyberg, A., 'Consumption and price of alcoholic beverages', Finnish Foundation of Alcohol Studies, 15, 1967.
Polites, G., 'Alcohol and other drug problems in industry—the employers' view', in *Alcohol in Australia*, Diehm, A., Seaborn, R. & Wilson, G. (eds), McGraw-Hill, 1978.
Randall, D. & Wong, M.R., 'Drug education to date: a review', *J. of Drug Educ.*, 6, 1976.

Ritson, B., 'Alcohol and education', in *Alcoholism and Drug Dependence*, Madden, J., Walker, R. & Kenyon, W. (eds) Plenum Press, 1977.

Senate Standing Committee on Social Welfare, *Drug problems in Australia—an intoxicated society? A report*, A.G.P.S., Canberra, 1977.

Smart, R.G. & Fejer, D., *Drug education: current issues, future directions*, Addictions Research Foundation, Ontario, 1974.

UNESCO, *Working Paper: Coordination of school and out-of-school education concerning the problems associated with the use of drugs*, Lisbon, 1980.

US National Commission on marijuana and Drug Abuse, *Drug use in America: problems in perspective. Second Report*, USGPO, 1973.

Unterberger, H. & Di Cicco., *Alcohol education re-evaluated*, cited by Blane, op. cit., p. 557.

9 Preventive strategies
Secondary prevention and professional training

Secondary prevention involves recognition of a problem and initiation of treatment. As we have seen, the last decade has produced a major shift in emphasis. Prior to the 1970s treatment was a specialist matter and community response to drug and alcohol problems consisted largely of voluntary services. These included AA, and facilities such as and shelters and hostels, generally run by religious organizations and local councils. Most tended to concentrate on specific target groups, chiefly the destitute or the homeless, and catered for only a minority of people with drug and alcohol problems.

By the early 1970s, economic pressures, changing views about alcohol and drug dependence, and disenchantment with the success of specialist treatment provoked most Western countries into policies that stressed a more comprehensive community involvement. In general, these policies implied that people with drug and alcohol problems should be helped in the context of their own families and lifestyles if at all possible, and that the provision of care should be primarily the responsibility of helping professions working directly in the community. An associated development was a reduced emphasis on the need for medical intervention and an expansion of the role of various forms of counselling.

Current strategies

Implementation of the new policies was envisaged as a two-tier structure. *Primary care* centres and workers were expected to respond to most misuse problems. Facilities were to be relatively simple. The common essential proposed was that the service should fit the needs of the clients. This meant, minimally, that people should be able to find treatment and care near where they lived and that the response should be prompt and relevant because disillusionment can set in quickly. Most frequently, this has taken the form of a building, perhaps with a few affiliated units, where day-care services of various kinds are offered by a team of primary care workers. The main tasks of the primary care workers were first, to recognise drug and alcohol misuse, its causes and effects, and to have adequate knowledge of the type of help required by the client or family. Second, they were to give as much help as possible, and to know where and when to seek more expert help. Third, they were to continue care and support during any specialist treatment, and, finally, ensure adequate follow-up.

The onus of primary care was thus placed mainly on helping professionals such as general practitioners, nurses, social workers and probation officers, who might be working in either a salaried or a voluntary capacity. In addition, because initial contact with drug and alcohol problems can occur in a wide variety of settings, such other professionals as police officers, teachers, magistrates, journalists and clergy were seen as having a responsibility of recognition, even though they might have little involvement in treatment.

Primary care centres were to be supplemented by *secondary care* facilities and personnel. The function of such secondary services was threefold. First, they were to provide support and advice to primary care personnel, regardless of their discipline. Second, they were to take responsibility for providing in-service professional training to their non-specialist colleagues and, to a lesser extent, for initiating, coordinating and monitoring relevant research. They were also to take charge of more general public education. Finally, they were to provide specialist treatment for clients with unusual problems.

Personnel operating at the secondary level were to differ from primary workers only in the degree of their specilisation in one or more areas. Their basic training was to be similar. Throughout, emphasis was placed on client care provided by teams of professionals whose orientation was to be as multidisciplinary as possible.

Implementation of this proposed program of care means that responsibility for the assessment and treatment of most people with drug and alcohol problems will fall on a heterogeneous body of non-specialist counsellors who may function in either a professional or a voluntary capacity. Their preparation for the task varies somewhat with the positions they hold, but it is in general very sketchy. Formally qualified personnel such as general practitioners and nurses will ordinarily have received minimal training in the specific problems associated with drug and alcohol misuse, and most other workers are even less qualified. A significant number of people employed as social workers in local social services have received no formal training although in practice they are required to deal with the same clients and problems as their fully qualified colleagues. The problem is even more severe in voluntary agencies, and it is acute for residential and day-care staff, of whom only about four per cent (other than those involved in child care) have any formal qualifications.

The need for courses at the specialist level may initially seem less pressing because fewer people are involved and most of these can be expected to have the kind of basic professional qualifications that would enable them to enter programs that might be offered by universities, postgraduate centres, vocational training schemes and various professional bodies. Nevertheless, the importance of adequate training for this group, however small, takes on a new urgency in view of the projected second role of such specialists as resource personnel, educators and supervisors for the primary care sector. It may prove more economical in both real cost and time to train a relatively small number of highly qualified specialists, who can then disseminate their knowledge further, than to attempt to train the much larger body of primary care workers directly.

Policy-making bodies recognised early that the professionals on whom these new responsibilities had fallen so suddenly might not have the skills to meet them, and their policy statements always speak generally of professional education. Emphasis is usually placed on the primary care sector, who need

> to gain greater understanding of the nature of dependence whether on alcohol or other habit forming substance, some skill in recognising alcoholism in its early stages and more knowledge of the scope of the social work techniques and the contribution of specialized treatment in the support facilities for alcoholics. (Department of Health and Social Security, London 1975)

In time, most policy-making bodies arrived at some variant of a sequence of three levels of training that increased in degree of specialisation.

The first level should be common to all relevant professional groups regardless of individual areas of specialisation. It should include knowledge of the effects of drugs and alcohol, and of the social and other factors that mould the onset of misuse. Training in the recognition of the problem and initiation of appropriate action in the context of the services available is also necessary. Ideally, such general training would establish the fact that drug misusers can be helped and would give trainees the basic ability and confidence to provide treatment and care. Further, when the team approach advocated as the optimal form of treatment is initiated, it would ensure that all the people concerned had a basic background of common knowledge, training and experience. This first level of training should be adequate to the needs of health educators, personnel and welfare officers, teachers, doctors other than general practitioners or psychiatrists, and some nurses, social and volunteer workers.

If contact with the problem is to go beyond general prevention, recognition and referral, and is to include actual provision of treatment and care, an additional *second level* of training is needed. This should include assessment of the extent and nature of the problem in individual cases, specific treatment strategies, goal setting, methods of evaluating progress and the knowledge of when and where to seek further help. General practitioners, prison medical officers, probation officers, district nurses, and most social workers, volunteer counsellors and nurses on general and psychiatric wards would require training to at least this level.

The first and second levels of training between them cover the needs of primary care workers. Care at the secondary level requires such specially trained persons as consultant psychiatrists, clinical psychologists, residential and day-care staff, and those social workers, nurses and volunteer counsellors who specialise in the care of people with drug or alcohol problems, either in private practice or in some institutional setting. Beside formal training in their various disciplines, such persons need all the skills provided by training at levels I and II, plus further work at a *third level* that would enable them to deal with more difficult problems where harm is extensive. Ideally, they should have a wide knowledge of different types of therapy, confidence in using them, and, above all, should be able to work in a multidisciplinary team. In addition, they should be able to advise, support and educate colleagues in their own and other disciplines.

A sub-group of secondary workers with somewhat special training requirements includes those the Advisory Committe on Alcoholism (1979) refers to as 'managers'. These are senior staff at area and regional levels responsible for the organization of such departments as social services, probation and community health, and that of certain voluntary agencies. These people are essential to the development of such services and their staff, and they also play a significant role in the design and operation of prevention campaigns. Unless they know the nature of the drug and alcohol problems in their locality and the practical needs of their staff in dealing with them, the necesary services and levels of training will not be achieved. The training of managers should therefore enable them to assess the extent, nature and changing trends of drug use in the community for which they are responsible, to develop multidisciplinary services to meet these needs and to assess their effectiveness. They also need to know the training needs of their staff and the educational opportunities available to them, and to take a special responsibility for community education.

Educational policy statements generally assume that most level III training will be gained through practical experience or internship. Similarly, there is a general feeling that all secondary level workers should spend a considerable part of their apprenticeship working in specialist secondary care facilities such as drug or alcohol treatment centres.

Problems of implementation

Implementation of all training goals in this area is hampered by major ideological and practical problems. The new emphasis on the multifactorial nature of drug addiction presupposes a multidisciplinary treatment approach, and it also markedly broadens the definition of what constitutes a professional worker in this field. On a practical level, the fragmentary nature of existing services makes provision of adequate and consistent training difficult.

Professionalism and multidisciplinarity

The need to change public attitudes toward people with drug and alcohol problems has already been discussed at length. Perhaps less obvious is the fact that similar changes must take place in the orientation of many health care professionals as well. In addition, the new emphasis on non-medical treatment of addiction means that people with a wide variety of basic professional qualifications will now need to add dealing with drug and alcohol problems to their professional expertise.

Many of the professionals now expected to deal with addictions have had very little in the way of drug or alcohol education to begin with. When they do have some related training, it is typically quite one-sided, because the information they will have been given will be that thought appropriate for members of their particular profession. Thus, most doctors will have been taught that there is a connection between alcohol intake and cirrhosis of the liver, and most police officers will have some concept of the contribution drinking makes to traffic accidents. In practice, though, these two professions share little common knowledge, and it is unlikely that they will communicate with each other or cooperate in the handling of excessive drinkers on any but the most superficial level.

Because professional training has been fragmented in this way, and because the subject does cut across a number of traditional disciplines, the view seems to have arisen that the study of drug addiction is an extremely fragmented area of knowledge. There is as yet no recognised body of common basic facts, and this presents a major difficulty for professional education programs. It is not necessary for police officers to have a detailed knowledge of cirrhosis, and doctors do not need special expertise in arresting drunk and disorderly people. It would be enormously helpful, however,

> for these professionals to be in possession of a body of common knowledge, which they were aware they shared with each other and with other professionals. Interdisciplinarity could thus become a reality instead of a laudable but unrealistic aim. What is required is that the area of common knowledge should be accurately defined and then presented, possibly in a number of quite different ways, so as to be relevant to the different professions. After all, the reason for such a proposal is an eminently practical one. The knowledge will be of use to them, not only in helping them to understand their own responsibilities, but also in assisting the development of an integrated community response. (Grant, 1977, p. 421)

The establishment of such a body of common knowledge has been side-tracked by two common misconceptions. The first is that although they are prepared to accept the concept of multidisciplinarity, many professionals continue to behave as though this obliged them to present a single multidisciplinary solution to the problem of addiction. This is clearly in the 'too hard' basket, and it has tended to inhibit creative effort. As Grant (1977) points out, adoption of the multidisciplinary viewpoint allows a rare and enviable flexibility. There is no obligation to argue that everybody can be helped by such techniques as hypnosis or methadone maintenance, and a range of different approaches becomes possible, to the greater benefit of clients.

The second misconception is one shared by all new and burgeoning areas of research: the tendency to assume that new knowledge is best and should always replace the old. The lure of frontiers and breakthroughs can fragment effort and divert necessary attention from analysis and evaluation of what has already been achieved, thus preventing the establishment of that much-needed body of common knowledge.

Two important questions emerge from this discussion. First, does multidisciplinarity mean that clients are to be treated by a team of people? This has clearly been the case in many instances, and the results are often negative. Multidisciplinary information and skills are required in dealing with drug users and their families, but no useful purpose is served by confronting these people with a bewildering array of different professionals, either en masse or in quick succession. Under such circumstances, multidisciplinary responses often degenerate into undisciplined ones, and the result is certain confusion of clients and possible antagonism or jealousy among the professionals.

The ideal practice is for the particular member of the multidisciplinary team who has the most background knowledge on and the strongest therapeutic relationship with the client to take prime responsibility for therapy, with the rest of the team acting in an advisory capacity. They may never see the client directly, and their only role may be to support the primary therapist.

The second question that arises is whether the area of drug and alcohol counselling is sufficiently distinct to warrant the creation of a new discipline with its own body of specialist workers. The overlap with problems encountered in more general forms of counselling is obvious and many take the position that the role of drug and alcohol services should be purely one of basic detoxification followed by referral to other agencies for more general types of treatment.

Others find this perspective untenable. Cartwright (1980), for instance, poses a twofold rationale for the need to deal with drug and alcohol problems as separate issues. First, he argues that the prime goal of therapy with addicts must be to alter behaviour, because if drugs are being used to cover fundamental difficulties, these will not emerge as long as the client continues the habit. Further, since all therapy works on the principle of cognitive reorganisation, that is, the enhancement of the client's ability to think and feel in an undisturbed fashion, therapy will be impossible as long as the client is under the influence of the drug. Once therapy can begin, Cartwright maintains that both the problems created by the drug use and the more fundamental problems that led to use must be attacked concurrently if success in one area is not to undermine success in the other.

His second point is that the presence of addiction creates such special conditions that normal treatment procedures must be modified. For one thing, anxiety in addicts must be managed especially carefully because excessive levels are likely to result in a return to the drug. Moreover, in dealing with, say, an alcoholic client, Cartwright believes that the emergence of the subject of alcohol in therapy and discussions concerned with alcohol itself must be given the highest priority when selecting material to work on. In his opinion, emergence of these topics signals potential relapse, and, should this occur, the entire therapy will, of course, receive a serious setback.

Whatever the validity of these reasons, there can be no doubt that the best interests of the client are not served by frequent changes in the nature of treatment, its location and the personnel providing it. Unless true multidisciplinarity and adequate integration can be achieved in both the physical facilities and staff available, the development of drug and alcohol specialists as a separate professional sub-group may be inevitable.

The issue may well be resolved by time. All newly developing disciplines are subject to unusually critical scrutiny and it is perhaps unfortunate that the subject matter of drug and alcohol services is not as academically respectable as one might wish. Quite apart from association with such scapegoats as temperance movements and various aspects of the counter-culture, drug and alcohol services deal with clinical material, and this is notoriously difficult to quantify and articulate in an academically acceptable theoretical framework. There are criticisms, for instance, that training courses for drug and alcohol counsellors degenerate into psycho-therapeutic groups in which the group leader merely exchanges patient and trainee and that the whole exercise quickly becomes irrelevant to the training goals. Some of these criticisms are valid.

On the whole, though, drug and alcohol services are experiencing the same problems that cause perennial difficulties for traditional psychology, which at least has the resilience of greater age. What is needed is a body of academic clinicians—people who carry on their helping role in the traditional manner but who are also able to present their theories as based on solid research that is adequately and appropriately quantified. Failure in this area leads to a lack of dialogue between a dogmatic, traditional public sector and an experimentally-minded private in-group who, to make matters worse, sometimes feel it necessary to misrepresent their aims and goals in the interests of funding and facilities. The ultimate loser is of course the client.

Status of existing services

The fragmentation of drug and alcohol education across several traditional professions has produced a body of equally fragmented services, each with its own policies and goals. Any doctor or police officer, however excellent their individual efforts on behalf of drug addicts, will be working in isolation and therefore at least to some extent in competition.

As already outlined in Chapter 7, the present arrangement of services is patchy and haphazard. Existing facilities are not being used effectively. There is duplication, confusion about role and goals, and decision-making processes are vague and bureaucratised. There is ignorance about, and in some instances reluctance to make use of, the range of services available. It would obviously be of value if each agency knew something of the others' activities and structures, but cooperation so far leaves much to be desired.

All services concerned with drug and alcohol problems carry out some basic training. Specialist medical services often have excellent in-service programs, but these are rarely if ever available to non-medical people, and most require that trainees be currently employed by that service.

Statutory services such as Social Services departments and Youth and Community services also provide in-house courses. These usually build on the basic, general skills the staff already have and are accustomed to using in the course of everyday duties. These are brief and often seek merely to build confidence. In some cases, a key person may be sent to a special program and later is expected to use this knowledge to educate colleagues. More rarely, staff may be sent to a voluntary agency for this purpose. Funding and staff incentives are usually provided from within the service.

Voluntary agencies, on the other hand, frequently experience considerable difficulties in training their staff because of limited resources and lack of access to suitable training programs. Supervision of newly qualified staff in field work is a special problem. Small voluntary agencies must typically make arrangements with a statutory service or with another, larger voluntary agency to ensure the necessary support.

Good programs are few and generally inaccessible. Where they have emerged, there is often the additional problem of what Grant (1977) has called 'coagulation'. An excellent program might develop at a specialist institution or, more typically, at a place where a number of interdependent facilities exist. The Addiction Research Foundation in Ontario is an example. Once the working model of such a program is established, it simply keeps on working:

> The services feed themselves, excellence attracting excellence, so that these centers survive, to some extent, at the expense of the rest of the country. Thus, the cumulating expertise coagulates, preventing the flow of excellence out from the centre toward the periphery. Of course, what we must not do is to destroy the excellence, for that is an essential component in the growth of service provision...
> [However]... one of the most urgent needs is not to develop new models, new approaches, but rather to ensure that people know about the existing models and approaches. Surprisingly often, whole sections of the community are starved of what they could so easily have, simply because the expertise has coagualted somewhere twenty miles away along the railway track. (Grant, 1977, p. 420)

Whether the main problem is fragmentation of services or coagulation of expertise, the remedy is not creation of new services, but coordination. Indeed, if new facilities and programs continue to emerge in the ad hoc and arbitrary fashion of the past decade, no real improvement can be expected. Nevertheless, coordinating these must not be seen as imposing some sort of 'party line'. The functions of the various services are not mutually exclusive, but most will have rather different educational requirements. People who are going to treat clients, carry out drug education in schools and administer detoxification centres are all going to need different skills, though there may be a common core.

> Once a coherent body of common knowledge has been established, it may be that some professions will require in addition only a relatively small input of specialized information whilst others will require more elaborate, detailed and experience-related programmes of great complexity. Only through the activities of an efficient co-ordinating

agency could such diverse educational modules be expected to bear meaningful relation to each other... A co-ordinator can open doors, which, without his intervention, are likely to remain not only closed, but firmly bolted, for years to come. (Grant, 1977, p. 422)

A caveat about coordination is in order, however. Coordinators and coordinating agencies run a real danger of attempting to pick up the burdens of a whole society under stress on the one hand and becoming bogged in a bureaucratic morass on the other. One cannot help but be impressed, but also rather depressed, by the number of organisations and facilities at least theoretically involved in alcohol and drug addiction. If a coordinator is worth employing at all, the job is likely to grow until enormous teams of ancillary staff and expensive administrative machinery only vaguely related to client needs and care are born, and in turn reproduce.

The organisational future of drug and alcohol services may well require the coordination of coordinators at local, regional and even national levels, and without due care this readily disintegrates into profligate waste of scarce resources. Part of the coordinating function should therefore be an educational one: the various services, facilities and programs must be impressed with the fact that it is their responsibility as well as the coordinator's to take steps to familiarise themselves with other professional organisations in their area and to establish and maintain appropriate channels of communication with them. Some suggestions on how this might be done can be found in Chapter 7.

Provision of training: what makes a successful professional?

When Shaw and his colleagues (1978) attempted to delineate the committed and successful professional in the field of alcohol addiction, four factors emerged:

1 Such people had *clinical knowledge* about alcohol and alcohol-related problems.
2 They had received *training in counselling*, and the hours of such training were generally closely related to their feeling of adequacy.
3 They were *experienced* in working with problem drinkers.
4 They worked in situations in which *role support* was available, either in the form of a specialist environment or of ongoing supervision.

These factors also interacted. Clinical information, for instance, did little to reduce anxieties about adequacy unless the worker also had some training in counselling and experience in working with drinkers. The single most critical factor turned out to be role support. Inexperienced workers who felt supported seemed committed to their work even when they were not too sure of their adequacy.

Reasonable role support is usually available in specialist environments. A social worker, nurse or psychologist operating within a psychiatric alcohol treatment unit can usually gain experience and pick up information and skills without carrying too great a burden of responsibility. When experienced staff who feel secure and comfortable when working with addiction problems are present, trainees are faced with minimal isolation and threat and can safely 'give it a go'. As their effectiveness increases client motivation improves, thus endorsing optimism and further reinforcing the trainee's role security and commitment.

Quite a different situation exists in the community. As we have seen, agents working in the community tend to be unsure of their rights and responsibilities; they often lack clinical information and training; and, most of all, they have little access to people with greater expertise who might advise them, clarify their position and encourage them in their work. As a result, they avoid recognising problems and responding to them as long as possible, and when these become too obvious to be ignored, the solution is rapid referral to some specialist. This, of course, precludes further experience on the agent's part. By safeguarding themselves against failure, community agents thus gain virtually no experience, develop no therapeutic skills and no realistic ways to handle addiction problems. Their clients usually sense this and cooperate poorly. This, of course, increases the agent's feelings of threat. It also reinforces their conviction that they cannot help such people, and activates the various self-defensive mechanisms that created the problem in the first place.

The general inadequacy of the community response to addiction, then, is not a matter of educational or personality deficiencies in the agents but rather of the development of a self-perpetuating negative spiral of ineffectiveness and low therapeutic commitment.

> So many agents travelled down this negative spiral on so many occasions that the safeguarding attitudes of pessimism and hostility towards clients with drinking problems became part of the mythology conveyed by members of each profession to new recruits. A stance of low therapeutic commitment was considered acceptable and indeed the 'realistic' perspective to adopt towards drinking problems. (Shaw et al, 1978, p. 243)

If, as current policies indicate, increasing responsibility for treatment is to fall on primary care workers in the community, this negative cycle must be broken and replaced by the more positive one described as possible in specialist situations.

All workers in the drug and alcohol field must have access to clinical information and counsellor training. Much of this can be obtained in fairly formal courses that either are already available or would be relatively easy to set up. The main problem, however, is to provide a situation where they can acquire experience under supervision and have access to known experts who can provide information, advice, and if necessary direct help and support in crisis situations. Very few opportunities for this exist outside specialist institutions, and the real challenge of professional education is to find ways in which the crucial elements of such environments might be transplanted into the working situations of general community agents.

Most attempts to do this remain strictly experimental. One of the most interesting is the concept of providing training through a 'community alcohol team' (Shaw et al, 1978). The concept is of course equally applicable to drugs other than alcohol.

The community alcohol team consisted of a consultant psychiatrist and a senior social worker. Because it was felt that role insecurity affected different professional groups in somewhat different ways, separate courses were provided for social workers, probation officers, general practitioners and nurses. The basic team was supplemented with senior members of whatever professional group the team was training at any given time. Each course involved 10 trainees and was divided into a series of two-hour sessions, most of which dealt with actual cases the trainees were managing.

Basically, each trainee presented the case history of a client's problems, the therapeutic goals and approaches being used, and an analysis of his or her personal difficulties in responding to that client. The rest of the group was then asked how each in turn would handle the case. The plan was to challenge each trainee's therapeutic position and clarify it, while allowing the rest of the group to generalise from each member's specific experiences to their own difficulties. The team and the group then worked out what seemed to be the most appropriate approach to the case and the trainee was asked to carry out these suggestions and report back to the group on the outcome.

Many trainees were reluctant to do this, but when they did try they unanimously discovered that the experience was not as difficult or as traumatic as they had feared it might be:

> their previously held safeguards had exaggerated the difficulties to justify to themselves why they should neither recognize nor respond to drinking problems. Support and supervision removed the anxieties which created such safe-guards. (Shaw et al, 1978 p. 178)

In any case, since each therapeutic approach had been developed as a cooperative effort between the team and the group, responsibility fo the possible failure of a proposed strategy would also have been shared.

At the end of the training courses, the trainees not only showed an increased sense of adequacy and therapeutic commitment as measured by various questionnaires, but also increased their recognition of related problems among other clients on their case-loads. Throughout, all were able to retain the main therapeutic responsibility for their clients.

This type of training presupposes that the trainee already has some basic knowledge and skills and is formally engaged in some kind of therapeutic relationship with a client. The course thus fits the requirements of level II training and would have to be preceded by some kind of level I preparation. Moreover, a brief training program such as this cannot be expected to change community agents immediately and completely from ineffective to effective counsellors. It was abundantly clear during the training courses that trainees still experienced profound difficulties in handling clients, despite the group's support and the team's supervision. Other evidence also suggests that trainee workers need to travel the positive cycle of rewarding experiences many times—perhaps with as many as 50 clients—before they come to feel completely secure in their role. It is therefore probable that the gains achieved during brief training programs will not be maintained, let alone increased, without continued role support.

One solution to this problem would be to second trainees to specialist institutions for fairly extended periods. Realistically, however, these facilities could physically meet the needs of only a fraction of the trainee population. An alternative plan might be to establish what amounts to a team consultation service in the community for this express purpose. A pilot project of this type (cf. Shaw et al, 1978) suggested that once such a consultation service developed beyond an embryonic stage it would deal with more clients (in terms of both professionals seeking support and help with case management and clients with direct problems of their own) than typical psychiatric specialist services.

The actual staffing and mode of operation of such team consultation services would need to vary from one to another according to specific local needs. Theoretically, staff could come from various sources, but in practice staffing is likely to present considerable problems. Most communities would not have enough professionals with the requisite training, experience and therapeutic commitment to act as team leaders, and it would probably be inappropriate for voluntary workers such as AA members to supervise professionals, even if AA members were willing to accept such a role.

This in effect places the burden of staffing such services on statutory bodies. Shaw and his colleagues have argued persuasively that statutory specialist centres, particularly those attached to psychiatric hospitals, should take on this role. The existing use made of psychiatric resources is, in their opinion, inefficient and inappropriate. Their costly facilities and manpower are being used to provide custodial and convalescent services that could often be taken over more economically by hostels or day-care institutions. Moreover, most of the specialist treatments for drug and alcohol problems (individual and group therapy, social retraining and the like) do not require a hospital setting. If suitable alternative venues were provided for these activities,

> there would be a case then for a general redeployment of psychiatric manpower, and it would seem reasonable to argue that agents working in psychiatric services should spend less of their time in highly labour-intensive care of a minority of clients with drinking problems and instead direct more effort toward helping general community agents become able to respond themselves at a primary care level to a much larger pool of clients... When general community agents felt that they were going to be adequately supported by readily available specialists, most of them were prepared to maintain responsibility for their own cases. In many such instances, it would be a far more valuable use of a specialist's time to spend an hour talking with a general community agent about the management of a case than just seeing the client for an hour in the psychiatric outpatient clinic. Clients would then also begin to receive more appropriate ongoing treatment from the agent most knowledgeable about their background and in the best position to help them on a long-term basis. (Shaw et al, 1978, pp. 248–49)

In the final analysis, therefore, effective professional education is not so much the provision of more specialist facilities or the development of the ultimately effective program. The greatest effect on clients in contact with helping agencies comes from the therapeutic commitment of the staff. As we have seen, this depends far more on their working conditions than on their formal clinical knowledge.

Unless the professionals, salaried or voluntary, who work with drug and alcohol problems are helped from their present position of unsupported insecurity into one in which role support is available and readily accessible, results cannot improve. If role support remains inadequate, government and community calls for a more active community response to drug and alcohol problems must

> 'continue to fall on the unreceptive ears of agents who see responding to drinking problems not as an interest, a duty or an obligation, but as an anxiety-provoking area which threatens their professional self-esteem. (Shaw et al, 1978, p. 253)

References

Advisory Committee on Alcoholism, *Report on Education and Training*, D.H.S.S./Welsh Office, 1979.
Cartwright, A.K., Unpublished working paper, 1980.
Department of Health and Social Security, *Better Services for the Mentally Ill*, H.M.S.O., Cmnd. 6233, London, 1975.
Grant, M., 'Developing a coordinated approach to inter-professional education', in *Alcohol and Drug Dependence*, Madden, J., Walker, R. & Kenyon, W. (eds) Plenum Press, 1977.
Shaw, S., Cartwright, A., Spratley, T. & Harwin, J., *Responding to Drinking Problems*, Croom Helm, London, 1978.

10 Main non-government and government contacts for alcohol and drug information

These are the main sources of information around Australia on various aspects of alcohol and other drugs.

Complete listings are published in the Australian Directory of Alcohol and Drug Services, published annually by the Australian Foundation on Alcoholism and Drug Dependence (AFADD). The Directory describes type of program, services available, admission and other requirements, size and type of facility, and full contact information. For single or bulk copies, contact AFADD, PO Box 477, Canberra City, ACT, 2601.

Main non-government alcohol and drug foundations and associations

National

Australian Foundation on Alcoholism & Drug Dependence (AFADD)
2nd floor, T&G Bldg
39 London Circuit   OR   PO Box 477
CANBERRA CITY, ACT, 2601   CANBERRA CITY, ACT, 2601
Tel: (062) 47 3939/8

Australian Capital Territory

Alcohol & Drug Problems Association of the Capital Territory (ADPACT)
Health Promotion Centre
Childers St
CANBERRA CITY, ACT, 2601
Tel: (062) 47 4747

New South Wales

Foundation for Research & Treatment of Alcoholism & Drug Dependence
of NSW (FRATADD)
37 Macpherson St
MOSMAN, NSW, 2088
Tel: (02) 90 6279, 908 3033, 908 3122

Riverina Foundation for Alcoholism & Drug Dependence (RFADD)
PO Box 248
WAGGA WAGGA, NSW 2650
Tel: (069) 21 4220

Northern Territory

Darwin & District Alcohol & Drug Dependence Foundation (DDADDF)
'Amity House'
79 Cavenagh St
DARWIN, NT, 5790
Tel: (089) 81 8030

Queensland

Alcohol & Drug Problems Association of Queensland (ADPAQ)
129 Leichhardt St
BRISBANE, QLD, 4000
Tel: (07) 221 3045

South Australia

SA Foundation on Alcoholism & Drug Dependence (SAFADD)
5 Rostrevor Ave
ROSTERVOR, SA 5073
Tel: (08) 337 3353, 51 2125

Tasmania

Tas. Foundation on Alcoholism & Drug Dependence (TASFADD)
PO Box 114
MOONAH, TAS., 7009
(002) 28 8256, 28 8351

Victoria

Vic. Foundation on Alcoholism & Drug Dependence (VFADD)
1st floor
153 Park St
SOUTH MELBOURNE, VIC., 3205
Tel: (03) 690 6000

Ballarat Regional Alcohol & Drug Dependence Association (BRADDA)
19 Windemere St North
BALLARAT, VIC., 3350
Tel: (053) 31 5333

Other non-government services—main capital-city contacts

Canberra (area code 062)

Alcoholics Anonymous 49 1340
Lifeline 82 2222
St Vincent de Paul 95 1138

Al-Anon 48 8651
Salvation Army 95 1256
Council of Social Service 48 7566

Sydney (area code 02)

Alcoholics Anonymous 799 1705
Lifeline 33 4141
GROW 516 3733
Salvation Army 212 2322

Al-Anon 233 4322
Narcotics Anonymous 908 2147 (AH)
NSW Temperance Alliance 267 8737
WHOS 438 4266

Darwin (area code 089)

Alcoholics Anonymous 85 1405
Salvation Army 81 2500

St Vincent de Paul 81 4374

Brisbane (area code 07)

Alcoholics Anonymous 221 7920
Lifeline 52 7527
Salvation Army 36 0222

Al-Anon 229 2501
St Vincent de Paul 37 2720
Qld Temperance League 221 1805

Adelaide (area code 08)

Alcoholics Anonymous 272 3868

Al-Anon 51 2959

Hobart (area code 002)

Alcoholics Anonymous 25 2440
Lifeline 34 5600
Salvation Army 28 1325

Al-Anon, PO Box 86, North Hobart
St Vincent de Paul 34 4594

Melbourne (area code 03)

Alcoholics Anonymous 41 5384
Narcotics Anonymous 754 5944
Salvation Army 328 1893
Al-Anon 62 4933
St Vincent de Paul 419 3644
Vic. Temperance Alliance 63 1285
Narcotics Anonymous 754 5944

Perth (area code 09)

Alcoholics Anonymous 325 3209
St Vincent de Paul 325 3474
Council of Social Services 321 9711

Al-Anon 325 3209
Salvation Army 325 3666

Note: About 1000 community health centres exist in cities and towns around Australia. Contact information is available from the nearest Health Department office or Telecom Directory Assistance.

Main government alcohol and drug organisations

Australian Capital Territory

Alcohol & Drug Dependence Unit
Health Promotion Centre
Capital Territory Health Commission
Childers St
CANBERRA CITY, ACT, 2601
Tel: (062) 45 4529

New South Wales

NSW Drug & Alcohol Authority
8th floor, Aetna Life Tower
Cnr Elizabeth & Bathurst Sts
SYDNEY, NSW, 2000
Tel: (02) 264 1161

Queensland

Alcohol & Drug Dependence Service (ADDS)
'Biala'
Cnr Roma & Saul Sts
BRISBANE, QLD, 4000
Tel: (07) 229 6566

South Australia

Alcohol & Drug Addicts' Treatment Board (ADATB)
3/161 Greenhill Rd
PARKSIDE, SA, 5063
Tel: (08) 272 6144

Victoria

Alcohol & Drug Services
10th floor, Enterprise House
555 Collins St
MELBOURNE, VIC., 3000
Tel: (03) 616 7777

Western Australia

WA Alcohol & Drug Authority
Salvatori House
35 Outram St
WEST PERTH, WA, 6005
Tel: (09) 321 2444

Northern Territory

NT Drug & Alcohol Bureau
PO Box 1701
DARWIN, NT, 5794
Tel: (089) 80 2911

Index

abstinence
  as an alternative lifestyle 184, 187; as a therapeutic goal 100–02, 116; disease concept of alcoholism and 47
addiction
  characteristics of 85–7; definition 83; genetic factors in 88–9; incidence of 120–1; learning and 84, 93–4; personality factors in 89–91, 94; physical dependence and 83; relationship to non-drug habits 85–6; social factors in 91–7; types of 96–7
adolescent drug users
  special problems of 122–3, 134–5; special techniques with 133–5; treatment model for 135–6
adulteration 24–5
'affective' approaches to drug education 170, 175
alcohol
  acetaldehyde production and 31–2; alternatives to drinking 187; amount consumed, effects of 35, 38, 187; Australian history, in 145–6; behavioural effects of 35–7, 39–41; beverages 30; blackouts 39; blood level 35–36; brain and 34; congeners 30, 38; content of beverages 30–1; diseases related to 33–5, 66–7; gastrointestinal system and 32, 35; 'grogstrife' and 40; hangover 38; heart and 33–4; intoxication 36–7; level of consumption in Australia 54–5, 187; liver and 31, 33; memory and 34, 39; metabolism 31; patterns of use in Australia 59–62, 185–7; physiological effects of 32–5; road deaths and 67, 186; social attitudes to 17, 184–9; standard drink 30–1; temperature and 32; tolerance to 31, 35; withdrawal from 38; women and 33, 36

alcohol misuse
  client attitudes to 43–4; consequences of excessive use 39–41, 70–1; costs of 186; diagnosis of 43–6; family and 112–14; genetic factors in 88; occupations at risk for 40; patterns of drinking 39, 85, 186–7; personality factors in 89; physical signs of 37; professional attitudes to 44–6; stereotypes and 47–9, 184–8; young drinkers and 111–12, 180, 187
alcoholics *see* alcoholism
Alcoholics Anonymous 47–8, 100, 103
  in Australia 145–6, 149–51
alcoholism
  definitions of 47–9; disease theory of 47–9, 83, 99–101; loss of control in 47–8, 83–4; stereotyping and 37, 47–9
alternatives theory 116, 136–8
aspirin *see* analgesics
assessment
  procedures 124–5; variables affecting 125
analgesics
  alcohol and 32; advertising and 75–6; diseases associated with 70; sale of 164; use in Australia 56, 77
Antabuse *see* disulfiram
'alconfrontation' 40
antidepressants,
  use in Australia 56

banana skin smoking 79
barbiturates
  as sedative hypnotics 41–2; metabolic effects of 21, 24; tolerance to 21 *see also* sedative-hypnotics
'barbiturate equivalents' 24
brain function 19–20

cirrhosis 33

'civilised drinking' 180–1
'coagulation' of treatment services 199
community-based treatment
   attitudes to 44–5; development of 103–4, 191–2; training for 192–4, 198–204; therapeutic commitment and 200–04
community drug education
   program guidelines 176–8; role of statutory bodies in 175–6, 178; specialist training and 194; status of 175–6 see also drug education
conditioned abstinence 95
conduct norms 91–2
controlled drinking
   as a therapeutic goal 101–2; indications for 102; predictors success in 101
consciousness-altering drugs see psychedelics
cross-dependence 23, 106
cross-tolerance 20, 106
counselling see individual counselling; 'real life' counselling; group therapy; family therapy
counsellors
   characteristics of 116–17, 142, 200; counselling skills of 126–9; group leadership and 141; personal problems of 124–6, 142; training of 193–4, 200–4

detoxification units 106–7
disulfiram (Antabuse) 32
   therapy with 109–10
doctor-patient relationship
   drug-taking and 75; in community drug and alcohol treatment 153–5
drugs
   advertising and 164–5, 181–4; commercialism and 75–7, 181–4; crime and 22, 69–70; definitions of 15–17; illegal 11–12, use in Australia 56, 58, 65, in education 176; prescription 11–12, 81, in education 176, patterns of use in Australia 64, extent of use in Australia 54–7; proprietary (over-the-counter) 81; social 81; socio-economic factors and 164–6, 179
drug action
   dose-dependent factors 20–1; receptors and 18; time-dependent factors 22–3; types of effects 18–20, 42; user-dependent factors 25–7
drug education
   'affective' approaches 170, 175; education and environmental manipulation 179; general problems of 167–9; 'one-night stands' in 176–7; program guidelines 176–8; role of statutory bodies in 175, 178; 'scare' techniques 169, 175; 'substance-focused' approaches 169, 175 see also school drug education, community drug education
drug educators
   characteristics of 177–8; specialist personnel as 193; tasks of 173
drug misuse 12
   diagnosis of 43–6; medical 82; misuse-addiction continuum 83; recreational 82; social definitions of 81–2; symptoms of 29ff, 42; use-misuse continuum 81–3
drug problem, the 11–12, 73–80
   biomedical factors in 74–5; 'dropping out' and 77–8; health and 76–7; mass media and 75–6; social factors in 76–82
drug-taking behaviour
   attitudes to 12, 15, 17, 93; availability and 179–80; legal restraints and 179–80, 186–8; peer groups and 91–5
drug-related death 12, 66–8
drug-related disease 67–70
drug use
   alternatives to 116, 184; cessation of 115–16; consumption and incidence of problems 179–81; initiation of 90–5; in schools 171–2; legal control of 186–8; levels of and education 176–7; maintenance of 90–5; medical 16–17, 74–5, 81; recreational 81; social attitudes to 78–80; symptoms of 29ff

early intervention
   controlled drinking and 102; occupational programs and 115, 188; services 146, 153
epidemiology
   definition of 51; methodological problems of 51–3
ethicals see prescription drugs
ex-addicts
   use of in drug education 177

family therapy
   family-focused management 112–14; importance of 112–14, 138
fatty liver 33
fillers 25

general depressant withdrawal 24, 38

general practitioners, as community resource people 153–5
genetic factors
  alcohol misuse and 88–9
  in addiction 88–9
'grogstrife' 40
group therapy
  adolescents, special problems for 138–9; advantages of 138; aspects of group life 141; open and closed groups 139–40; stages of group development 140–1; with young drinkers 111–12

halfway houses 107
hallucinogens see psychedelics
hepatitis 33
heroin
  antagonist therapy in misuse 109; initiation into use of 94; maintenance therapy in misuse of 108–9; withdrawal 23 see also narcotics
heart attack, alcohol and 33–4

individual counselling
  mistakes in 129; procedures of 126–9; success of 110–11, 129

Korsakoff's psychosis 34

legal controls, nature and effects of 179–81, 186–9
loss of control, in alcohol misuse 47–8, 83–5

maintenance therapy 99, 108–9
mass media
  the drug problem and 75–6; prevention and 181–4; public image of use/misuse and 184–7
'mateship' 92
marijuana
  attitudes to 17; mass media and 76; tolerance to 21
'maturing out' 87
methadone 23, 106, methadone maintenance 108–9
mind-altering drugs see psychedelics
'minimisation' in prevention 162–3
multidisciplinarity 195–8
multiple drug use 24
motivation
  effects on drug users 25–6; for cessation of drug use 84–5, 114–16; for drug misuse 84; of professional drug and alcohol workers 43–6, 200–4

narcotics
  dependence on 83; genetic factors in misuse of 88–9; legal use in Australia 56–7; maintenance therapy with 99, 108–9; personality factors and 89; social attitudes to 80; symptoms of use 42; tolerance to 20–1; withdrawal syndrome 23
narcotic antagonists
  use in therapy 109
nicotine see tobacco
non-purposive withdrawal symptoms 22
non-voluntary clients
  referral of 123–4
  special techniques with 130–3
normality
  definition of 16

occupational drug and alcohol programs
  principles of 115, 188; success of 115–16
'one-night' stands
  in drug education 176–7
opiates see narcotics
over-the-counter drugs see proprietary drugs

peripheral (poly)neuritis 34
placebo effects 26–7
physical dependence
  addiction and 83; definition of 22; management of 106–7; rate of elimination and 23; withdrawal syndromes in 22–3
potentiation 24
prevention
  education as a means of 167; environmental manipulation as a means of 179–89; evaluation of programs for 165–6; general problems in 161–66; setting goals for 161–63
primary care 191–204
primary prevention see also school and community education; mass media; legal controls
professional training
  'coagulation' and 199; effectiveness of 203–4; existing services and 198–200; experimental programs of 201–4; fragmentation of 195; model of 193–4; multidisciplinarity and 195–6; need for core knowledge and 195–6; problems of implementation 44–6, 195–204; professionalism and 197–8; specialist facilities and 203–4

psychedelics 22, 25–6, 42
  social attitudes to 80; 'talk down' procedures 105–6
psychological dependence
  addiction and 83; definition of 22
purposive withdrawal symptoms 22

referral
  as a means of avoiding responsibility 45–6; feedback on outcome of 157–8; procedures of 156–7
referral services
  evaluation of 156; feedback on 157–8; setting up of 155–6
reverse tolerance 21
'real life' counselling
  special techniques in 130–5
role legitimacy 44–5

sampling
  controlled drinking and 101; effects on the characteristics of addiction 87–90
'scare' techniques in drug education 169, 175
school drug education
  curriculum and 174;
  evaluation of 170–2; in Australia 170; role of schools in the community 174; teachers and 172–3 see also drug education
secondary care 192–204 see also treatment; treatment services
secondary prevention 290–306
  current strategies 191–3
  professional training and 193–4, 200–4
  see also treatment, treatment services
sedative-hypnotics
  functional similarity among 41; legal use in Australia 54, 56; potentiation among 24; social attitudes to 80; symptoms of use 41–2; use of 26–7 see also barbiturates; tranquillisers; alcohol
smoking see tobacco
special vulnerability 180–1 see also disease theories of alcoholism
specialist treatment
  attitudes to 45; effectiveness of 103; role of 192, 203–4; therapeutic commitment and 201–2; training for 192, 194, 198–204
stereotyping 37, 47–9, 97, 185–9
stimulants
  social attitudes to 80; symptoms of use 42

stimulus flooding 78
subcultures
  role in drug use 91–3
'substance-focused' approaches in drug education 169, 175

'talk down' procedures 105–6
'therapeutic commitment'
  improving 200–4; status of 46
thiamine
  alcohol-related disease and 34
tobacco
  diseases related to 66–7; level of consumption in Australia 54–5; patterns of use in Australia 62–3
tolerance
  general description and mechanisms 20–1
tranquillisers
  as sedative-hypnotics 41; attitudes to 17; barbiturate equivalents 24; illegal use in Australia 58; legal use in Australia 54, 56; potentiation 24 see also sedative-hypnotics
treatment
  by multidisciplinary teams 196; client-related variables in 114–16, 121–2; drug-free 110–14; model of 135–6; of acute withdrawal 106–7; of drug emergencies 105–6; pharmacological 108–10; symptomatic and curative 78–9; therapeutic success of 114–18, 121; therapy-related variables 116–18, 121–2 see also counselling
treatment services
  'coagulation' of 199; coordination of 199–200; development in Australia 145–6; finding services 150–5; fragmentation of 198–200; government organisations 147–8; non-government organisations 148–50; primary care facilities/workers 191–2, 198–9; professional training and 198–204; secondary care facilities and workers 192, 198–9; setting up and operating services 155–9; state foundations 148–9

voluntary referral 107, 123
voluntary services 148–50
  training problems of 191–2, 199, 203–04 see also treatment; treatment services
Wernicke's disease 34
withdrawal reactions see physical dependence